Experimenters, Rebels, and Disparate Voices

Recent Titles in
Contributions in Drama and Theatre Studies

Experimenters, Rebels, and Disparate Voices

The Theatre of the 1920s Celebrates American Diversity

Edited by Arthur Gewirtz and James J. Kolb

Prepared under the auspices of Hofstra University

Contributions in Drama and Theatre Studies, Number 99

Westport, Connecticut
London

Library of Congress Cataloging-in-Publication Data

Experimenters, rebels, and disparate voices : the theatre of the 1920s celebrates
American diversity / edited by Arthur Gewirtz and James J. Kolb.
    p. cm. — (Contributions in drama and theatre studies, ISSN 0163–3821; no. 99)
    Includes bibliographical references and index.
    ISBN 0–313–32466–2 (alk. paper)
    1. American drama—20th century—History and criticism. 2. American drama—Minority
authors—History and criticism. 3. Lawson, John Howard, 1894—Criticism and
interpretation. 4. Experimental drama, American—History and criticism. 5.
Theatre—United States—History—20th century. 6. Pluralism (Social sciences) in
literature. 7. Difference (Psychology) in literature. 8. African Americans in literature. 9.
Ethnic groups in literature. 10. Minorities in literature. 11. Dissenters in literature. I.
Gewirtz, Arthur. II. Kolb, James J., 1944– III. Series.
   PS351.E97   2003
  812'.5209920693—dc21   2002072543

British Library Cataloguing in Publication Data is available.

Library of Congress Catalog Card Number: 2002072543
ISBN: 0–313–32466–2
ISSN: 0163–3821

First published in 2003

Praeger Publishers, 88 Post Road West, Westport, CT 06881
An imprint of Greenwood Publishing Group, Inc.
www.praeger.com

Printed in the United States of America

The paper used in this book complies with the
Permanent Paper Standard issued by the National
Information Standards Organization (Z39.48–1984).

10 9 8 7 6 5 4 3 2 1

Copyright Acknowledgments

The editors and publisher gratefully acknowledge permission for use of the following material:

Extracts from the Introduction to *Appearances* by Garland Anderson (p. 97), reprinted with permission of The Free
Press, an imprint of Simon & Schuster Trade Publishing Group from *Black Theatre USA: Plays by African
Americans 1847 to Today*, Revised & Expanded Edition, edited by James V. Hatch and Ted Shine. Copyright ©
1974, 1996 by The Free Press.

Extracts from the Sophie Treadwell Papers, located at the University of Arizona Library Special Collections, Ms.
124 (lectures and notes) and 8 ("Lonely Lee").

The following chapters were originally published in the *Journal of American Drama & Theatre* and are used here
with permission of The City University of New York: "Glitter, Glitz, and Race" (*7,3*, 1995) and "Disparate Voices"
(*7,1*, 1995) by Freda Scott Giles; "Garland Anderson and Appearances" (*6,2&3*, 1994) by Alan Kreizenbeck; and
"The Idiosyncratic Theatre of John Howard Larson" (*8,1*, 1996) by John D. Shout.

Illustration from *Continental Stagecraft* by Kenneth Macgowan, copyright © 1922 by Harcourt Brace & Company,
reproduced by permission of the publisher.

Contents

Contents

Introduction

Arthur Gewirtz and James J. Kolb

The twenties was an extraordinary time in the American theatre. After some two decades of ferment from native and foreign influences and the intensely transforming experience of World War I, the theatre burst forth into something new and exciting. The sense of change did not come immediately but quickly enough. On 16 December 1924 the playwright Sidney Howard wrote to his friend the critic Barrett H. Clark: "There's rather a showing, these days, for American plays, isn't there? There may not be any *great* ones—though Stallings and Anderson are pretty near—but there are four of them, doing big business and earning at least serious respect, and that's *not* bad."[1] Interestingly, not only is there awareness of a new artistic era in this comment but also awareness that art could make money.

Art theatres—institutions dedicated to the production of dramas that were nothing but beautiful and true—hardly ever showed a profit and broke even only with the help of private donors. But the Theatre Guild, an art theatre transmuted more or less from the prewar Washington Square Players, generally flourished on Broadway (although it sometimes approached the line of extinction), battling away with the money-loving producers. Increasingly, the producers stopped their mere commercialism; they, perhaps following the lead of the Theatre Guild or perhaps sensing a fresh spirit, also climbed aboard the new gravy train—albeit sometimes a bit cautiously. John D. Williams presented Eugene O'Neill's first full-length Broadway play, *Beyond the Horizon*, early in 1920 for a series of special matinees. But no such timorousness prevented George C. Tyler from producing in 1921 and 1922 the first plays of George S. Kaufman and Marc Connelly, who though more attuned to the popular ear than, say, Eugene O'Neill, still showed a merry satiric spirit that might have frightened away both producers and widespread audiences just a short time before. Nor were Brock Pemberton, the much maligned William Brady, a firm called Stewart and French, the quintessentially commercial Shubert Brothers, and Arthur Hopkins (who showed the courage of his high principles even before the 1920s) afraid to produce the serious endeavors of Zona Gale, Sidney Howard, Elmer Rice, Rachel Crothers, Philip Barry, and Maxwell Anderson.

The playwrights themselves had no intention of starving. Americans all, they wished to live the good life, many of them supporting themselves and their families by other means before their early plays succeeded. No twenties version of Alphabet City for them. Once their work brought in the cash, they aimed to go forward, not backward. They desired financial and artistic solvency. Even though they had learned from the European masters—the Ibsens, the Strindbergs, the Hauptmans—and had absorbed the pioneering writings and practices of the New Stagecraft of Gordon Craig, Adolph Appia, Max Reinhardt, and their American protégés, they now desired to create a world of profit as well as of delight.

These commercially successful ventures did not prevent the continuation or the founding of art theatres that preferred to survive on their own but generally lost money. In fact, many of the same artists who worked in the art theatres also worked on Broadway. A good example is the Experimental Theatre, founded by Eugene O'Neill, Robert Edmond Jones, and Kenneth Macgowan as a successor to the Provincetown Playhouse, which closed its doors in 1922 after seven years of exciting and tumultuous work. The Triumvirate, as the founders of the Experimental Theatre were known, intended to produce significant plays of foreign and native extraction with Jones, a protégé of Reinhardt, as its influential designer. But Jones already had started a major career on Broadway as an artistic partner of producer-director Arthur Hopkins, and O'Neill himself was by this time an important Broadway force, having had three commercial successes uptown, two of them transferred from the Provincetown on Macdougal Street. The line between Broadway, where the money was, and the art theatres was hardly distinct. This was true as well of the actors in the Experimental Theatre. None was expected to give up a good commercial gig to remain downtown in artistic but needy splendor. Writers, directors, and designers easily and hopefully shuttled among the various art theatres and their money-paying counterparts.

Despite their sharp desire to stay alive, healthy, and comfortable, these were high-minded, high-spirited, hardworking men and women. Many wrote, designed, and acted in works that would probably succeed only in the art theatres and did the same for works that they thought would succeed both artistically and commercially on Broadway. One must remember that there was no government support for the arts in the twenties, nor were any of the New York art theatres backed by huge corporations. There was no comfortable place for a producer or director or writer to settle in and have his deficits somehow rectified. (Only later in the nineties, when large-scale support was drying up, were art theatres, which enjoyed such backing for about thirty years, beginning to face the problems of their counterparts in the twenties.) Art theatres such as the Neighborhood Playhouse, the Civic Repertory Theatre, and the New Playwrights Theatre were all privately supported, and when costs climbed too high or a depression rolled in, the theatres folded. But theatre was bountiful in the twenties. These joyfully toiling men and women, though they were a minority, achieved their goal of reshaping the American theatre. Art remained on Broadway—more or less. Art theatres continued to be founded, sending their most popular work to commercial precincts to garner prestige and cash, as they still do.

The large-scale, lasting, and influential achievements of theatrical practitioners in the twenties and the consciousness of some that 1924 was a pivotal date inspired us to call a conference at Hofstra University on 3, 4, and 5 November 1994. But we, the directors of the conference, knew well enough that art did not overpower the flourishing theatre of the twenties. Glitter and glitz, always an accompaniment of the theatre, and the newly developing musical comedy, with an astonishing array of composers and lyricists, kept bouncing along. No theatre conference of the twenties could afford to bypass those. And so the conference in its attempt to be comprehensive came to be called Art, Glitter, and Glitz.

But as we thought more about the theatre of the period, we became aware of another of its aspects, that its practitioners and its subject matter spanned a diverse spectrum. New York City itself contained a various population, as Elmer Rice indicated in his 1929 Street Scene where he showed a tenement inhabited by people of several European national extractions. Ann Douglas, recently writing of "mongrel" Manhattan in the twenties, reminded her readers of another way of New York's cross-pollination, that which derived from the Black community in Harlem.[2] But beyond the subject matter provided by a hugely mixed population, the writers, producers, designers, and directors came from widely scattered parts of the United States and from backgrounds different from each other. Eugene O'Neill, from Connecticut of a theatrical family, spent part of his early manhood seafaring. Sidney Howard, from California of an upper middle class family, became an ace pilot in World War I. Maxwell Anderson, from a midwestern farm family, wrote for a newspaper and aspired to be a poet. Robert Edmond Jones, from rocky New England and Harvard, studied under Reinhardt in Germany. Lawrence Langner, a major force in the Theatre Guild, was not American at all; born in England, he became and remained all of his life a successful patents attorney while carrying a full load at the Guild. Helen Hayes, born in Washington, D.C., spent virtually all of her life in the theatre.

It is such variousness that suggested the subtitle for our conference: The Theatre of the 1920s Celebrates American Diversity.

Of course, no call for a conference knows what the turn-out will be. We were surprised by two things: the number of responses and their diversity. We did not realize the amount of research that was proceeding on the theatre in the twenties, especially by young people, and we did not realize that the subject matter crossed an even wider spectrum than we at first thought it did. While we had hoped to receive work on African American theatrical activity, we did not expect so wide and so unusual a range of material as, for example, a paper on the controversy among African American theatre critics in the twenties, and one on the indomitable San Francisco bellhop turned playwright, Garland Anderson, and one on significance of the drama program at Howard University. Another surprise was the essay on Chinese dramatists whose plays though unacted were at least published.

This volume is devoted to those persons and groups who did not usually draw the attention of numerous playgoers. Yet these individuals and organizations were important because their activities often occurred in barely visible pockets of America or in barely visible corners of the American psyche. These

Photo 1. George Kelly, *The Show-Off.* Playhouse Theatre, 5 February 1924. Used by permission of the Billy Rose Theatre Collection, The New York Public Library for the Performing Arts, Astor, Lenox and Tilden Foundations.

Photo 2. Maxwell Anderson and Laurence Stallings, *What Price Glory?* Plymouth Theatre, 5 September 1924. Used by permission of the Billy Rose Theatre Collection, The New York Public Library for the Performing Arts, Astor, Lenox and Tilden Foundations.

Photo 3. Eugene O'Neill, *Desire Under the Elms*. Greenwich Village Theatre, 11 November 1924. Used by permission of the Billy Rose Theatre Collection, The New York Public Library for the Performing Arts, Astor, Lenox and Tilden Foundations.

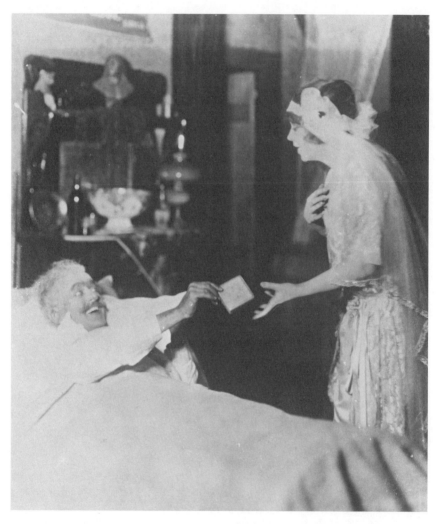

Photo 4. Sidney Howard, *They Knew What They Wanted*. Garrick Theatre, 24 November 1924. Used by permission of the Billy Rose Theatre Collection, The New York Public Library for the Performing Arts, Astor, Lenox and Tilden Foundations.

sometimes obscure productions in comparatively obscure places meant theatre for these audiences. Those who went to Fourteenth Street in Manhattan to see the Civic Repertory Theatre, not so obscure in either profile or location but certainly without the glitter of Broadway or the glamour of its audiences, seemed to have remembered the experience all of their lives. African American productions in various parts of the United States kept theatre alive for its audiences in Harlem and elsewhere. This work helps give us a complete picture of theatrical activity in the twenties. But more important, they help us to understand why, as the Broadway theatre shrank, little flare-ups of serious theatre burst out in a small Greenwich Village theatre or in a church basement in what is now called the East Village; or in this or that college campus in any part of the United States, midwest or southeast; or in an auditorium in a northwestern city or one in a small town. These eventually became a conflagration of activity in the eighties and nineties and are now the chief source of serious drama on Broadway. This is not a direct result of the off-beat voices of the twenties, but without these voices remembered, the rich vein of talent that is now being tapped throughout the United States may never have been developed in all its diverse and splendid forms. For what knowledgeable person can see a modern stage set without thinking of the cry for the New Stagecraft in the twenties; or hear August Wilson calling for an exclusively Black theatre without thinking of the arguments about the theatre during the Harlem Renaissance; or listen to discussion of feminist drama without thinking of Susan Glaspell or Sophie Treadwell. It is such ancestors of current work as these that this volume hopes to illuminate and celebrate.

EXPERIMENTERS, REBELS, AND DISPARATE VOICES

The accounts of discordant voices—that is, those which differed from those most often heard—show them to possess a variety that validates the conference's subtitle.

Among the most clangorous of the discordant voices was that of John Howard Lawson, represented by three chapters here and a fourth in Part II, where Anne Fletcher discusses the work of designer Mordecai Gorelik, who created the sets for most of Lawson's dramas of the twenties. Beverle Bloch concentrates on the most prominent of Lawson's dramas in that decade, *Processional*, while John D. Shout and Michael C. O'Neill take different views of Lawson's career.

Robert Edmond Jones was an experimenter of a different sort, shifting in the mid-twenties from the role of stage designer to that of director of Provincetown Players productions. Jane T. Peterson assesses his efforts at achieving a "poetic, total theatre."

Perhaps the aspect of the theatre of the twenties that has been most ignored is the contributions of African Americans, and as Ann Douglas has demonstrated, much more remains to be done. In a very small way we have tried to compensate for the lack by including five chapters directly pertaining to black theatrical activity.

Two chapters are by Freda Scott Giles. In one she details the rise and fall of the production of *Harlem*, a play by a black man and a white man. In "Disparate Voices: African American Theatre Critics of the 1920s," from which we have filched part of the title of this section, she recounts the story, virtually unknown until now, of the crosscurrents of African American theatrical criticism.

Alan Kreizenbeck offers the astonishing biography of Garland Anderson who, when only a bellhop in a San Francisco hotel, determined to, and succeeded in, getting his play, *Appearances*, on Broadway. He also made sure that it was presented in London. In a more comprehensive chapter about African American contributions to the theatre, Jeanne-Marie A. Miller discusses early serious African American plays on Broadway. Finally, Scott Zaluda explores the role of theatre and drama in a community, as exemplified by the drama program at Howard University.

Comparatively few papers came into the conference on another subject that has been insufficiently treated, women in the theatre. We tried to compensate for that lack in part by an exhibition about some of the prominent young actresses of the period: Katharine Cornell, Clare Eames, Lynn Fontanne, Helen Hayes, Eva Le Gallienne, and Pauline Lord.

Estelle Aden presents a chapter on Eva Le Gallienne's courageous founding and leadership of the Civic Repertory Theatre, one of the great art theatres of the decade, which folded in the Great Depression.

Only two women dramatists are represented in this volume: Sophie Treadwell and Susan Glaspell. Perhaps because of the recent admired productions of *Machinal* in this country and in England, Sophie Treadwell is apparently receiving feverish attention. Kornelia Tancheva counters the usual feminist readings of *Machinal* by insisting that the play's success at its original production came about precisely because it was not understood as feminist, and it is our currently anachronistic perspective that makes us see it as such. Jerry Dickey discusses an important and unusual summer in the life of Sophie Treadwell.

Susan Glaspell, a founder of the Provincetown Players, should be receiving a good deal of research and criticism. Steven Frank in his chapter illuminatingly compares her obscure but magnetic drama, *The Verge*, with the motion picture *The Cabinet of Dr. Caligari*. At the conference there was a reading of the Glaspell drama, which suggested that if this and her other plays are not produced, they should at least be studied.

"Aliens Then and Now" perhaps should be the heading for the next group. Beverlee Bronson Smith tells us how aliens were kept in that position on the stage in "They Knew What They Wanted: American Theatre's Use of Nonverbal Communication Codes to Marginalize Non-Native Characters in the 1920s." Dave Williams, in his chapter about plays in English by and about Chinese appearing in the little-known magazine *Poet Lore*, demonstrates that they showed the viewpoints of the dominant white Anglo Saxons of this country.

THEATRE AND SET DESIGN

The three chapters in this section concern a set designer, a producer of a major theatrical exhibition, and the beginnings of twentieth-century theatrical architecture.

We have already come across Mordecai Gorelik's work in the discussions of John Howard Lawson's dramas. Anne Fletcher explains why Gorelik, an immensely talented set designer, is not as well known today as such contemporaries as Robert Edmond Jones, Norman Bel Geddes, or Aline Bernstein.

Even less known today is Jane Heap, editor of the *Little Review* and a "'lesbian modernist' who helped shape this century's concepts of modernist art, literature, and performance." In his chapter John Bell tells of her effort to present the pivotal International Theatre Exposition of 1926.

William F. Condee introduces us to the work of the writers and architects who helped shape the new theatres of the twentieth century. Mainly unsuccessful in their efforts to alter the design of theatres in their time, they were nevertheless influential in the period since World War II.

In this volume a good deal of writing appears on the great array of the art, glitter, and glitz in the theatre of the twenties. The chapters show the immense variety and sometimes depth of the scholarly work being done, but much more research and critical analysis remains to be done. We notice that only three chapters, all excellent, on little-known subjects, are included in the final section. But large areas in the field continue to be unexplored. Robert Edmond Jones has here received a fair amount of attention, but the designers mentioned earlier as well as such others as Lee Simonson and Jo Mielziner also deserve investigation. The new art of direction arising in the United States in the twenties also requires research and thought. Some of the major dramatists of the twenties—Susan Glaspell and Sidney Howard, for example—should be brought out from under the shadow of Eugene O'Neill, and such a beginner as S. N. Behrman from the late part of the decade requires analysis. We hope that this book, a modest attempt to bring together some of the current investigation on the theatre of the twenties, will stimulate other such collections.

NOTES

1. The four plays to which Sidney Howard alludes are certainly *What Price Glory?* by Maxwell Anderson and Lawrence Stallings and undoubtedly *The Show-Off* by George Kelly, *Desire Under the Elms*, by Eugene O'Neill, and his own *They Knew What They Wanted*. See Photos 1-4. Emphases in the quote are Howard's.

2. Ann Douglas, *Terrible Honesty: Mongrel Manhattan in the 1920s* (New York: Farrar, Straus, Giroux, 1995). The subtitle of Douglas's book refers to the significant interplay of black and white culture which she explores at some length. Of course, she uses mongrel ironically.

Part I:

Experimenters, Rebels, and Disparate Voices

1

Searching for "The Big American Play": The Theatre Guild Produces John Howard Lawson's *Processional*

Beverle Bloch

From its inception the Theatre Guild, America's premiere art theatre, elected to produce a majority of plays by European dramatists. In the guild's formative years, this policy was not questioned. However, by the mid–twenties, the guild's scanty production record of American plays was beginning to attract negative comment. An example of this sentiment can be found in an article titled "American Playwrights Not Welcome Here?" published in 1923.[1] In it Walter Prichard Eaton noted that out of twenty-five plays produced by the Theatre Guild in its first five seasons, only four had been by American dramatists.

Eaton's article was symptomatic of a new interest in native American drama. By the mid-twenties, theatregoers had come to accept the burgeoning experimental drama offered by the Theatre Guild and other art theatres, but they were weary of European dominance. Barrett Clark, writing for *The Drama* in November 1924, gives voice to these sentiments:

On my return to America last winter from a two year's stay in France and Germany, I was ready to be convinced of what I was practically certain, namely that New York was the most important theatrical center in the world. . . . A glance at the papers on the day of my arrival was enough to show me that our theatrical capital was producing more and better plays than any two European cities.[2]

Clark's attitude reflected America's new, post–World War I image of itself. The war had decimated Europe, but the United States was now on its way toward becoming a world power. As the United States took its first steps toward its new position in the world, growing interest in self-definition began to manifest itself in publications concerned with American theatre. According to Oliver M. Sayler, the theatre had ceased to be "a harmless adjunct to life, a game played according to traditional rules," and had become instead "the most provocative of the arts."[3] In an article titled "Our Anniversary, 1907–1924," James O'Donnell Bennett, writing for *The Drama*, noted: "Most of us date back to the time when the stage was the nation's entertainment. We have come into a time when it is more and more valiantly becoming the nation's heart-searcher and mind dis-turber."[4]

Sensing a growing interest, theatrical producers began to look for the "Big American Play." When four Broadway producers were asked to talk about the kinds of plays they wanted to produce, in 1924, only one of the men mentioned commercial concerns. Two of the producers said they wanted to produce Ameri-can plays by American authors about American life, and the fourth, Lawrence Langner of the Theatre Guild, used his allotted space to defend the Theatre Guild's policy of refusing to produce American plays that were not up to their standards.[5]

Langner's response was the second time the guild's position vis-à-vis American dramatists had been printed in *Theatre Magazine* that year. The Janu-ary issue of the magazine had carried an article by Theresa Helburn, titled "Our Door Is on the Latch."[6] In it Helburn responded to the Eaton article, stressing the guild's interest in finding plays by American playwrights that were of suffi-cient quality to be produced. Perhaps the public debate over the guild's policy toward American dramatists had some influence on the guild board's decision to produce Sidney Howard's *They Knew What They Wanted* after it had been turned down by twelve other producers. The Howard play was scheduled for the second slot of the 1924–1925 season. A similar influence may have been operat-ing when they chose the third offering of the season, *Processional*, by John Howard Lawson. It is easy to imagine that the guild board members, tiring of being called "Un-American," responded positively when they received a copy of Lawson's play, subtitled "A Jazz Symphony of American Life." However the decision was actually made, it is certain that the Theatre Guild optioned *Proces-sional*, scheduling it for a January opening in 1925. A letter from Helburn to her colleague Lawrence Langner, dated 7 November 1924, notes: "We are going to do *Processional* next though Maurice [Wertheim] is somewhat skeptical about it. The rest of us are willing to take the chance."[7]

Processional takes place on the Fourth of July, during a mining strike. The basic events of the play revolve around protagonist "Dynamite Jim" Flimmins, a hard-drinking, sexually aggressive coal miner. Jim escapes from jail, kills a soldier, rapes a woman, and flees to avoid capture. When Sadie, the rape victim, becomes pregnant, she is hounded by the Ku Klux Klan. The Klan catches Jim and blinds him, but he escapes. In the last act of the play Jim returns and mar-ries the pregnant Sadie, rescuing her from the Klan. As the whole town gathers to celebrate the wedding, all conflicts including the strike are miraculously set-tled, and the play ends with a celebration of hope and unity.

The basic structure of *Processional* is a movement from diversity to unity. At the end of the play, the negative energy of the rape is transformed by the wedding ceremony, the communist worker gives up Bolshevism, the strike ends, and we learn that the Klan has disbanded and former Klan members are now "loyal workmen" (211).[8] Comparable to ritual, the play represents a kind of synecdoche. If the play works, the drama on the stage is reenacted in the audi-ence and in society at large. One indicator of the ritual's power is audience in-volvement so strong that the audience joins in the procession at the end of the play. As scripted, *Processional* displays the potential to create a powerful theat-rical experience. Asking the Theatre Guild to produce it as written was quite another matter entirely.

A close examination of Lawson's stage directions reveals a kind of drama-turgy that is completely unconventional for its time. There is no curtain, and Lawson stipulates that both the stage and auditorium be brightly lit. A drop curtain, visible as the audience filters in, sets the tone of the first act. Joyously theatrical, it is precisely described in Lawson's stage directions:

A drop curtain like those used in the older vaudeville theatres represents a town street painted with brick buildings, signs of Central Hotel, Palace Movie, Quick Lunch, etc. In the center of the curtain is the door of Cohen's General Store, with show window painted on the curtain. The tone is that of the usual vaudeville drop, except that it is more startlingly crude, vigorous, in color contrast, blaringly Ameri-can. (3)

As the stage directions indicate, the setting is two-dimensional with no attempt at illusion. A painted show window, obviously fake, adjoins a practical door and window. The contrast between the two will be heightened every time a char-acter uses the practical scenery, calling attention to the theatricality of the play and reminding the audience that they are in a theatre. There is no obvious be-ginning to the play, and no concrete division between the audience and the ac-tors. The first character to enter does so through the audience, and Lawson makes use of entrances through the aisles of the theatre throughout the course of the play.

Particularly effective is Lawson's use of the "jazz miners," nine ethnically differentiated characters who make their first entrance through the audience, play-ing a variety of instruments and singing. Functioning both as characters in the play and as a kind of "Greek chorus," the miners go back and forth through the house, drawing the audience into the world of the play. Representing a stylistic innovation for contemporary drama of the period, the jazz miners play a major role in creating a direct relationship between the actors and audience. The play ends with blind Jim and pregnant Sadie center, while the jazz miners and all the other characters in the play march around them, forming a procession that leaves through the audience, "disappearing at the rear of the theatre" (218).

Although the guild would later stress the experimental nature of the offer-ing, preproduction time allotted for *Processional* was one month, the same amount of time allotted to all plays produced by the guild. The large cast in-cluded actors from a wide variety of backgrounds, ranging from light opera and musical comedy to drama. Notable in the cast were George Abbott, Sanford Meisner, and Lee Strasberg. Lawson was an integral part of the production team, which included Director Philip Moeller, Executive Director Theresa Helburn, and scene designer Mordecai Gorelik, who designed both sets and costumes.

Gorelik's inclusion on the team was a last-minute decision and a lucky break for Lawson. Gorelik had no problem understanding what Lawson meant by burlesque technique, as he had designed sets for burlesque "in the sewing room of a supply house in Tin Pan Alley."[9] In addition, Gorelik shared Law-son's dislike of realistic staging with its "unwieldy, expensive, three dimen-sional scenery."[10] Although Theatre Guild board member Lee Simonson was the guild's first choice to design *Processional*, he was ill and Theresa Helburn ac-cepted Gorelik's designs. In *Calendar of Commitment*, Lawson's unpublished autobiography, Lawson notes that Gorelik's sketches caught the cartoon spirit of the play, even anticipating the actual blocking of the scenes.[11] Unfortunately, Lawson's dealings with Moeller and the rest of the guild board were much less harmonious.

From the beginning of the rehearsal period, Lawson found himself embroiled in a controversy over his choice of style. According to his comments in his autobiography, Lawson believed that direct communication between the actors and the audience was the key to achieving the strong, emotional, audience response that he sought. As a result, he was committed to staging *Processional* in a nonillusionist style, which would allow for this type of interaction. "I had planned the play so that a great deal of the action takes place in the auditorium, as well as on the stage. This concept of theatrical communication was the driving force of the play."[12] Although the guild board had experience with experimental staging, they were nonplussed by Lawson's desire to experiment with the very nature of the actor/audience relationship. In theory, the guild board disagreed with Lawson's plan to "have the actors confront the audience," because they considered this a "rape of the spectators."[13] They also had more practical objections. As written, *Processional* begins with a newsboy selling his papers in the audience. Soon afterward, the Miner's Jazz Band enters through the audience doors, marching down the aisles to the stage. The guild board was unanimous in rejecting this action because "latecomers would get entangled with the actors in the aisles."[14] When Lawson pointed out that the use of the aisles set a tone for the whole play and was especially related to the procession at the end "when the whole cast follows the jazz band through the audience and into the lobby, apparently on their way to the street," the guild board solved the problem by rejecting Lawson's ending because "it would interfere with commuters hurrying to catch the last suburban trains."[15]

To clarify his stylistic intentions, Lawson took Executive Director Helburn to a performance of Minsky's Burlesque to show her an example of nonillusionistic theatre utilizing direct interaction between the performers and the audience. Helburn enjoyed the burlesque show and considered Lawson's "running commentary in extremely highbrow terms" as part of the fun.[16] Though Helburn expressed doubt that the style of the burlesque show had any relevance to the guild production, she was the one primarily responsible for engineering a stylistic compromise. The miner's band would enter from the orchestra pit, using steps that led from the pit to the stage. In addition, the acting area was slightly extended into the audience.[17]

Looking back at the production, Lawson credited Gorelik's scenic investiture with helping to unify the acting style and make it less naturalistic. As written and realized, the first and second acts used no props or furniture. There was nothing for the actors to sit on or lean against. An actor who attempted to behave as if the setting were real would constantly bump into the obviously false drops. Thus, the most "natural" position for the actors during the production was to face the audience with their backs to the drops. In this sense, Gorelik's settings did amplify the inherent theatricality of Lawson's script.

One last stylistic compromise involved the use of the Miner's Jazz Band. The guild board complained that the actors in the band were not musicians, and they played atrociously.[18] When Lawson refused to have the music played by real jazz musicians and mimed by the actors, the guild board insisted on hiring real jazz musicians to play before and after the production, and between the acts, while the actors continued to furnish the music during the play. This last change might seem minor, but it was one more dilution of the style Lawson was trying to create—a style that depended on lessening the separation between the actor and the audience. The addition of "sweet jazz" at the beginning and end of the production and between the acts added one more layer of separation. Thus, the compromises engineered by the guild board served to dilute the effect of Lawson's nonillusionistic staging, creating a hybrid somewhere between nonillusion and illusion. Despite its toned down theatricalism, *Processional* caused an incredible stir. An excerpt from an article by John Dos Passos, written in May 1925, gives an idea of the production's effect:

So accustomed are we to the conventions of the so called realistic drama, in which the semblance of actuality is carefully maintained by the use of minutely ordered scenery, and action that at least seems plausible, that when the actors scrambled out of the orchestra pit at the opening of John Howard Lawson's *Processional* to the strains of a raucous jazz band, the audience fairly gasped, and some of them at least remained holding onto the edges of their seats as the play whizzed round various theatrical curves, until the end of the performance.[19]

Although early reviews seemed to indicate a unified negative response from the audience, critical response was arrayed over a wider spectrum. Heywood Broun found the new piece "wholly engrossing, extraordinarily poignant, and altogether one of the finest things which has yet come out of the native theatre."[20] Stark Young wrote, "As a drama it throws off astonishing suggestions of living stuff; it is full of strong, wounded, indomitable life. However unequal it may be, it is always creative and streaked with genius."[21] Other reviews found less to recommend. In an article titled, "'Processional' Is a Discordant Jumble," Burns Mantle remarked: "They have gone back to the jumble drama at the Theatre Guild. And this 'Processional' is the weirdest jumble of them all. . . . It is wild and discordant. It is rough and primitive. It is satire and muttered raving. It is life out of focus, like Caligari's dream."[22] From Alan Dale of the *American* came the pronouncement, "The only thing in its favor was that you could come when you pleased, leave when you pleased and miss nothing."[23] *Post* reviewer John Anderson added, "[Lawson] had nothing to say. Jazz had nothing to say, and both of them said it violently for two-and-a-half hours."[24] Other reviewers commended the guild for producing the play, while warning potential audience members to stay away.

Newspapers across the nation reprinted the first night reviews, stressing the controversial nature of the offering. Often the reviews were reprinted verbatim, but enterprising editors revised the titles, further enhancing the play's reputation. Burns Mantle's review was printed in the *Cleveland Ohio News* retitled "Guild Trots out Its Padded Cell Play."[25] The same review in the *Denver Post* bore the headline, "Life out of Focus Is Shown in Latest Production That Came from Diseased Brain."[26] A reporter from the *New York Telegram* compared the reception of *Processional* to the riot that greeted Synge's *Playboy of the Western World*,[27] while an article in the *St. Paul Minnesota Pioneer Press News* summed up the controversy with the following: "The Theatre Guild's new *Processional* reaches a high place as the most irritating and the most questioned, discussed and defended of all plays."[28]

Processional's merits were debated in newspapers all over the country, as those who had seen the offering made their views known. Noting that his favorable review of *Processional* had garnered a huge negative response, Gilbert Gabriel devoted a follow-up column to his readers' comments concluding, "There is hope for a play which drives grown men to letter writing."[29] And Carlton Miles noted, in an article published in the *Minneapolis Journal*, that *Processional* was quickly becoming "the play all America loved to argue about."[30]

As the controversy escalated, the Theatre Guild scheduled an open forum at the Klaw Theatre on a Sunday afternoon, inviting Dorothy Parker, Fannie Hurst, and Elmer Rice to defend the play, while Robert Lytell of the *New Republic* and John Anderson of the *New York Post* led the attack against it. On the afternoon of the debate, every seat was quickly filled, and thousands had to be turned away.[31] Some interested parties who could not get in continued the debate on the sidewalk outside the theatre. The 25 February edition of the guild bulletin carried an apology to those subscribers who came too late to get seats, along with this description of the forum:

The discussion of *Processional* was a most stimulating event. We wish it could have been broadcast to all our members who were not quite sure what the play signified. They would have heard Mr. John Anderson of the Post, attack it with a vigor which was only equalled by the vehemence with which Mr. Elmer Rice, author of *The Adding Machine* defended it. . . . And there were violent speeches from the balcony; volleys of applause for those who hailed the play as the beginning of a new American art form, and a somewhat fainter measure for those who confessed that they did not know what it was all about. All in all, it was a thrilling experience for the Guild. A play which can stir up such a volume of feeling, both for and against, must surely be entitled to a hearing.[32]

When *Processional* ended its six-week run at the Garrick Theatre, the guild moved the production to a Broadway house, the Comedy Theatre, for a week. Newspaper articles, based on guild publicity, stressed the idea that Broadway audiences were "finding new places to laugh," and "responding to the entertainment value of the play."[33] In addition, several critics viewed the show for a second time and found that it had improved. An item in Franklin P. Adams's column in the *New York World* proclaimed, "Feb. 28. To the theatre, again to see 'Processional,' and liked it far better now, it being better acted than on its first night, and the riotousness and beauty of it much more sharply outlined."[34] Alexander Woollcott did a complete turnaround, urging his readers to see *Processional* before it closed. Noting that his early negative assessment had changed, he confessed:

I did not have the clairvoyance to see that out of the faltering stumbling muddle of unpreparedness which marked the first performances there would emerge a sardonic comedy which, however gauche and brash and at times cheap, still contains a rare and exhilarating quality of beauty and high excitement . . . the curious pace and idiom of the play (at first caught by only two of the company, June Walker and Donald MacDonald) has since spread by infection to most of the others in the troupe.[35]

Favorable publicity, word of mouth, and the revised critiques combined to attract large audiences so that the last three performances played to standing room crowds while many more potential audience members had to be turned away.[36] Although the production had to leave the Comedy after one week, another theatre was found to continue the run. In all, *Processional* played ninety-four performances, and by the time it closed, new voices had been added to the discussion of *Processional*'s merits with a resulting change of focus regarding relevant criteria.

Supporters of the play, including Elmer Rice, Sherwood Anderson, John Dos Passos, and Thornton Wilder, hailed *Processional* as a new American art form, claiming that Lawson's merger of form, content, and dramaturgy was innovative and significant. Anderson also praised Lawson's nonillusionistic dramaturgy which he compared to the dramaturgy of Eugene O'Neill:

Surely the plays of Mr. Eugene O'Neill and remarkable play, "Processional," by Mr. Lawson are great steps toward breaking down the toppling wall between the audience and the players on the stage. One begins to really feel the reactions of this new kind of play come up out of the mass of people sitting in the theatre and watching the play. The imaginations of the people in the audience are released. Life comes into this kind of theatre and the old dead wall between the players is swept away.[37]

In an article for *Vanity Fair* John Dos Passos concurred, stressing the importance of *Processional*'s use of nonillusionistic dramaturgy in a serious play:

Processional is the first American play in our generation in which the convention of the invisible fourth wall has been frankly and definitely abandoned. In other plays, the subterfuge of a dream has been used to placate the critics whenever the author felt he needed to be positively theatrical. . . . Meanwhile burlesque, musical comedy, and vaudeville have preserved, but more or less flippantly, the real manners and modes of the theatre. In *Processional* these are employed with passionate seriousness. The actors are actors, you feel the boards of the stage in every line, events take place against painted scenery, behind footlights, in the theatre. There is no attempt to convince the audience that, by some extraordinary series of coincidences, they have strayed into a West Virginia mining town in the middle of an industrial war. They are in a theatre seeing a show.[38]

By the end of the play's run, the overall assessment of the production was positive, and each of the collaborators benefited from their participation. For Lawson, it was a chance to have his play produced by a theatre with a production capacity beyond that of any experimental or avant-garde theatre. It also gave him a chance to collaborate with designer Mordecai Gorelik, the beginning of a long association which would eventually lead both Lawson and Gorelik to the Group Theatre. The Theatre Guild received an extraordinary amount of favorable publicity and was able to document its support for American playwriting. Although the Theatre Guild may not have been the ideal producer for Lawson's purposes, it is doubtful that Lawson could have found the kind of support he needed at any other theatre in the United States at that time.

NOTES

1. Walter Prichard Eaton, "American Playwrights Not Welcome Here?" *Theatre Magazine* October 1923: 9.

2. Barrett Clark, "The Broadway Season Begins in Earnest," *The Drama* November 1924: 28.

3. Oliver M. Sayler, *Our American Theatre* (New York: Brentano's, 1923) 1.

4. James O'Donnell Bennett, "Our Anniversary, 1907–1924," *The Drama* November 1924: 27.

5. Lawrence Langner, "What We Are Looking For," *Theatre Magazine* March 1924: 22.

6. Theresa Helburn, "Our Door Is on the Latch," *Theatre Magazine* January 1924: 56.

7. Theresa Helburn, Helburn Correspondence File, Theatre Guild Archives, Yale University, New Haven.

8. John Howard Lawson, *Processional* (New York: Thomas Seltzer, 1925). Page references appear in the text.

9. Mordecai Gorelik, "Up from Burlesque," *New York Evening Post* 8 October 1922: 5.

10. Mordecai Gorelik, "On Processional," *New York World* 8 February 1925: 9.

11. John Howard Lawson, *Calendar of Commitment*, Box 100, Folder 4, ts., John Howard Lawson Papers, Southern Illinois University, Carbondale, 108.

12. John Howard Lawson, *Rebellion in the Twenties*, Box 99, Folder 13, ts., Early Draft, John Howard Lawson Papers, Southern Illinois University, Carbondale, 224A.

13. Lawson, *Rebellion* 225.

14. Lawson, *Calendar* 107.

15. Lawson, *Calendar* 107.

16. Theresa Helburn, *A Wayward Quest* (Boston: Little, Brown, 1960) 244.

17. Lawson, *Rebellion* 247.

18. Lawson, *Rebellion* 247.

19. John Dos Passos, "Is the Realistic Theatre Obsolete?" *Vanity Fair* May 1925: 114.

20. Heywood Broun, "The New Play," *New York World* 13 January 1925, Package #1, John Howard Lawson Papers, Southern Illinois University, Carbondale.

21. Bernard Beckerman and Howard Siegman, eds., *Selected Reviews from the New York Times 1920–1970* (New York: Arno, 1970) 52.

22. Burns Mantle, "'Processional' Is a Discordant Jumble," *Daily News* 13 January 1925: 16.

23. Alan Dale, "'Processional' Presented by Guild," *American* 13 January 1925: 16.

24. John Anderson, "The Play," *New York Post* 17 January 1925, Package #1, John Howard Lawson Papers, Southern Illinois University, Carbondale.

25. Burns Mantle, "Guild Trots out Its Padded Cell Play," *Cleveland Ohio News* 18 January 1925, Pressbook, Theatre Guild Archives, Yale University, New Haven.

26. Burns Mantle, "Life out of Focus Is Shown in Latest Production That Came from Diseased Brain," *Denver Post*, n.d., Pressbook, Theatre Guild Archives, Yale University, New Haven.

27. Gilbert Gabriel, "Rhapsody in Red: John Howard Lawson's 'Processional' Produced by the Theatre Guild," *New York Telegram* 13 January 1925: 2.

28. "Theatre Guild Produces Wild 'Processional': Queer Drama of Strike and Jazz in Coal Mining Town," *St. Paul Minnesota Pioneer Press News* 18 January 1925, Pressbook, Theatre Guild Archives, Yale University, New Haven.

29. Gilbert Gabriel, "Disturbing the Public," *New York Telegram* 25 January 1925, Package #1, John Howard Lawson Papers, Southern Illinois University, Carbondale.

30. Carlton Miles, *Minneapolis Journal* 6 February 1925, Pressbook, Theatre Guild Archives, Yale University, New Haven.

31. "Firm Friends and Fiery Foes of Processional Fight It Out," *New York World* 30 January 1925, Package #1, John Howard Lawson Papers, Southern Illinois University, Carbondale.

32. *Guild Bulletin*. 25 February 1925: 2, Pressbook, Theatre Guild Archives, Yale University, New Haven.

33. "Processional Seeks New Houses to Conquer," *New York Telegram* 2 March 1925, Package #1, John Howard Lawson Papers, Southern Illinois University, Carbondale.

34. Franklin P. Adams, "The Conning Tower: The Diary of Our Own Samuel Pepys," *New York World* Package #1, John Howard Lawson Papers, Southern Illinois University, Carbondale.

35. Alexander Woollcott, "A Belated Cheer for 'Processional,'" *Sun* 26 February 1925: 22.

36. "Processional Seeks New Houses to Conquer."

37. Sherwood Anderson, "A Drama Convert Gives Reason," *New York World* 15 February 1925, Package #1, John Howard Lawson Papers, Southern Illinois University, Carbondale.

38. Dos Passos, "Is the Realistic Theatre Obsolete?"

2

The Idiosyncratic Theatre of
John Howard Lawson

John D. Shout

How much do any of us remember about John Howard Lawson? How much did we ever know? As a Marxist playwright in the 1930s, he would come up with *Success Story, The Pure in Heart*, and *Gentlewoman*, doctrinaire works, more or less, though not forthright enough to please the purists of the Left. These plays would also receive a tepid response from the mainstream press, leading to a nasty exchange between dramatist and critics that diverted readers for a few weeks in 1934. Two years after this, Lawson would turn out *Theory and Technique of Playwriting*, a standard text on the subject that hung on into the 1960s. The following year he would reinstate himself with the Left through *Marching Song*, a radical drama that in 1937 looked unfortunately anachronistic (though paradoxically it would have proved very timely a few months later with the General Motors strikes in the news); it would prove the swan song of the idealistically driven Theatre Union. Lawson periodically shifted to Hollywood and would contribute screenplays for the likes of *Algiers, Counter-Attack*, and *Action in the North Atlantic*. Refusing to cringe in front of the House Un-American Activities Committee (HUAC), he would take the First rather than the Fifth Amendment and would do time as one of the newly dubbed Hollywood Ten. And ultimately Lawson would wind up a Hollywood adjunct, advising would-be filmmakers to get seriously involved in game shows.

Lawson's output in the 1920s, however, was considerable, and in the decade in which the American theatre was being shifted in a new direction with every other opening, his influence may well have been pervasive. There were five Lawson plays on professional stages between 1923 and 1928, and even if none of the five is now part of whatever canon there is for American drama, they startled audiences with surprises and dissonances that would in time become standard features of theatre grammar. Those who found the stage an exciting milieu in those years were as likely to talk up Lawson as they were Rice or O'Neill. They would, some of them, persist in their enthusiasm, leading a frustrated Robert Garland in 1934 to label Lawson, rather snidely, "America's most promising playwright. Day after day, week after week, month after month, year after year he keeps on promising."[1] But once the promise was visible and exciting.

Roger Bloomer was Lawson's breakthrough, a commercial failure in its midtown production by the Equity Players in March of 1923 but much better received a few weeks later when offered at the Greenwich Village Theatre, which had at least some grasp at this startling sort of drama. When published, *Roger Bloomer* would include a foreword in which John Dos Passos, Lawson's one-time army buddy and a sometime collaborator, would insist that "there *is* going to be a theater in America" if only because the pace will require "other safety valves than baseball and the movies and the Ku Klux Klan" (v).[2] *Roger Bloomer* may seem an odd sort of "safety valve," but it is purely American and answers to the complaint, later in the foreword, that "the New York theater to-day has no more to do with the daily existence of the average New Yorker . . . than it has with the pigtail of the living God at Lhasa" (viii).

Critics much later would debate whether *The Hairy Ape* (a year earlier), *Roger Bloomer*, or *The Adding Machine* (two weeks later) ought to be acclaimed as the first American play entirely "in the new mode." The value of such a title is dubious since pure expressionism was on its way to obsolescence, but expressionism may not be *Roger Bloomer*'s exact descriptor anyway. The first act provides a rather astute caricature of what drives Roger to the breaking point: a stultified existence of rigid propriety in aspiring middle-class America. If Lawson intends to be the American Georg Kaiser (or perhaps, given Roger's half-articulated longings for a sexual ideal, its Wedekind), his milieu is that of Sinclair Lewis and Sherwood Anderson. Roger's nemesis is a father who finds it "disagreeable" that his son is "different from other people." Roger's vague ambition to possess women's souls sets him up as a pretty confused guy, but the play implies that 1920s America has made him that way.

So in act 1 we get a detailed, hyper-realistic look at Roger's home life in Excelsior, Iowa: the empty conversations over dinner (with virtually identical meals every evening), the upwardly mobile father who longs to send his son to "Yale College," the dead-end lives of the sales staff at Everett Bloomer's department store, the supposed role-model Yalie, Eugene, whose aspirations are limited to succeeding with the right crowd, and so on—all of it providing plenty of justification for what Dos Passos termed "the commonest American theme—a boy running away from home to go to the Big City" (vi).

The remaining two acts present the various disillusionments of Roger's New York experiment, and here Lawson finds the techniques of the European expressionists more useful. A business office, "where they make the money," includes clerks who "all move in unison like wax-works throughout the scene, turn over papers, pick up telephones, rise and walk with the appearance of organized haste, giving impression of choral movement" (105). The boss, Mr. Ramsey, who refuses to hire Roger because he doesn't fit in with the "gigantic exchange of energies" that is Wall Street, is given to spouting vast sums of foreign currencies at random over his Dictaphone. At the depth of his misfortunes, Roger identifies with pitiless, impersonal New York, and in a long soliloquy he tells the city all about it: "I am yours, oh city of slaves . . . I am one of the millions, servants of death and time, hungry, moaning for bread" (117).

Roger's partner in despondency is Louise Chamberlain, likewise an escapee from Excelsior and no happier in New York than Roger; but preoccupied with her living standard, she steals some bonds and then, pursued amorously first by her boss and then by Roger's erstwhile chum Eugene, she becomes convinced of her unworthiness and commits suicide. In lines very reminiscent of Wedekind, she mutters, "All a joke anyway: I'm caught in a net, more subtle than Law, wider than Time, that's all there is to this pure love stuff! What are we anyway? Just two children caught by this terrible Sex joke, that's all there is" (181).

Roger is improbably imprisoned as a material witness in Louise's death, a plot turn that allows the play to resolve in a nightmare in which Lawson at last employs his full arsenal of expressionistic techniques. All of the figures in Roger's life writhe or shimmy past him with threats or cynical rejections until the spirit of Louise rises from her bier to protect Roger and to admonish him: "In yourself you must find the secret" (224).

In *Theory and Technique of Playwriting* Lawson remarks that expressionism "reflects the confusion of a rebellion without a defined objective,"[3] a confusion readily apparent in Roger himself and implicit in the structure and widely varied techniques in his play. Some of the time his distress is an obvious product of his booboisie environment, but his subsequent dissatisfaction with both P. B. Shelley and the *Police Gazette* as an articulation of what he is looking for in women (as well as poor Louise's inability to supply that impossible feminine ideal) can hardly be blamed on the America of Warren G. Harding. (In fact, whenever he muses on women or sex Roger sounds thirteen rather than eighteen, and the whole play seems to be about arrested development. It can't have helped the uptown production that Henry Hull, the original Roger, was fully thirty-three.)

As frustrating as this incoherence might have been to playgoers in 1923—most of whom couldn't have entered the theatre well versed in expressionistic language—in fact there is a logic to it. The judge who passes sentence on Roger orders him to "organize your ideas, young man! What use are you to Society?" (188), and Louise's spirit at the finish proclaims Roger's liberation thus: "Away, ghosts of yesterday, for the young are coming marching" (222). *Roger Bloomer* makes sense only as the inarticulate discontent of youth with their elders' demand that they organize their ideas: so of course their rebellion can't very well be coherently explained. The ending may still seem rather preposterous, but the expressionists liked to juxtapose nightmares with the loftiest optimism. Expressionism, when it goes all the way, is probably not for anyone much over twenty-five.

If you had been looking for an evening of theatre early in 1925, you might have happily settled on *Othello* with Walter Hampden, fresh from his much-acclaimed Cyrano, but if you were a reader of Robert Benchley, you would certainly have considered a Theatre Guild offering of John Howard Lawson's *Processional*. "Enough inspiration, originality, poetry and sincerity to make fifteen Othellos," pronounced Benchley, while Heywood Broun, nearly as enthusiastic, called *Processional* "one of the finest things that has come out of the native theatre." Still, Broun had to acknowledge that he had seldom seen "first nighters more mystified and annoyed." And you might also have read Winchell: "I have never seen anything so bad, which is being pretty kind to it."[4] There were very few who sat on the fence for *Processional*.

Many viewers were surprised by Lawson's willingness to bring the vitality of what later generations learned to call popular culture to the serious theatre. In his preface to the published edition Lawson would be explicit about this: "It is only in the fields of vaudeville and revue that a native craftsmanship exists.

Here at least a shining if somewhat distorted mirror is held up to our American nature. Here the national consciousness finds at least a partial reflection of itself in the mammy melody, the song and dance act and the curtain of real pearls" (vi).[5]

This invocation of the popular is evident in various ways. There is ethnic comedy—cartoon representatives of Jew, Black, and Pole of the sort that were becoming an embarrassment to the more proper theatre of the mid-1920s. There is a newspaperman who is supposed to be a journalistic version of George M. Cohan. There is a jazz band entering through the house, and, although the term *jazz* could mean practically any music that wasn't strictly European in 1925, this very American ensemble included a banjo, bassoon, accordion, and harmonica, as well as the instruments one would expect (in fact, bandleader Ben Bernie dismissed the whole show on the grounds that they didn't play very well). Mordecai Gorelik, who did the scenery, insisted that the design of the play have the open contrivances of "theatricalism" as inspired by Meyerhold but acknowledged that his own source was "cheap burlesque."[6] Affection for the low-brow, which has provided the basis for all sorts of "serious" American theatre since the 1920s, has a startling fruition here, but there is a fair question how connected it is to *Processional*'s particular story.

Processional is set in West Virginia where a miners' strike is in progress, and the protagonist is a rough-hewn working-class rebel called Dynamite Jim Flimmins. Jim is incarcerated and busts loose, finds an outlet for his passions in the seventeen-year-old flapper Sadie Cohen, and then, running afoul of the KKK as well as of mining interests, ends up blind. *Processional* is on its way to being a bona-fide didactic labor play—and would become one a decade later in Lawson's *Marching Song*. Some elements are already in place in the agit-prop caricatures of "The Man in the Silk Hat" (representing capitalist interests), and the Sheriff (who stands for hired goons). But Jim is no idealized labor martyr: his anger is too random and unfocused just as Roger Bloomer's was. If *Processional* is muddled, as it now seems to be, its very muddle might be indicative of an era when the enemies of the Left were clearly understood but its heroes were not. Dynamite Jim is all energy and libido, but he is also stuck with a puritanism (mixed with an Oedipal impulse) that turns him against his mother when she uses sex to distract his pursuers. In traditional terms Jim seems the perfect match for Sadie Cohen who is just as confused about what she wants as Jim is. The same inexplicable conscience is working here that operated in *Roger Bloomer*: and, as in the earlier play, it is mixed up with undefined resistance to the establishment. Still, the resistance is pursued with all the vitality that Lawson finds in popular entertainment of his time—with what is new. He mistrusts American standards but loves American schlock with equal intensity, which is not a bad start for lively political theatre.

The Garrick Theatre/Theatre Guild program proclaimed that "Mr. Lawson employs the various techniques of the theatre, ranging all the way from vaudeville to tragedy," and *Processional* invites the question whether such a mix is advisable. For most of the play—as would continue to be his undoing—Lawson just imposes too much plot, so that there's no time to explore the possibilities that abound once popular theatre has been allowed in. But in his fourth act he gets it right. Starting with a Klan rally bent on protecting the community's morals by punishing Sadie Cohen (who is carrying Jim's child), Lawson goes on to expose the King Kleagle who, with his hood off, turns out to be the Man in the Silk Hat. But this fearsome situation is less threatening than it sounds: the Kluxers with their illuminated crosses and American flags (burlesque gimmicks) are altogether inept and take frequent pratfalls. When the blinded Jim returns and he, Sadie, and Mrs. Flimmins are most at risk, Lawson suddenly invokes the most artificial of happy endings: the Man in the Silk Hat proclaims a strike settlement ("We want to open up the mines, make concessions, boom business, sign contracts" [211]), pardons all the strikers, disbands the Klan, and reminding us that this is Mother's Day, reads a telegram from Calvin Coolidge "stating that all men are brothers" (214). All this harmony will be cemented with Jim and Sadie's marriage, albeit with a dog rather than a marriage license. One who found this intoxicating was Thornton Wilder: "A jiggling parade is formed, the entire cast links arms and the whole house is invited to come along, God knows where."[7] Lawson was at his best when he was able to lighten up. The original Dynamite Jim was none other than George Abbott, and he may have been on target in *Mr. Abbott* to limit his comments on the production to one observation: he called his co-star, June Walker, "one of the cutest little ingenues you ever want to look at."[8]

Processional was alone among Lawson's 1920s plays in being treated to a full-scale revival—in 1937, in a Federal Theatre production. In the wake of the Depression the extravaganza felt very different, and the director, Lem Ward, offered an appropriately sober revisiting: "The play is essentially a conflict of two philosophies which were prevalent in the post-war period in the United States—idealism as against cynicism. It is the cynicism of the Mencken school in conflict with the idealism of certain Utopian labor leaders and social workers, which is represented in the clash of the characters, with each other, with their environment and with the economic and social conditions of the time."[9] An astute summary, no doubt, but also a basis for a tiresome production since there is no special insight to be found among Lawson's depictions of the conflict. This play probably just had to be let fly as the guild did in 1925. *Processional*'s original director was the imaginative Philip Moeller who had staged that other landmark of expressionism in 1923, *The Adding Machine*, and he apparently knew that in a play like this one, style was what mattered.

It is necessary to mention—but to rush quickly past—*Nirvana*, the Lawson disaster of 1926. Although he never let this misbegotten effort reach publication, we know that it brought together a variety of discontented people—unhappy for ideological, sexual, or religious reasons, or just because they said they were unhappy. Ultimately this led to the most disconsolate character being shot into space in search of a new god. Lawson, if we can believe the reviewers, was really not focusing this time.

But he managed to focus very well the next time, with the suddenly established New Playwrights League, a bunch of variously aligned or unaligned radicals who had finagled financing from the unlikely figure of Otto Kahn. They would assert their position with a manifesto—as every noncommercial theatre did then: they would be a "theater which is as drunken, as barbaric, as clangorous as our age."[10]

These were not Lawson's words—his colleague with the New Playwrights, Em Jo Basshe, wrote "The Revolt on 52nd Street"—but Lawson's *Loud Speaker*, the first offering of the group, fit the description to a T. In *Loud*

Speaker Lawson let his imagination for the possibilities of popular theatre run wild, but this time without undirected hostility. Joseph Wood Krutch, always a Lawson promoter, emphasized this in his introduction to the published edition: "What Mr. Lawson has done is to take both the mechanics and the philosophy of the revolutionary drama and to use them joyously" (ix).[11] Krutch would go on to call the play "American *commedia dell'arte*."

The satire takes off from the published epigraph, Calvin Coolidge's demand that we "look well to the hearthstone, therein all hope for America lies." The hearthstone Lawson finds useful as both a political and a domestic target. Harry U. Collins, a successful businessman, is now, inevitably, a candidate for New York State governor, hopping about with varied platitudes for each ethnic constituency and watching his home life break up as his wife embarks on spiritualist odysseys and his flapper daughter looks for thrills. Meanwhile, he is haunted by memories of a long-ago fling with a beauty pageant competitor and is terrified that the rapacious press will get hold of his past. Apparently falling to pieces, Harry gives a drunken radio appeal to the voters in which he abandons the usual boilerplate in favor of seamy bluntness: "I'm too good to be governor, I get more satisfaction out of telling the American people to go to hell" (139). This is enough to sweep Harry into office and reunite his family, at least temporarily.

None of this story is presented for more than a minute with anything like seriousness; instead Lawson assaults the audience with burlesque-style gags, many of them openly corny—Johnnie, the journalist/juvenile: "She conceived a hopeless passion for me." Clare, the world-weary flapper: "Any passion for you would be hopeless" (108). Others are snappy twits at Mencken's Boobus Americanus: "To think I thought religion could save my soul, when all I wanted was publicity!" (120). Anything with pretension is promptly leveled, again in the burlesque spirit: the feminine ideal (which had so obsessed Roger and Jim) here is a beauty queen whose banner reads "Miss New Lots Avenue." And when the young lovers, Johnnie and Clare, try to be ardent, they mess up so badly that they decide to shoot craps instead. There is political humor, certainly, with the characteristic vote-scrounging politicos presented at their most ludicrous, but, in *commedia* fashion, the laughs come first, and each of the clowns has plenty of opportunity for *lazzi*.

Mordecai Gorelik gave Lawson a varied set of platforms connected by ladders, stairways, and chutes (the latter inspired by Coney Island[12]), all of it in the Meyerhold constructivist manner, and Lawson worked them directly into his script: the platforms might be rooms in Harry's house and a second later gathering places for his various constituencies. Simultaneous staging goes on, sometimes with three platforms representing three separate plot strands at one time. Here—and elsewhere—Lawson anticipates Brecht (whom, in the sober 1930s, he would condemn as "unmarxist").[13]

For his denouement Lawson went expressionist with a dream sequence brought on by Mrs. Collins's mysterious astral lover. Harry imagines himself an impotent governor, a stooge of various power interests, and, a victim of his waning physical abilities, falling ingloriously from an unlit rostrum. Abruptly the action switches to China (calling attention to the uninhibited theatrics with Johnnie's line, "Anything's possible nowadays: look at the theatre" [182]), where Clare and Johnnie's romance is amounting to no more than Harry's ambitions. Gerald Rabkin, in *Drama and Commitment*, would have us take seriously Johnnie's vision of a "new religion," but actually the play is twitting that too and is derisory to the finish.[14]

Harry Wagstaff Gribble, who directed, had to struggle to find a style for this material, and, though he aimed at laughs (apparently), he also imposed full-scale choreography and went along with Lawson's request for "a Negro Jazz orchestra" above the stage. The mix led to confusion, even though *Loud Speaker* is Lawson's most coherent script, the one least cluttered with contradictory intentions. But the prevailing adjective among the critics once again was "muddled," and *Loud Speaker* had a very short run. For the New Playwrights, though, that was proof of their integrity.

Lawson's other New Playwrights script, *The International*, which appeared early in 1928 under his own direction, ought to have been a pinnacle achievement. He had a mixed theatricalist-constructivist scheme in mind, but this time for a global scenario: his play would leap from New York to Tibet to Paris. The subject would be *vast*—an intercontinental conflict pitting American and British oil interests against Soviet-Trotskyite ideologues. Characteristically, Lawson would demand a continuous musical score with "special emphasis on broken rhythms, machine noises and chanting blues," and, in addition, there would be a double chorus, "a combination of jazz treatment with the dignified narrative strophe and antistrophe of Greek drama" (7).[15] *The International* would be Lawson pushed to the limit, a backdrop larger than America and an arsenal of theatrics incorporating classical as well as popular culture. The sorry fact is that he couldn't handle it, and the massive production was required to conceal some pretty shallow thinking. Charles Brackett's response in the *New Yorker* was characteristic: finding the play "bewildering," he could only conclude that he had spent "three hours in one of those penitential seats."[16]

Lawson attempts to build out from young David Fitch, the son of an international oil manipulator, who, despite his worldly upbringing, is as guileless as Roger Bloomer. Determined to go his own way, David becomes a boy-hero out of the dime novels, getting entangled with revolutionaries in Tibet, the primary arena for the first half of the play before matters get altogether apocalyptic. Thereafter, Lawson tries to juggle his own radical sympathies with David's Bloomer-like Oedipal hostilities and his yearning for a feminine ideal (here an anarchist called Alise, tougher but no more divine than Louise or Sadie). This leads to an absurd impulse to define a kind of universal itch that would make everyone, regardless of class, a revolutionary. Thematic words emerge from the act 3 chorus: "We got the bad mad bad glad blues" (223), but the source, nature, and cure of those blues remain undefined.

Lawson is still a perceptive scenarist sometimes, using a simple map on a roller to create a global backdrop (though he is indebted to Erwin Piscator for this) and ingeniously employing malfunctioning cannon to evoke a spontaneous revolution. And the ironist who played a range of games in *Loud Speaker* is sometimes on target, as when the High Lama studies "an occidental treatise on Love" which turns out to be an Elinor Glyn novel. On the downside there is such a heavy-handed device as the slashing of the revolutionary Alise's palms by a Mussolini worshipper, thus providing her with instant and very obtrusive stigmata, and left-wing allusions to Sacco and Vanzetti that some middle-of-the-road supporters of the pair must have found exploitative. *The International* is not quite as incoherent as Charles Brackett thought (though Lawson's direction was apparently less than lucid), but it was ill planned, never an argument for revolution, never an explanation for revolutionary impulses, merely a panorama of global anxiety. Woollcott understood that *The International* was structured as a musical with heavy condensation to allow for numbers, except that there weren't any numbers, only more anxiety.[17]

The lesson Lawson apparently took from his twenties experiments was the necessity of being explicit in his didacticism. But that lesson did not exactly suit his temperament: *Gentlewoman* and *Success Story* are hardly confusing, but rumbling among their protagonists' speeches is still a discontent which they don't articulate, just as Roger, Jim, and David couldn't articulate theirs. The likelihood is that revolutionary politics—of whatever stamp—just wasn't Lawson's *cri de coeur* and that he never found his real fury.

In a piece called "The New Showmanship" that appeared in 1927, Lawson praised such dramas as *The Hairy Ape*, *The Adding Machine*, and Francis Faragoh's *Pinwheel* (as well as his own *Roger Bloomer*), asserting that "to my way of thinking and seeing, this work . . . is a hundred times more real than the mechanism of the drawing room conversation patter play."[18] His adjectives of choice for this new theatre were "dynamic" and "pictorial," and his theatre was certainly both of these, but he also called for a "return to theater values"—an emphasis on storytelling—and here Lawson faltered, for he didn't care about his stories and he didn't know when to stop telling them. A decade later, in *New Theatre*, Charmion Von Wiegand mused on Lawson's failure to follow up on the exhilaration she had found in *Roger Bloomer*. Lawson's undoing, she concluded, was simply "an abundance of gifts."[19]

NOTES

1. Robert Garland, *New York Evening Post* 4 August 1934.

2. John Dos Passos, "Foreword," *Roger Bloomer* by John Howard Lawson (New York: Thomas Seltzer, 1923). Page references to both foreword and play appear in the text.

3. John Howard Lawson, *Theory and Technique of Playwriting* (1936; New York: Hill and Wang, 1960) 119.

4. All reviews cited by Percy Hammond, *New York Herald Tribune* 1 April 1934.

5. John Howard Lawson, *Processional* (New York: Thomas Seltzer, 1925). Page references to both preface and play appear in the text.

6. Mordecai Gorelik, *New Theatres for Old* (1940; New York: Dutton, 1962) 308–309.

7. Thornton Wilder, "The Turn of the Year," *Theatre Arts* 9.3 (March 1925): 153.

8. George Abbott, *Mr. Abbott* (New York: Random House, 1963) 108–109.

9. John O'Connor and Lorraine Brown, *The Federal Theatre Project* (London: Eyre Methuen, 1980) 95.

10. Malcolm Goldstein, *The Political Stage* (New York: Oxford University Press, 1974) 16.

11. Joseph Wood Krutch, "Introduction," *Loud Speaker* by John Howard Lawson (New York: Macaulay, 1927). Page references to both introduction and play appear in the text.

12. Joseph Wood Krutch, *The American Drama Since 1918* (New York: George Braziller, 1957) 243.

13. Letter to the editor, *Theatre Workshop* September 1937.

14. Gerald Rabkin, *Drama and Commitment* (Bloomington: Indiana University Press, 1964) 139.

15. John Howard Lawson, *The International* (New York: Macaulay, 1927). Page references to play appear in the text.

16. Charles Brackett, *The New Yorker* 28 January 1928: 26.

17. Alexander Woollcott, *New York World* 16 January 1928.

18. John Howard Lawson, "The New Showmanship," *New York Sun* 2 February 1927.

19. Charmion Von Wiegand, "Playwright into Critic," *New Theatre* April 1936.

3

Glitzing the Proletariat: John Howard Lawson's Plays of the 1920s

Michael C. O'Neill

Perhaps best remembered as one of the "Hollywood Ten" who was cited for contempt of Congress by the House Un-American Activities Committee (HUAC) in 1947, John Howard Lawson established his reputation as an innovative dramatist in the 1920s among critics and audiences eager to create a new American theatre. Lawson claimed at the HUAC hearings that he was part of "the great Voice of democracy" and that the committee was "conspiring against the American way of life."[1] Four decades earlier, his plays had embodied similarly broad strokes of American allegory in staging and ideas that prompted many critics to hail Lawson as the country's most promising playwright. By 1947, as Lawson again returned, however briefly, to the national spotlight, it was clear that this promise had never been fulfilled. Why?

Until his 1934 declaration in the leftist publication, *New Masses*, that he would use his art to serve the revolutionary working class, Lawson's search for meaningful theatrical forms and methods mirrored those of most of his contemporaries. Anita Block in 1939 noted that Lawson had been part of a postwar group of "young playwrights critical of their America and convinced, as the European moderns were before them, that the theatre must be used as a medium for self-criticism."[2] Late in his life Lawson described his World War I experiences to interviewers Dave Davis and Neal Goldberg as the foundation of his radical thinking, and European influences on Lawson that include Antonin Artaud, Sigmund Freud, and Henri René Lenormand have been examined by his contemporaries and critics alike. Like Eugene O'Neill and Elmer Rice, Lawson used expressionism in his plays of the 1920s, making him, according to Malcolm Goldstein, "a major contributor . . . to the expressionist substratum of American drama."[3] Joseph Wood Krutch places Lawson among a group of American writers who, in their search for new techniques to convey their radical thinking, adopted expressionism partly because it had been taken up in post-revolutionary Russia as "the most typical contribution of the revolutionary spirit in dramatic art."[4] John Dos Passos described Lawson's expressionistic *Roger Bloomer* (1923), begun and perhaps completed during Lawson's "Lost Generation" experience in Europe with Dos Passos, as "only a beginning" to fusing diverse elements into a genuine American style—something Dos Passos himself attempted in *U.S.A.*[5]

Like O'Neill, Lawson consciously worked to introduce new techniques to the American stage in the 1920s. Louis Broussard notes that the staging of *Roger Bloomer* "became in the long run more influential than its ideas."[6] Although Walter Eaton claims in his history of the Theatre Guild's first decade that Lawson's method in *Processional* (1925), still considered his best work, was never imitated, the play did help validate popular American theatrical styles in more serious drama.[7] Both *Loud Speaker* (1927) and *The International* (1928) reinterpreted ancient theatrical devices for modern effects; the former, as Krutch has observed, superimposed the stock characters of the *commedia dell'arte* on Jazz Age types, and the latter turned the Greek chorus into competing groups of Broadway chorus girls.[8] *Loud Speaker* also used the techniques of Vsevelod Meyerhold in its constructivist setting and staging. Malcolm Goldstein observes that *Processional*, which more successfully achieved the fusion with which Lawson experimented in *Roger Bloomer*, moved with the currents of intellectual life in the 1920s by incorporating into its form political allusions to labor unions and the Klu Klux Klan, as well as such elements of popular culture as jazz, vaudeville, comic strips, burlesque, ethnic stereotypes, and the Fox Trot.

Lawson's innovations, however, are coupled with a morally unambiguous and often sentimental adulation of the common man. Contextualized by a popular culture that Lawson viewed from a distant and elitist perspective, this generic proletarian figure—a glitzed-up American Everyman—remains at the center of Lawson's plays. In reviewing *Loud Speaker* in 1927, Dana Skinner, who usually was sympathetic to Lawson, wrote that if he would "content himself with writing a play of character and emotional struggle, he would rapidly emerge as one of the finest playwrights we have."[9] Lawson's inability to do this stems, in part, from his confusion of the proletariat experience with the trappings of common American customs, music, speech, and behavior that fueled the innovations in his plays. As Gerald Rabkin has noted, Lawson's commitment to the working class was "an obvious excrescence which has little relation to the artist's experience."[10]

A child of wealth and privilege, Lawson enrolled at Williams College at the age of fifteen, the youngest member of his class. After graduation he joined the Red Cross as an ambulance driver in France and Italy and returned in 1920 to the United States eager to merge his radical political thinking with the radical techniques of the avant-garde he had observed while abroad. The result, *Roger Bloomer*, which opened three weeks before Rice's *The Adding Machine*, contains over thirty scenes and an extended dream sequence to portray a young Iowa man's rebellion against society and his search for love that can transcend sex. As late as 1934, Harold Clurman, in his foreword to Lawson's *With a Reckless Preface*, had generally high praise for Lawson's attempt in *Roger Bloomer* to treat startling subject matter with expressionistic techniques in a purely American context; however, the tendency in expressionism to emphasize allegorical figures and types over individualized characters proved a convenient vehicle for Lawson's uncomplicated morality and his romantic view of a universal American young man.

According to Lawson's stage directions, "Roger Bloomer must be played by an actor of sturdy virile appearance, giving [the] impression of [an] average American boy" (xi).[11] Everett Bloomer, Roger's father and the owner of the biggest store in Excelsior, Iowa, introduces Roger to the son of his merchant friend Poppin, a Yale varsity athlete named Eugene who admonishes Roger to "stick to the guys with money and an American name and you can't go wrong" (44). Living by his motto, "To sell big and sell cheap" (8), and worshipping his heroes, Washington and Woolworth, Everett Bloom eats steak and potatoes prepared every night by his subservient wife. Roger revolts against these American bourgeois types when he falls in love with a hardened proletariat woman named Louise, who, having been fired as a department store clerk by Everett, establishes a common bond with Roger. He claims they share a hate for his father and a desire "never to be satisfied with things as they are" (72); for Lawson, Roger's interpretation of his relationship with Louise is more crucial than the elements of that relationship itself, because the central concern of *Roger Bloomer* is a generational conflict in general terms. In descriptions that echo O'Neill and T. S. Eliot, respectively, Roger is derided in the play as a "dreamy kid" (77) and "a straw man" (171); an alienated hero with a modernist sensibility, Roger is a relative of James Joyce's Bloom—a Bloomer blooming into universal manhood. About Roger's dreams and aspirations, the Babbitt-like Eugene comments for the entire American bourgeoisie, "There's nothing in that stuff—too European. It isn't safe!" (50). Roger is less important as a developed character than he is a soldier in a fight Lawson arms with European theatrical innovations that he hopes will dazzle the audience into seeing that old ways of thinking are as obsolete as old ways of doing theatre.

Roger, who claims "I want women's souls" (53), follows Louise to New York, which is peopled with more types: the lecherous landlady, "looking very much as if she were a piece of the wallpaper come to life" (85), who tries to seduce Roger and represents the carnality he despises; Louise's prudish mother, who embodies Victorian morality and fails to understand Roger's interest in her daughter; a dictatorial judge resembling the owlish college examiner who failed Roger in Iowa and quizzes him about being a socialist; members of Eugene's posh men's club snoring rhythmically with newspapers over their eyes; Louise's co-workers, who "all move in unison like wax-works" (106); and Louise's bang-for-the-buck boss, Mr. Runsey, who replies to Louise's rejection, "I wouldn't marry you for a million dollars," with a capitalistic counter-offer, "How about a million and a half?" (161). Like the central figure in most expressionistic plays, Roger encounters each of these types on his journey to self-discovery through the maze of New York City; as Runsey tells him after turning down his job application, "Take a look at the big buildings, see your real size" (109).

However, until the final dream sequence, Lawson relies little upon the violent dislocations of time and place normally associated with expressionism. The third act of the play eschews all but the most superficial innovations, turning instead on the melodramatic plot devices of embezzlement, attempted suicide, sexual blackmail, and Louise's dying confession of true love. Nonetheless, Lawson continues to use allegorical figures and representative types as characters, because they help him clearly delineate an American landscape of good and evil that no longer supplies a viable moral code for Roger, his American "every youth." Before Roger is thrown into jail, the Judge asks him, "Have you any idea of right and wrong?"—and Roger answers, "No, sir; but, by God, I intend to find out" (187).

Once he is imprisoned, Roger dreams "a nightmare of pursuit" (196) in three strophes that explode the conventions and proprieties already satirized by Lawson in preceding sections of the play. This final, and most purely expressionistic part of *Roger Bloomer*—it is a dream, after all—conjures up images of death, obscenity, and heredity from Roger's psyche, and ends with Louise in a synthesizing vision as "Virgin Harlot" (222) helping Roger defeat his inner demons with these words: "Away! Away, ghosts of yesterday, for the young are coming marching, marching; can't you hear the echo of their feet, can't you hear them singing a new song?" (222). Roger awakes from his dream, leaves prison through the intervention of his father's lawyer, and walks into manhood.

The implausibility of this deus ex machina subverts the convention and, furthermore, *Roger Bloomer* ends on a decidedly optimistic note, unlike most expressionistic plays of this—or any other—period; Louise's final speech foreshadows the call to arms of Lawson's most emphatically dogmatic Marxist play, *Marching Song*, some fourteen years later. Moreover, Louise finally equates Roger with an entire generation that will inevitably triumph over the stifling forces of mindless capitalism, bourgeois morality, corrupting education, sexual propriety, and the exploitation of the common man—each of which is represented by a particular character type in the play. The great paradox of *Roger Bloomer* is that Lawson employs the outward trappings of American behavioral stereotypes to delve into the inner world of Roger, who, according to Lawson, is "the most normal person in the play" (xi). John Farrar wrote of the 1923 production, "*Roger Bloomer* is weak chiefly because of Lawson's seeming inability to understand his hero, or at least, to give his audience the impression of understanding him."[12] Roger remains an embodiment of youthful American idealism who, as a consequence of Lawson's romantic conception of him, is primarily a representative type—an assertion made clear by Louise's final speech. Lawson's attempts to give Roger depth and complexity as a character falter in awkward monologues and contrived melodramatic scenes, indications that Lawson may have failed to grasp the details of the common man's experience.

Presented by the Theatre Guild, *Processional: A Jazz Symphony of American Life in Four Acts* derived its technique from vaudeville, jazz, and burlesque. In his preface to the play, Lawson claims, "I have endeavored to create a method which shall express the American scene in native idiom, a method as far removed from the older realism as from the facile mood of Expressionism" (v).[13] Attacked by George Jean Nathan as sloppily constructed and derivative, *Processional* nonetheless challenged audiences to consider the stage as a metaphor for the confusion of American life.[14] The W.P.A. (Works Progress Administration) Federal Theatre Project revived a rewritten, more Marxist version of *Processional* in 1937, but critical reaction favored the noisier, more boisterous production of 1925, in which, Thornton Wilder noted, Lawson "intermingles strips of vaudeville patter, exciting drama and burlesque, a Klu Klux Klan ballet and a negro-song-and-dance."[15]

Despite Lawson's considerable innovations in *Processional*—Barrett Clark enthusiastically and inaccurately prophesied that "*Processional* will in the years to come be regarded as marking an epoch in the American drama"[16]—the play's central character is yet another romanticized version of the common man caught up in a struggle defined by allegorical types with antecedents in American popular culture. Aptly named for the working class about to explode, Dynamite Jim, originally played by George Abbott, is the center of a battle waged in the West Virginia coal mining country, peopled not only with bosses who caricature the upper classes but also with workers whose racial and ethnic stereotyping is implicitly celebrated within the play's vaudeville form. The Sheriff is portrayed as a vaudeville stage magician whose best trick is making the law appear and disappear at will. The Man in the Silk Hat plays both the mining boss and Uncle Sam, thus making the interests of industry and government one and the same. Lawson reserves special venom for the ineffectual bourgeoisie through the liberal reporter Phillpott, who explains, "Being a good middle-class man, I'm sorry for everybody, but I never know what to do about it" (162). The processional jazz band that begins the play with "The Fourth of July Blues" includes: Jake Psinski, "a Pole" (6) and leader of the union; Rastus Jolly, "a Negro . . . who plays a banjo and sings most of the time for good measure" (6); Alexander Gore, "a man of the hayseed type" (7); and, Dago Joe, "a sleek greasy Italian" (7). The cops in the play are Irish; the town shopkeeper is a Jew. The theatricality of all this role-playing in American life is celebrated in the final scene when Rastus arrives safely under a Ku Klux Klan hood, and Jim, blinded by the Klan, marries Sadie Cohen, who is carrying his child, as the groom's gentile mother and the bride's Jewish father dance together.

As Roger Bloomer is Lawson's romanticized embodiment of the feelings and aspirations common to a generation, so Dynamite Jim is Lawson's idealized version of the common man. Strip away Lawson's wildly inventive dialogue, Mordecai Gorelik's overtly theatrical settings and costumes, Philip Moeller's busy direction of a boisterous cast that included Lee Strasberg and Sanford Meisner in bit parts, and a live jazz band—and what remains is the formula Lawson used throughout the 1920s: theatrical innovation surrounding an idealized, only partially realized, common man. The difficulty for audiences with *Processional*, Stark Young suggested, lay precisely in Lawson's inability to see social struggle in America in anything but the broadest terms; audiences, he wrote, are unfamiliar with characters battling "against forces spelled with a capital letter" (1). Skinner, one of Lawson's most consistent supporters among the critics, noted that the play's "outward circumstances are chaotic," but Lawson's main allegory is simple: through three figures—a man, his mother, and a girl—*Processional* is an allegory of crime, punishment, and redemption that "holds true of the nation at large."[17]

However, H. I. Brock, in contending that "Americans don't see their culture the way outsiders might,"[18] suggested that Lawson misread his audience by assuming that Americans would choose to recognize, as Lawson himself had done, the significance of jazz and vaudeville as expressions of American culture rather than simply to respond to these elements of *Processional* as familiar entertainment. This observation points to a deeper, more problematic strategy in the play. Unlike the characters *Processional* celebrates, Lawson, despite his politics, was never a member of the working class, and his years in Europe and in intellectual pursuit influenced his construct of American popular culture, rightly or wrongly, from the perspective of an outsider. *Processional*, like Lawson's other plays of the 1920s, is an implicit attempt to fashion elements of popular culture into a proletariat mythology that, ironically, remained outside the immediate experience of its creator.

Nevertheless, Lawson explicitly demonstrated this same commitment to the working class by helping to form the Workers' Drama League in 1926 and by joining forces with Em Jo Basshe, Francis Edwards Faragoh, Michael Gold, and Dos Passos in 1927 to establish the New Playwrights Theatre, a venture bitterly fictionalized by Dos Passos in his novel, *Most Likely to Succeed* (1954). A trio of experiments—*Nirvana* (1926) and two productions by the New Playwrights Theatre, *Loud Speaker* (1927) and *The International* (1928)—helped fuel Lawson's ongoing artistic and increasingly ideological quarrel with those he attacked as proponents of a bourgeois theatre.

Nirvana (1926), described by Lawson in a program note as "a comedy of the uncertainties and aspirations of the thinking man as he confronts the enlarging universe," seemed to invite critics to fault the play for its pretensions. Clurman comments that "*Nirvana* is the most confused of Lawson's plays because he is a poet and not a thinker, and in it he has tried to handle ideas most directly."[19] This conflict between Lawson the innovative theatrical poet and Lawson the radical social thinker with visions of an idealized proletariat intensified as the decade came to a close. *Loud Speaker*, with incidental music by Eugene L. Berton and lyrics by Edward Eliscu, used Mordecai Gorelik's inventive constructivist setting of slides, stairways, and platforms to present a farcical fable about a contemporary politician who, after getting drunk before a radio broadcast, tells the audience what he really thinks and gets elected as a result.[20] *The International*, staged by Lawson and choreographed by Don Oscar Becque, portrayed a young man's travels around the world in search of a solution to end oppression. Although both plays continued Lawson's use of allegorical character types, *Loud Speaker* relies less upon a central figure than does *The International*. With its title alluding to the revolutionary anthem, *The International* fused dance, ingenious settings by Dos Passos, and chanting that Lawson describes as "a weaving of jazz rhythms with orchestral backgrounds"[21] to create an innovative theatrical environment for David Fitch, Lawson's proletariat Everyman. David journeys to Tibet where his encounters with Alise, Tim, Henley, and Karneski allow Lawson to move from satirizing American politics, as he does in *Loud Speaker*, to presenting universal political arguments and points of view. *The International* ends in a disturbing apocalyptic vision as David dies in Alise's arms, Tim is shot getting out of an overturned taxi, people are gunned down as war breaks out in the streets of New York City, and Karneski is leading hordes to victory in Asia.

It is fitting that Lawson's proletariat hero, David Fitch, leaves America in a play where Lawson himself abandons the proletariat mythology he tried to create from American popular culture in the 1920s. Lawson's innovations for the stage ceased after *The International*; he began writing screenplays, returning to New York throughout the 1930s with realistic social dramas that no longer centered on an abstract character whom he framed with the glitz of innovation and in whom he expected the common man to see himself reflected. Increasingly prolific as a Marxist commentator and critic, Lawson the poet gradually succumbed to Lawson the dogmatic thinker. His plays of the 1920s may be considered preparation for his dedication to class struggle and revolutionary theatre, but they also provide valuable insight into an American theatre beginning to define itself during the decade. Despite their innovations, Lawson's plays of the 1920s have been generally neglected, a fate not shared by O'Neill or by Rice. Like them, Lawson shaped the popular cultural experience of his times into innovative theatre, but his vision of the 1920s American Everyman—blooming proletariat youth, dynamite common man—remained only an abstraction.

Assessing Lawson's plays now inevitably reaffirms an American dramatic tradition that, when all the glitter and glitz of innovation fades, defines its broadest social themes through the specifics of individually realized lives. The mixed popular reception of Lawson's plays in the 1920s and, with very few exceptions, our neglect of his work ever since can thus be linked in part to characters who only broadly represent, to use Lawson's words to HUAC, "the American way of life." His stage characters remain vehicles weighed down by a political and social agenda that Lawson was never able to embody, as were O'Neill and Rice, in vivid portraits of individuals that seemed to arise from and connect with the particulars of American experience. Whereas many of Lawson's contemporaries continued to grow and experiment in a variety of directions, Lawson himself seemed to lose his capacity for innovation once the techniques of expressionism became widely recognized and accepted. Despite his bow to the increasingly prosaic theatre of the 1930s in *Success Story* (1932), *Gentlewoman* (1934), and *The Pure in Heart* (1934), Lawson's Marxist agenda never changed. Our theatre likes its politics and its social consciousness, if it likes either one at all, to be performed in the arenas of our theatricalized national life—where, in 1947, Lawson finally had a brief, starring role. To Lawson's credit, he did battle with limited success in the 1920s against this dichotomy between art and politics in our theatre; it was his misfortune—and ours—that he lacked the artistic ammunition to prevail.

NOTES

1. Robert Vaughn, *Only Victims* (New York: Putnam's, 1972) 315.

2. Anita Block, *The Changing World in Plays and Theatre* (Boston: Little, Brown, 1939) 225.

3. Malcolm Goldstein, *The Political Stage: American Drama and Theater in the Great Depression* (New York: Oxford University Press, 1974) 10.

4. Joseph Wood Krutch, *American Drama Since 1918* (New York: George Braziller, 1957) 243.

5. John Dos Passos, "Foreword," *Roger Bloomer* by John Howard Lawson (New York: Thomas Seltzer, 1923) viii.

6. Louis Broussard, *American Drama: Contemporary Allegory from Eugene O'Neill to Tennessee Williams* (Norman: University of Oklahoma Press, 1962) 51.

7. Walter Prichard Eaton et al., *The Theatre Guild: The First Ten Years* (New York: Brentano's, 1929) 84.

8. Joseph Wood Krutch, "Drama: Harlequinade," *Nation* 124 (23 March 1927): 324; Joseph Wood Krutch, "Introduction," *Loud Speaker* by John Howard Lawson (New York: Macaulay, 1927) ix–xiii.

9. Dana Skinner, "The Play: 'Loud Speaker,'" *Commonweal* 5 (16 March 1927): 524–525.

10. Gerald Rabkin, *Drama and Commitment* (Bloomington: Indiana University Press, 1964) 294.

11. John Howard Lawson, *Roger Bloomer* (New York: Thomas Seltzer, 1923). Page references appear in the text.

12. John Farrar, "To See or Not to See," *Bookman* 57 (May 1923): 319.

13. John Howard Lawson, *Processional: A Jazz Symphony of American Life in Four Acts* (New York: Thomas Seltzer, 1925). Page references appear in the text.

14. George Jean Nathan, "The Theatre," *American Mercury* 4 (March 1925): 372–373.

15. Thornton Wilder, "The Turn of The Year," *Theater Arts Monthly* March 1925: 152.

16. Barrett H. Clark, "'Processional' and Some Others," *Drama* 15 (March 1925): 130.

17. Dana Skinner, "The Play: 'Processional,' " *Commonweal* 1 (4 February 1925): 354.

18. H.I. Brock, "American Dance of Life Rhymed to Jazz," *New York Times* 1 February 1925, sec. 4: 18.

19. Harold Clurman, "Foreword: A Preface to John Howard Lawson," *With a Reckless Preface: Two Plays* by John Howard Lawson (New York: Farrar and Rinehart, 1934) xxi.

20. John Howard Lawson, *Loud Speaker* (New York: Macaulay, 1927).

21. John Howard Lawson, *The International* (New York: Macaulay, 1927) 7.

REFERENCES

Basshe, Em Jo. "The Revolt in Fifty-Second Street." *New York Times* 27 February 1927, sec. 7: 4.

Clurman, Harold. *The Fervent Years*. New York: Da Capo, 1983.

Krutch, Joseph Wood, with Dave Davis and Neal Goldberg. "Organizing the Screen Writer's Guild: An Interview with John Howard Lawson." *Cineaste* 8, No. 2 (1977): 4–11, 58.

Lawson, John Howard. " 'Inner Conflict' and Proletarian Art." *New Masses* 17 April 1934: 29–30.

Sievers, W. David. *Freud on Broadway: A History of Psychoanalysis and the American Drama*. New York: Hermitage House, 1955.

Valgemae, Mardi. *Accelerated Grimace: Expressionism in the American Drama of the 1920s*. Carbondale: Southern Illinois University Press, 1972.

Williams, Jay. *Stage Left*. New York: Scribner's, 1974.

Young, Stark. "Stalking New Gods: Note on 'Processional.' " *New York Times* 25 January 1925, sec. 7: 1.

4

Direction by Design(er): Robert Edmond Jones and the New Provincetown Players

Jane T. Peterson

In 1941 Robert Edmond Jones published *The Dramatic Imagination*, a compilation of musings, lectures, and essays distilled from over three decades of work in the American theatre. The slim volume both articulates and reflects the style that prompted John Mason Brown to refer to the designer as "our stage's high priest of evocation."[1] Jones's theatrical ideals soar far above the mundane tools (fabric, gel, and paint) of his trade; his vision shimmers with the incandescence of the poet.

Through the art of stage design Jones sought a theatre that could "express our newly enlarged consciousness of life."[2] Beginning with his designs for Harley Granville-Barker's 1915 Broadway production of *The Man Who Married a Dumb Wife*, Jones led the vanguard of artists determined to infuse the principles of the European New Stagecraft into the professional American theatre. Combining scenery, lights, and costumes into a unified evocation of mood and atmosphere, Jones strove for a total, poetic theatre. By stripping the stage to its essentials in an effort to capture the essence of a play, Jones challenged the Belasco-bound realism of the Broadway theatre in the late 1910s and 1920s. His success can be gauged by the fact that in May 1920 (a mere five years after his Broadway debut), Robert Edmond Jones became the first American designer to have his drawings, photographs, and models exhibited in a one-man show at New York's Bourgeois Galleries. While critics were generally unanimous in their praise of Jones's contributions to the evolution of a new era in stage design, reviewer Oliver Sayler foreshadowed the shift in direction that Jones's career was soon to follow:

> Not so very long ago, in a moment of impatience and discouragement that comes to all artists, Robert Edmond Jones said to me, "What are the designers of scenery who have caught the spirit of the new theatre going to do? Must we quit for a while and sit back and wait for the producers to catch up with us?"
>
> "No," I replied. "That's no solution. You yourselves will simply have to learn to produce."[3]

Sayler's suggestion may have nurtured the seed of a preexisting ambition, but it was not until the season of 1923–1924 that Bobby Jones was fully able to exercise his prerogatives as a producer/director.

This chapter examines Robert Edmond Jones's directorial career during his three seasons (1923–1926) at the Experimental Theatre, a reorganization of the Provincetown Players. Was the designer/director's dream of a poetic, evocative theatre created *from* the mind and *by* the hand of a single guiding spirit actualized in the plays he directed? Was Robert Edmond Jones able to concretize his vision of a theatre that could "express our newly enlarged consciousness of life"? By focusing on selected productions, one can compare the artist's intentions with the critical evaluation of the final product in an effort to assess the success or failure of Jones's directorial endeavors.

Bobby Jones's career as a theatre director is intimately tied to the history of the Provincetown Players. His association with the Provincetown group began with his staging contributions for the two one-act plays (Neith Boyce's *Constancy* and Susan Glaspell and George Cram Cook's *Suppressed Desires*) performed in Hutchins Hapgood's house during the summer of 1915. It was from that modest beginning that the Provincetown Players were born. However, while the Provincetown Players went on to help redefine the American drama within the context of the little theatre movement, Jones's design career took a more professional turn.

Broadway producer/director Arthur Hopkins had been among the audiences dazzled by Jones's designs (sets, lights, and costumes) for Harley Granville-Barker's *The Man Who Married a Dumb Wife* in January 1915. The evocative simplicity of style, in sharp contrast to the busy detail that crowded most Broadway stages, appealed to the producer. Hopkins hired Jones and their frequent and fruitful collaboration over several decades allowed the designer's innovative ideas to be infused into the commercial theatre. In an era when authenticity and realism prevailed, Jones sought something much more elusive and prided himself on the absence of historical accuracy: "As a matter of fact . . . there is absolutely nothing historical about what I have done in *The Man Who Married a Dumb Wife*. I read the play carefully and I have tried to do with colors and design what the actors do with speech. I have tried to catch the spirit of the work even as the actors by voice inflection convey a subtle meaning."[4] Jones's proclamation of suggestion over imitation was a principal tenet of the European visionaries (Gordon Craig, Adolph Appia, and Max Reinhardt) who had ushered in a new era of the theatre by shattering the conventions of nineteenth-century theatrical realism in favor of symbol and simplicity.

Between 1915 and 1923 Robert Edmond Jones and Arthur Hopkins collaborated on a total of twenty-eight productions that helped transform the American stage.[5] From the gritty, if simplified, realism of O'Neill's *Anna Christie* (1921) to the light, comedic spirit of *The Laughing Lady* (1923) with Ethel Barrymore, they demonstrated that their combined arts and talents easily accommodated the entire spectrum of the drama. The Jones-Hopkins team brought innovative, serious drama to a Broadway stage dominated by "the hokum [and] tricks"[6] of *The Bat* (1920) or the "riotous entertainment"[7] of *Abie's Irish Rose* (1922). Their *The Tragedy of Richard III* (1920) and *Hamlet* (1922) were not only successful explorations of the unit set but were honest attempts to create a respectable repertoire of plays for John Barrymore.

While Jones maintained his professional association with Arthur Hopkins during the 1921–1923 seasons, it was his collaborations with two other significant theatre personalities that influenced the immediate trajectory of his career.

The Hopkins-Jones team produced two Eugene O'Neill premieres (*Anna Christie* in 1921 and *The Hairy Ape* in 1922), fostering a close working relationship between the young playwright who was redefining American dramaturgy and the young designer who was reimagining the uses and functions of stage design. Jones also toured theatres throughout Europe with theatre critic and novice producer Kenneth Macgowan during the spring and early summer of 1922. *Continental Stagecraft,* published that same year and illustrated by Jones, described contemporary theatrical practices they had observed on the continent. It was through Eugene O'Neill and Kenneth Macgowan that Bobby Jones's career reconnected to the Provincetown Players and the little theatre movement.

By 1922 the artistic objectives of the original Provincetown Players were in flux. The commercial success of several Provincetown productions, including O'Neill's *The Emperor Jones* (1920), spawned factionalism within the group. In an effort to redefine their mission, George Cram Cook, the group's founder and guiding spirit, undertook a bold initiative which ultimately changed the shape of the Provincetown Players. At the conclusion of their 1921–1922 season, Cook announced that "our faith needs quickening through 'leisure.' . . . To that end therefore, the quickening of faith and the freshening of spirit—we have decided on what, mechanically looked at, from a practical standpoint, is an absurd thing—a year of rest."[8] When various efforts to fill the void left by the original Provincetown group had failed, playwright Eugene O'Neill and Robert Edmond Jones allied themselves with Kenneth Macgowan to form the Experimental Theatre, Inc. for the 1923–1924 season. The new incarnation of the Provincetown Players, with a permanent acting company of ten to be augmented by guest artists engaged for specific productions, drew on the talents of many of the original Provincetowners. Jones was installed as "artist and stage-director-in-chief,"[9] giving the designer a unique and enviable opportunity to "carry through to realization his original vision."[10]

Although Robert Edmond Jones was not untried as a director, his previous experience was decidedly limited. His first professional directing assignment had been a historical, if short-lived, event: Ridgely Torrence's *Three Plays for a Negro Theatre*, which opened at the Garden Theatre on 5 April 1917. These plays marked the first time that African American actors had performed on Broadway in dramatic roles and has been referred to as "the most important single event in the entire history of the Negro in American theatre."[11] This directorial debut was followed by a season of summer stock at the Pabst Theatre in Milwaukee in 1918, where Jones was one of three directors in addition to being responsible for designing the scenery.

Strindberg's *The Spook Sonata*, the play chosen to inaugurate the Experimental Theatre's opening in January 1924, was Jones's first directorial assignment for the group. The choice of the Strindberg play was in keeping with the spirit of the organization as O'Neill envisioned it: "a new organization whose *emphasis* shall be upon *experiment in production*, utilizing any play, ancient or modern, foreign or native, to that end. . . . I mean experiment in acting, directing, scenery—everything. It is to be a directors' theatre, as it had been a playwrights'."[12] In keeping with this new emphasis on experiment in production, Jones supervised the redecoration of the Provincetown Playhouse: "an inner portal was added to the tiny stage, and the walls of the theatre were ornamented with 'Venetian mirrors' that were made of tin and decorated with the caps of beer bottles."[13]

Because Jones shared the responsibilities on *The Spook Sonata* with James Light (directing) and Cleon Throckmorton (design), one cannot fully attribute the guarded success of this production to Jones. However, Jones's penchant for mood and atmosphere was indelibly stamped on the Strindberg play. It was judged by most critics to be a "thoroughly well-conceived presentation . . . the intention is to evoke an impression, a mood."[14] To that end masks were used on various characters and "a complete freedom in the use and dramatic variety of the lighting" was employed.[15] Old Hummel's retreat into the closet to hang himself, for example, was accentuated by the sudden disappearance of the figures on stage and the scene being bathed in red.

The Experimental Theatre's second production was a revival of Anna Cora Mowatt's *Fashion* (1924). This romp through 1845 New York society adroitly blended the historical with the comedic. Nineteenth-century theatrical conventions were spoofed: an ornately painted curtain rolled up from the bottom and was lighted by tin footlight reflectors while "actors trumpet their asides at the audience through their hollowed palms."[16] Although *Fashion* was a box office hit, critics were mixed in their assessment of Jones's success. Alan Dale claimed that "this revival is mordantly disappointing, for it seemed like bad burlesque . . . the actors over-acted, over-emphasized the absurdities, over-did everything."[17] While Heywood Broun specifically mentioned Jones's direction as "a beautiful job,"[18] the *Christian Science Monitor* countered with the opinion that "the stage direction leaves much to be desired and a great opportunity is lost thereby."[19]

Jones's next directorial outing was considerably more stormy: a collaboration with O'Neill on *The Ancient Mariner* (1924), a dramatized version of Coleridge's poem. As the lines were recited by the Mariner, the actions described were enacted by a chorus of sailors whose faces were hauntingly covered with death masks. Although the piece appealed to Jones's proclivity for evocative, poetic theatre, most critics concurred that the experiment was a noble failure. Several moments were described as thrilling and memorable, but one critic hints at a directorial weakness that was to plague Bobby Jones throughout his tenure as a director of the Experimental Theatre: a static, sculptural quality created by a "series of finely arranged tableaux and shadow plays."[20]

The next Jones-O'Neill collaboration, *Desire Under the Elms* (1924), was a natural match. Both artists had roots in the rocky New England soil: Jones on a New Hampshire farm and O'Neill in New London, Connecticut. Jones translated his own feelings about New England ("violent, passionate, sensual, sadistic, lifted, heated, frozen, transcendental, Poesque"[21]) into the settings and direction of the production. Critics immediately recognized the importance (and unevenness) of O'Neill's play, but they did not necessarily enjoy the experience. One such critic who could not wait to escape the "cantankerous, cancerous proceedings" gave the most vivid description of the production. "The atmosphere is persistently dark green; there are long pauses in the dialogue, to suggest intense thought. Everybody is exquisitely miserable and there is a dangling dank despondency about them all that could be funny, but isn't. The theatre is dimly lighted."[22]

For the 1925–1926 season Macgowan, Jones, and O'Neill were no longer in association with the Experimental Theatre, Inc. However, they continued their association as a producing organization at the Greenwich Village Theatre, where they presented O'Neill's *The Fountain* (1925) and *The Great God Brown* (1926).

The notices for *The Fountain* were mixed with many critics praising O'Neill for his new departure into history and poetic romance but felt that "despite occasional flashes of poetic beauty and dramatic intensity *The Fountain* is more a pageant than a play. It serves as an excellent framework for the pictorial talents of Robert Edmond Jones. It is a gorgeous feast for the eyes, but a rather lean diet for the ears."[23] The majority of critics judged the play as one of O'Neill's more insignificant efforts, but John Mason Brown was particularly stinging in his evaluation. "O'Neill builds a long-winded and tiresome play . . . the dialogue has a dullness equaled only in the third-rate historical tragedies of the early American theatre."[24] Brown went on to praise the designs but felt that Jones was clearly out of his element in terms of the direction.

[H]e has dived beyond his depth, and the play has suffered at his hands. Mr. Jones naturally sees more in the theatre than he hears. As with all designers turned directors, the result has been some haunting visual effects. His single groupings are beautifully composed, but from grouping to grouping, when the director must manage tempo and take care of the pacing of the play at hand, there is little continuity. All the fine groupings in the world belong only to pageantry and masques unless they spring from action and seem inevitable, not posed.[25]

Alexander Woollcott commented on Jones's "increasing skill as a director"[26] but criticized the vision scene as "partak[ing] perilously of a pageant organized by the Miami Ladies Auxiliary."[27] The tempo and pacing of the play were also hampered by the excruciatingly long changes between the eleven scenes.

The last play that Bobby Jones directed for the triumvirate was O'Neill's *The Great God Brown* which opened in January 1926. A run of 171 performances attests to the production's success even though most critics were ambivalent, citing the play's imaginative richness along with its unevenness. For example, O'Neill and Jones took the use of masks much further than they had in *The Spook Sonata* or *The Ancient Mariner*, employing them to indicate the various selves (public and private) that one presents to the world. Many critics, however, felt that the device "grew wearisome and eventually cumbersome"[28] by the end of the play. While one critic credited Jones's staging with "partially clarifying the O'Neill mysteries,"[29] the director's contribution was of little concern to most reviewers.

Although Jones maintained associations with O'Neill and Macgowan, the production of *The Great God Brown* ended his stint as director and designer for the triumvirate. Jones resumed his professional career as a Broadway designer, making only brief forays into the role of director during the remainder of his professional career.

How successful was Robert Edmond Jones as a director for the Macgowan-O'Neill-Jones productions from 1923 to 1926? There is no unequivocal answer. If one is to judge by box office receipts, his success was mixed. *Desire Under the Elms* ran 208 performances, *Fashion* and *The Great God Brown* each ran more than 150 performances, and *Patience* played 104 times. However, *The Spook Sonata* eked out a mere 24-performance run, while *Michel Auclair* sustained only 19 performances and *The Saint* closed after 17 shows.

To evaluate Robert Edmond Jones's success on the validity of his interpretations of the text, one must examine his goals and objectives. Jones's working method was to immerse himself in the play—to absorb the atmosphere, mood, and tone of a piece—then to translate that mood into the concrete terms of the actor and the decor. As a designer his "translations" were generally praised for evoking the spirit and atmosphere of the play regardless of the critical reception of the production. For example, despite the mixed reception for *The Fountain*, his designs were unanimously commended. His costume for the Duenna was said to "embody the time, the race, and the spirit of the romance of greed, lust and the fruitless quest for lost youth,"[30] even if the production was sluggish and dull.

His ability to translate his interpretation of the play to the actors was not always as successful as his ability to mold light, color, and mass into an articulate design concept. Not all actors understood Jones's ethereal style. A young Harold Clurman, working as an extra on *The Saint* (1924), "realized immediately that he had made no connection to his actors. . . . They did not speak his language, and he had been at no pains either to teach it to them or to translate himself into a language that might affect them."[31] On the other hand, Mary Morris, the original Abbie in *Desire Under the Elms*, recalled her positive experience of working with Jones as a director.

He speaks in flashing images, in moving figures, with an expansive understanding and a vivid passion for life with all its tragedy and beauty. Those first days of talk about the play, whatever it might be, about the characters, about what a true "incarnation" of them might mean, are unforgettable. Life took on another dimension and man's stature was enhanced. . . . He believed that the director, like the actor, exists to "reveal" and never, *never*, to "exhibit" *himself*.

Jones's direction was full of rare and original "images." If you understood them, you entered into a deep experience as an actor trying to make them come true. There was always a worship of beauty, a reverence and passion for life in all its manifestations—even the most tragic—in Jones's whole approach. This is why he is so *right* to direct an O'Neill play.[32]

As suggested above by Morris, the close association among Macgowan, Jones, and O'Neill clearly nurtured O'Neill's already evolving dramaturgy. Like the original Provincetown group before it, the Experimental Theatre, Inc. and the Greenwich Village Theatre in turn provided O'Neill the artistic freedom to explore new dramatic terrain within a safe producing environment. There is little doubt that the art theatre aesthetic undergirding the work of Robert Edmond Jones and Kenneth Macgowan inspired O'Neill's more daring theatrical explorations. *Desire Under the Elms* (1924) was a foray into intensified "psychologic" realism; an innovative use of masks was employed in the expressionistic *The Great God Brown* (1926); and *The Fountain* (1925) was O'Neill's attempt at a "'retheatricalized' poetic, total theatre."[33]

This "poetic, total theatre" was certainly a part of Jones's vision—a vision that often transcended the prosaic language of the theatre and the streets. His project of concretizing that vision in the productions he directed was only partially successful. In a world of limited budgets, small theatres, and amateur actors, however, it was not always possible to bring to life on the stage the world Bobby Jones envisioned.

The theatre of the present offers to the creative artist an undreamed of opportunity, if he can grasp it, to discover the movements of the titanic forces that urge and guide our own time, and to reveal them to his fellow men in the flux and flow of life on his stage. If into the theatre there came such a revelation and release of the spiritual energies of the world made manifest in us and through us, fulfilling in us their own transcendent destinies, it would fuse the numberless aspirations of today into one common ideal and would illuminate all art, all science, all philosophy and all religion with the blinding certainty of a new era of spiritual freedom as with the light of a strange new dawn.[34]

The "release of spiritual energy" and the fulfillment of "transcendent destinies" may require more than canvas, light, and actors. That the productions Jones directed did not accomplish all that he believed the theatre was capable of achieving is not a measure of failure. Rather, the theatre is a far better place for Robert Edmond Jones's attempts to realize his ideals.

NOTES

1. Jero Magon, "Farewell to a Great Designer," *Players Magazine* March 1955: 130.

2. Robert Edmond Jones, *The Dramatic Imagination* (New York: Duell, Sloan and Pearce, 1941) 19.

3. Oliver M. Sayler, "Robert Edmond Jones: Artist of the Theatre," *New Republic* 23 June 1920: 122.

4. Robert Edmond Jones quoted in "The Gentleman of the Decoration," *New York Times* 14 February 1915, sec. VII: 4.

5. Ralph Pendleton, "A Chronology," *The Theatre of Robert Edmond Jones*, ed. Ralph Pendleton (Middletown, CT: Wesleyan University Press, 1958) 146–183. The figure of twenty-eight collaborative productions encompasses the period between 1915 and 1923. Jones and Hopkins were to join forces again later in their careers.

6. Robert Benchley, rev. of *The Bat*, by Mary Roberts Rinehart and Avery Hopwood, *Life* 9 September 1920: n. pag.

7. "Mister Hornblow Goes to the Play," rev. of *Abie's Irish Rose*, by Anne Nichols, *Theatre Magazine* August 1922: 95.

8. George Cram Cook, "Provincetown Valedictory," qtd. in Sarlos, *Jig Cook and the Provincetown Players: Theatre in Ferment* (Amherst: University of Massachusetts Press, 1982) 142.

9. Jackson R. Bryer, ed., *"The Theatre We Worked For": The Letters of Eugene O'Neill to Kenneth Macgowan* (New Haven: Yale University Press, 1982) 69.

10. Sayler, "Robert Edmond Jones" 122.

11. James Weldon Johnson, *Black Manhattan* (1930; New York: Da Capo, 1991) 175.

12. Bryer, *"The Theatre We Worked For"* 48.

13. Mordecai Gorelik, "Life with Bobby," *Theatre Arts* April 1955: 95.

14. Harold Kellock, "Inward Bound and Outward Bound," rev. of *The Spook Sonata*, by August Strindberg, *The Freeman* 23 January 1924: 472.

15. Stark Young, *"The Spook Sonata,"* rev. of *The Spook Sonata*, by August Strindberg, *New Republic* 23 January 1924: 231.

16. John Corbin, "Spoofing the Eighteen Forties," rev. of *Fashion*, by Anna Cora Mowatt, *New York Times* 5 February 1924: n. pag. Most of the following reviews are taken from clipping files in the Billy Rose Collection of the New York Public Library or the files in the Museum of the City of New York Theatre Collection. Page numbers were not found with most clippings.

17. Alan Dale, "Fashion's Revived from New York Days of 1845," rev. of *Fashion*, by Anna Cora Mowatt, *American* 5 February 1924: n. pag.

18. Heywood Broun, "At Provincetown Theatre, *Fashion, or Life in New York*," rev. of *Fashion*, by Anna Cora Mowatt, *World* 5 February 1924: n. pag.

19. F. L. S., "*Fashion*," rev. of *Fashion*, by Anna Cora Mowatt, *Christian Science Monitor* 8 February 1924: n. pag.

20. E. W. Osborn, "*George Dandin*" "*The Ancient Mariner*," rev. of *The Ancient Mariner*, by Eugene O'Neill, *Evening World* 7 April 1924: n. pag.

21. Elizabeth Shepley Sergeant, *Fire Under the Andes: A Group of Literary Portraits* (1927; Port Washington: Kennikat, 1966) 40.

22. Alan Dale, "*Desire Under the Elms* by Eugene O'Neill Is Story of New England Farmhouse; Cast Includes Mary Morris," rev. of *Desire Under the Elms*, by Eugene O'Neill, *American* 14 November 1924: n. pag.

23. Robert Coleman, "Author Explains Play," *Daily Mirror* 14 December 1925: n. pag.

24. John Mason Brown, "The Director Takes a Hand," rev. of *The Fountain*, by Eugene O'Neill, *Theatre Arts Monthly* February 1926: 77.

25. Brown, "The Director Takes a Hand" 77.

26. Alexander Woollcott, "The Stage," rev. of *The Fountain*, by Eugene O'Neill, *World* 11 Dec. 1925: n. pag.

27. Woollcott, rev. of *The Fountain,* 11 December 1925, n. pag.

28. Alexander Woollcott, "The Stage," rev. of *The Great God Brown*, by Eugene O'Neill, *World* 25 January 1926: n. pag.

29. "*The Great God Brown* Is Fascinating Enigma," rev. of *The Great God Brown*, by Eugene O'Neill, *New York Herald* 25 January 1926: n. pag.

30. Photo caption, *Theatre Arts Monthly* February 1926: 79.

31. Harold Clurman, *The Fervent Years: The Story of the Group Theatre and the Thirties* (New York: Knopf, 1945) 8.

32. Eugene Robert Black, "Robert Edmond Jones: Poetic Artist of the New Stagecraft," diss., University of Wisconsin, 1955, App. 1: iii–vi. Emphases are in original text.

33. Bryer, *"The Theatre We Worked For"* 69n.

34. Robert Edmond Jones, "A Note on the Theatre," *Provincetown Playbill* for *The Spook Sonata* 1924: 3, 4.

5

Glitter, Glitz, and Race: The Production of *Harlem*

Freda Scott Giles

In his first autobiography, *The Big Sea*, Langston Hughes provided a definitive portrait of Wallace Thurman: "He was a strange kind of fellow, who liked to drink gin, but didn't like to drink gin; who liked being a Negro, but felt it a great handicap; who adored bohemianism, but thought it wrong to be a bohemian. He liked to waste time, but he felt guilty wasting time. He loathed crowds, yet hated to be alone. He almost always felt bad, yet he didn't write poetry."[1]

Thurman did write two of the most highly regarded novels of the Harlem Renaissance period, a seminal era for African American arts and letters marked by its inception at the end of World War I and by its decline at the Great Depression: *The Blacker the Berry* and *Infants of the Spring*. He also wrote, in collaboration with William Jourdan Rapp, a playwright of Irish German extraction, a financially successful Broadway play, *Harlem*, which gained him both positive and negative notoriety, raised and dashed his hope for financial stability, and strained his chronically fragile health to the breaking point.

Born 16 August 1902 in Salt Lake City, Utah, Thurman suffered through a childhood marked by the disintegration of his parents' marriage, frequent moves from city to city throughout the midwest and west, and debilitating illnesses, including being caught in the great flu epidemic in 1918. He managed to finish high school, then matriculated at the University of Utah in Salt Lake, where the pressures of the hostile racial environment combined with those of his premedical studies precipitated a nervous breakdown. Thurman eventually completed his undergraduate studies at the University of Southern California. He supported himself as a student by working as a postal clerk and remained at the post office for the year following his graduation.

Thurman called his decision to become a writer a "sudden inspiration."[2] Stimulated by what he had learned of the New Negro movement centered in New York, he tried starting a magazine, *The Outlet*, to encourage this movement on the West Coast. His effort was unsuccessful, but his friendship with a struggling young poet who worked beside him in the post office, Arna Bontemps, helped him remain enthusiastic. Bontemps, as soon as he gained publication, moved to New York, and Thurman migrated soon after, in 1925.[3]

Among Thurman's first friends in New York was Theophilus Lewis, theatre critic for *The Messenger*, the journal published by the Brotherhood of Sleeping Car Porters. With Lewis's help, Thurman gained editorial positions with *The Messenger* as well as with two white liberal publications, *The Looking Glass* and *The World Tomorrow*. By 1926 Thurman was familiar with most of the writers of his generation, and his Harlem apartment, popularly known by the appellation he had given it, "niggerati manor,"[4] became the scene of frequent raucous gatherings of uptown black and downtown white bohemians.

Thurman invited some of the most gifted of the younger generation of black writers to contribute essays, short stories, and poetry to his next effort at magazine publishing, *Fire*, which debuted in November 1926. Though Langston Hughes, Zora Neale Hurston, and Countee Cullen were among the contributors, this beautifully produced magazine illustrated with the artwork of Aaron Douglas, priced at a dollar per copy, proved an impossibly hard sell. *Fire* also ignited the wrath of powerful critics, such as W.E.B. Du Bois, editor of the NAACP's journal, *The Crisis*; critical denunciations, particularly from the more conservative among the black literary establishment, flew hot and heavy. *Fire*'s first issue was its last, and Thurman, severely wounded emotionally and financially, was forced to spend the next several years paying off printing and start-up costs.

Thurman's contribution to *Fire* had been a short story, "Cordelia the Crude." Written in the first person from the perspective of a struggling writer, it chronicles a brief encounter with a young woman transformed by life in Harlem from a naive Southern migrant to a sexually precocious "chippie." In order to ease the sting of his rejection of her sexual advance, the writer presses two dollar bills into her palm; ironically, this gesture inspires Cordelia to enter a life of prostitution.

Sketching out a three-act melodrama, Thurman turned the short story into a play scenario also entitled "Cordelia the Crude." He created a family for her, the Masons, recent émigrés from North Carolina, and surrounded them with a variety of characters from the working class and Harlem underworld, including a bisexual male hustler and his sidekick, a gigolo known as a "sweetback."[5]

In order to shape these ideas into dramatic action and dialogue, Thurman turned to William Jourdan Rapp, a friendly acquaintance since 1925, when Thurman, new to the New York scene, had sought out Rapp for advice on how to gain employment as a writer.[6] Rapp had been a feature writer for the *New York Times*, an editor at *True Story* magazine, and a collaborator on several produced plays such as *Whirlpool*, *Substitute for Murder*, and *The Holmses of Baker Street*. A play under his sole authorship, *Osman Pasha*, a drama of the Turkish Revolution, was produced in 1925.[7]

Thurman and Rapp spent a year rewriting *Cordelia the Crude*, with a new title for each draft: *City of Refuge* (from a short story about Harlem by Rudolph Fisher), *Black Mecca*, and finally *Black Belt*, which began to make the rounds of agents and producers in 1927.[8] Cordelia's family name is now Williams and she is crowded into a railroad flat with her two younger sisters, younger brother, unemployed father, and overworked mother. Unlike her older brother, who has his own family and has brought everyone to Harlem, Cordelia, seventeen, is described as "selfish, lazy, sullen."[9] Among the four boarders who also share the flat is Basil Venable, an honest, hard-working Barbadian student, who is in love with Cordelia. The Harlem underworld is represented by Roy Crowe, a Harlem "sheik" (a ladies' man, no longer bisexual), gambler, and numbers runner, and his cohort, Kid Vamp.

The action revolves around Cordelia's efforts to avoid entrapment in a life like her mother's:

I got all I needs but freedom. Jes' cause I don' wanna tend to babies, slave, cook an' wash for pa or some white women don' mean I don't know what's best for me. I ain't cut out for dat. I'm cut out for something big, something more exciting and beautiful. . . .

All black women don' have to be sudsbusters and kitchen mechanics. And don't tell me to be no schoolteacher! I've had enough of kids right here! . . . I'm going on de stage.[10]

She sees Roy Crowe as her ticket out, and dances wildly with him at the rent party[11] in the Williams' apartment, which serves as the climactic scene in act 1; the action culminates in a fight between Basil and Roy. Cordelia leaves the party with Roy; act 2 is set in his apartment. Roy's hidden agenda is to seduce her and become her pimp. Kid Vamp murders Roy and attempts to frame Basil, who has followed Cordelia. The truth is revealed in act 3, when the action returns to the Williams flat, where the rent party is just breaking up. Kid Vamp is killed by the police. Cordelia storms out of the apartment vowing to make her own way in the world.

A number of producers expressed interest in *Black Belt*, including one who wanted to rescript the play into a vehicle for entertainer George Jessel,[12] but the play was finally optioned by Crosby Gaige under the title *Black Mecca* in January 1928. A cast was assembled but dismissed when the producer's partner, Al Lewis, decided that there was no "wow" in the third act; the playwrights produced several rewrites but could not satisfy Lewis.[13] The option was allowed to expire, and the script went back into circulation until it caught the attention of a neophyte producer, Edward A. Blatt, who bought the option and hired Chester Erskin to direct. *Harlem*, as the play would soon be known, was the first Broadway credit for both.[14]

Blatt searched for investors while Erskin, Thurman, and Rapp set out in search of a cast. Believing that *Porgy*, which had opened in 1927 and was still running successfully on Broadway, had tied up the most viable acting talent, the trio scoured Harlem cabarets, shows, and any place where they thought talent might be found.[15]

Erskin found Cordelia in the chorus at the Alhambra Theatre in Harlem. She was Isabell Washington, who had followed the footsteps of her sister Fredi, who would later become best known for her searing performance in the 1934 film, "Imitation of Life." Isabell would go on to develop a stage career and to become the first wife of Adam Clayton Powell, Jr., noted Harlem minister and politician.

Richard Landers, hired to play Basil, was the Trinidadian son of a politician. Veteran actors Inez Clough and Lew Payton were selected to play Ma and Pa Williams. After the show opened, a story was circulated that Erskin discovered the other Williams children in an uptown Chinese restaurant. The cast was filled out with community theatre actors, school teachers, a dentist, and two female boxers among the company of sixty, two-thirds of whom were employed solely for the rent party sequences.[16]

After a successful tryout at the Boulevard Theatre in Jackson Heights (Queens), New York for the week commencing 11 February 1929, *Harlem*, now subtitled *An Episode of Life in New York's Black Belt*, opened at the Apollo Theatre on Forty-second Street on 20 February. The initial response of the downtown critical establishment was quite favorable. Brooks Atkinson in his *New York Times* review called *Harlem* "Perhaps the most informalist melodrama in months with its high jinks, sizzling dancing, kicks on the shins and family jars. . . . It is a rag-bag drama and high-pressure blow-out all in one." Atkinson also noted that police department censors were on hand to scrutinize the dancing in the rent party scenes and that despite the threat of censorship, the company, particularly Isabell Washington, "performed with an abandon seldom seen before."[17]

Reviews in most of the daily papers were similar; some critics were so taken with the glossary of Harlem slang included in the program that they reprinted it. *Variety* and *Billboard* augured box office success. A cautionary note was sounded by Burns Mantle in the *Daily News*. While he admired the vitality of the play and the quality of much of the acting, he expressed concern for the reaction of the police commissioner to the dancing and the protests from Harlem against "the transplanting of this sector of cheaper Harlem in the Times sq. [*sic*] district. . . . So much of a message as they had to deliver, which appears to be a plea that the southern black should be urged to stay where his soul is comparatively safe rather than be brought north . . . is so completely buried under the surface showiness of the play that it emerges as a mere whisper."[18]

Harlem's producers may have anticipated a negative response from the African American community; in any event, they made a concerted effort to discourage the potential black audience, as reported by the *New York Age*, a leading African American weekly newspaper:

"Harlem," the new play . . . is not for Negro theatregoers, said the press representative, C. A. Leonard, to a representative of The Age. No advance publicity was sent to any of the Negro papers, nor were any sent tickets for the opening. . . . When inquiry over the telephone . . . was made, Mr. Leonard replied that the show was primarily for "white consumption.". . . The attitude is one of marked contrast to that adopted by Lew Leslie, producer of "Blackbirds," and David Belasco, when he produced "Lulu Belle" . . . in which a large number of colored people appeared.[19]

Members of the black press who did attend the opening were confined to the balcony. Thurman himself was denied access to center orchestra seats.[20] Shortly after the *Age*'s report appeared, its dramatic editor, William E. Clark, was invited to review *Harlem*; he was conservatively favorable, calling the play "an entertaining melodrama of one phase of Negro life in New York City."[21] Other African American papers, such as the *Chicago Defender* and *Pittsburgh Courier*, expressed reservations concerning the images projected by *Harlem* but recognized that some exaggeration was needed to make the play commercial.

Theophilus Lewis staunchly defended the play, citing the forcefulness of the character of Cordelia as a welcome contrast to the passivity or indolence with which the usual stage Negro was portrayed. Lewis saw the success of *Harlem* as opening up commercial possibilities for other African American playwrights.[22] There were those, however, who viewed the play as detrimental and dangerous, as expressed in this letter to the editor of the *New York Age*: "I consider it is the most degrading show ever produced by colored artists. Instead of it being something to help raise the race's name in the theatrical world, it is putting the black man down where the white man wants him."[23] This view might serve as a telling contrast to an opinion on *Harlem* printed in the *New York Times*:

The novels and plays about Harlem . . . reveal and revel in a primitive folk. It is a civilization still happy in the joyous rhythms . . . that have been vanishing, alas, out of our less primitive white civilization. . . . Suppose 135th Street, as currently portrayed, does look like a very short step away from the Congo? Think of the kick our own rarer, truly civilized spirits get therefrom! Esthetically envisaged, Harlem is being glorified, not libeled.[24]

Thurman and Rapp felt compelled to respond to the criticisms leveled at their play; both individually and as a team, they produced articles and essays in support of the veracity of *Harlem*'s situations and characters. Meanwhile, the play had garnered audience support to the extent that a second company was formed and a tour launched. *Harlem* traveled to Detroit and Chicago, and there were indications that West Coast and European tours were in the offing. The controversy over the depiction of Harlem's nightlife and underworld seemed only to fuel interest in the play. Then things began to fall apart.

During the year leading to the production of *Harlem*, Thurman had had his first novel, *The Blacker the Berry*, published, started another unsuccessful literary journal, married Louise Thompson, an educator and political activist, and six tempestuous months after the marriage, become embroiled in a lengthy and acrimonious divorce proceeding. Further exhausted and depressed by the controversy over *Harlem*, Thurman traveled west, hoping to get some rest, distance himself from his problems, and break into screenwriting by selling *Harlem* to Hollywood. According to Edward Blatt, screen rights to the play were eventually sold to Universal Studios; no film was made.[25]

In letters to Rapp, Thurman expressed distrust for *Harlem*'s producers, which, in Detroit and Chicago, included the Shuberts. Thurman feared that he was being underpaid his royalties but was hesitant to voice his doubts openly. The show's cast, however, became increasingly less hesitant in expressing its dissatisfaction, and dissension led to rebellion in New York after the show moved to the Times Square Theatre, managed by Jed Harris, two doors away from the Apollo.

According to an account given by *Harlem*'s stage manager, Helmsley Winfield, to the *Amsterdam News*, another major African American paper, the cast had agreed to open in Queens at a much lower than average salary with raises promised if the show succeeded on Broadway. Two months after the Broadway opening, no raises were forthcoming. Verbal and written inquiries on this matter gained no response from the producers. Finally, in desperation, the ensemble in the rent party scene refused to perform, staging a wildcat strike in the middle of a show. An agreement was hastily reached that the cast would join Actors Equity and receive a raise. It was soon discovered that a pay cut forced upon the principal players compensated fully for the raises given the rent party ensemble. Prior to the strike, Isabell Washington earned seventy-five dollars per week; after the strike each principal player lost ten to fifteen dollars per week. A lead performer in *Porgy* could earn up to two hundred dollars per week.[26] Tensions mounted. Resentment over the preferential treatment afforded the sole white cast member, who, though he played a very secondary role as a police detective, was assigned the star dressing room and featured in the show's publicity, added to the smoldering hostility.[27]

On 6 May 1929, director Erskin called the company together and, following "a tirade of profane abuse," notified them that *Harlem* would close on 11 May. Calling them a "bunch of crafty niggers," Erskin bid the cast "go back to Harlem . . . and starve."[28] The original Broadway production of *Harlem* closed after ninety-three performances, just shy of the benchmark of one hundred which was the measure of a hit show at that time. The tour ended in Chicago on 22 June 1929. Though Blatt and Erskin publicly insisted that faltering box office receipts closed *Harlem*, Irving Salkow, Blatt's business manager, told the *Daily News*: "They thought they had a whip hand and could make all kinds of demands because the show was a sell-out. But when they thought they were indispensable, and dared us to close the show, Mr. Blatt obliged. . . . Now they can all go back to Harlem and stage their own rent parties and see how much they make. They couldn't appreciate what we were doing for them."[29]

Paradoxically, Thurman sided with the producers, firing off angry telegrams to newspapers and threatening legal action for libel. Blatt and Erskin retained five members from the original cast, added a few actors from the touring company, filled out the ensemble with new performers, and revived *Harlem* at the Eltinge Theatre, a Shubert house on Forty-second Street, on 21 October 1929. The show closed after two weeks,[30] then played one week at the Windsor Theatre on East Fordham Road in the Bronx, followed by another one-week booking at Werber's Flatbush Theatre in Brooklyn. *Harlem* never played its namesake community.

Robert Levy, the producer for the Lafayette Players, the African American stock company housed in Harlem's Lafayette Theatre, opened a production of *Harlem* at the Music Box Theatre in Los Angeles on 7 October 1932. Reviews were lukewarm, and the show limped through a two-week engagement. Thurman's second novel, *Infants of the Spring*, had been published that same year.

Thurman, the first African American editor at McCauley's, a major publishing concern, rose to editor-in-chief. His friendship and collaboration with Rapp continued; they had completed a second play, *Jeremiah the Magnificent*, a drama based on the rise and fall of Marcus Garvey, in 1930. This play was never produced. Thurman also worked on a novelization of *Harlem* with Rapp's wife, Virginia, which was never completed. In the fall of 1932 Thurman and Rapp set to work on a dramatization of Thurman's third novel, *The Interne* [*sic*], a story of corruption in a large urban hospital; there is no evidence of an extant script.

In 1934 Thurman returned to California under contract with Foy Productions Ltd. to write screenplays for two films, *High School Girl* (1935) and *Tomorrow's Children*, which was censored in New York because of its topic, sterilization. Life in Hollywood proved detrimental to Thurman's health, which was further endangered by his increased consumption of alcohol. He eventually returned to New York, gravely ill and deeply depressed. He collapsed and was taken to City Hospital on Welfare Island, which had ironically served as his model for *The Interne*. Louise Thompson, despite their divorce, returned to nurse him. Thurman succumbed to tuberculosis on 22 December 1934 and was buried on Christmas Eve.[31]

Much has been written about the literary gifts Wallace Thurman possessed and the personal demons which beset him. He struggled with his desire to break new literary ground, his thirst for fame and its rewards, and his ambivalent feelings concerning his view of himself and his race as well as his race's view of him. *Harlem* had made him famous and infamous. Those who defended the play praised his vivid characters and his exposure of real problems in the African American community, such as limited employment opportunities, strife between African Americans and West Indians, overcrowded living conditions, crime, and the impact of life in Harlem on a family fresh from the South. Those who condemned *Harlem* excoriated it for fostering stereotypical images of near-savages dancing to jungle music and for perpetuating the myth of Harlem as an exotic wonderland of unrepressed sensuality, a myth that had already made Harlem the playground of white cafe society after dark.

Thurman was the fourth African American playwright to have a nonmusical play produced on Broadway and the first to have his play approach hit status. For this he paid a price, commercializing the play for a predominantly white audience to the extent that he risked confirming their prejudices and potentially alienating the black audience, which was deeply concerned with countering exaggerated and denigrating depictions of African American life. But Thurman's goal was not simply to sell a play; he was attempting to strike a blow for his creative freedom. He felt that despite the risk, there should be no limits or taboos, spoken or unspoken, on what he could write. His rationale for creating the troubled families, alienated, confused youth, slick, dangerous underworld characters, and desperate dreamers who populated *Harlem* remained the same as when he had created Cordelia for *Fire*: "It was not interested in sociological problems or propaganda. It was purely artistic in intent and conception. Its contributors went to the proletariat rather than to the bourgeoisie for material. They were interested in people who still retained some individual race qualities and who were not totally white American in every aspect save color of skin."[32]

NOTES

1. Langston Hughes, *The Big Sea* (1963; New York: Thunder's Mouth Press, 1986) 238.

2. Wallace Thurman Papers, James Weldon Johnson Collection, Yale University.

3. Arna Bontemps, "The Awakening, A Memoir," in *The Harlem Renaissance Remembered*, ed. Arna Bontemps (New York: Dodd Mead, 1972) 15.

4. Theophilus Lewis, "Harlem Sketchbook," *Amsterdam News* 5 January 1935: Thurman papers, Johnson Collection.

5. Wallace Thurman, "Cordelia the Crude," ts., Johnson Collection.

6. William Jourdan Rapp, autobiographical statement, Thurman papers, Johnson Collection.

7. Obituaries of William Jourdan Rapp, Thurman papers, Johnson Collection.

8. William Jourdan Rapp, notes, Thurman papers, Johnson Collection.

9. Wallace Thurman and William Jourdan Rapp, *Black Belt*, ts., Thurman papers, Johnson Collection.

10. Thurman and Rapp, *Black Belt*.

11. A house party at which admission was charged and food and drink, which during Prohibition included bootleg liquor, were sold.

12. William Jourdan Rapp, notes, Thurman papers, Johnson Collection.

13. Wallace Thurman and William Jourdan Rapp, "Detouring Harlem to Times Square," *New York Times* 7 April 1929, sec. 10: 4.

14. *Harlem* marked the beginning of successful careers for both Erskin and Blatt. Erskin directed the stage version of *The Last Mile*, which brought him, along with cast members Spencer Tracy and Clark Gable, to Hollywood, where he became a producer, writer, and director. Erskin also claimed to have rewritten and redirected Langston Hughes's first Broadway play, *Mulatto*; Hughes detested the changes. Blatt became an independent theatre producer after working with producer/managers Herman Shumlin, Jed Harris, and Martin Beck.

15. Wallace Thurman, notes, Thurman papers, Johnson Collection.

16. Thurman, notes.

17. Brooks Atkinson, "The Play," *New York Times* 21 February 1929: 30.

18. Burns Mantle, " 'Harlem' Reveals Harlem in the Grip of a Turbulent and Ginny Jamboree," *New York Daily News* 21 February 1929: 21.

19. "Negroes Not Wanted as Spectators of Play, 'Harlem,' Says Producer," *New York Age* 2 March 1929: 1.

20. In a letter to Rapp, Thurman stated, "Five times I have bought seats for myself to see Harlem—including opening night—and tho [*sic*] I asked for center aisle seats (as much as a week in advance) not yet have I succeeded in not being put on the side in a little section where any other Negro who happened to buy an orchestra seat was also placed." C. A. Leonard, the show's publicist, composed a fabrication for his article, "Dramatizing New York's Black Belt," which appeared in the June 1929 edition of *Theatre Magazine*: "Whenever Wallace Thurman, the young Negro co-author of *Harlem*, goes to the Apollo Theatre to look his show over, he voluntarily buys a seat in the balcony. . . . His chief concern when going to the theatre is that some white spectator might object to his sitting in the orchestra. He wants to spare such a spectator the possible embarrassment of discovering that he is the co-author, and for that reason, if not another, has a perfect right to sit wherever he darn well pleases." Thurman was treated as a second-class citizen as a playwright, as well; Rapp was given primary credit in all publicity releases.

21. William E. Clark, " 'Harlem,' " *New York Age* 23 March 1929: 6.

22. Theophilus Lewis, "If This Be Puritanism," *Opportunity* April 1929: 132.

23. Paul Bebee Grymes, "Says 'Harlem' Degrades," *New York Age* 27 April 1929: 4.

24. "A White Man's Holiday," *New York Times* 5 March 1929, *Harlem* clipping file, Schomburg Collection, New York Public Library.

25. Edward A. Blatt clipping file, Billy Rose Theatre Collection, New York Public Library.

26. "Thurman Play Finds Trouble Casting," *Pittsburgh Courier* 10 March 1928, sec. 2: 2.

27. "Director of 'Harlem' Calls Members of Cast 'Artful Niggers,' " *New York Age* 11 May 1929: 1.

28. Ibid.

29. "Play 'Harlem' Shut in Race-Cash Fight," *Billboard* 11 May 1929: n. pag.

30. The stock market collapsed on Friday, 28 October 1929.

31. Lewis, "Harlem Sketchbook."

32. Wallace Thurman, "Negro Artists and the Negro," *New Republic* 52 (31 August 1927): 37.

6

Disparate Voices: African American Theatre Critics of the 1920s

Freda Scott Giles

Among the observations Jennie M. Waugh included in a 1930 retrospective, "The Last Decade on Broadway," published in the journal *The Drama*, was that

> An interesting trend in subject matter has been the use of negro life and prob-
> lems. The negro has always had a place in the lower type of plays and musical re-
> views. During the last decade the negro has been accepted by outstanding native
> dramatists as material for the higher type of legitimate drama. . . . The growing popu-
> larity of native life in its various settings as subject matter is significant in that it
> brings us closer to the "great American play."[1]

As examples of this trend, Waugh listed Eugene O'Neill's *The Emperor Jones*, Paul Green's *In Abraham's Bosom*, and DuBose Heyward's *Porgy*, three among a substantial number of critically and commercially successful plays by Euro American playwrights that explored African American subject matter. The 1920s was a period of fruition of the efforts of a generation of American play-wrights who sought to throw off imitation of European models and develop a substantial body of work based on indigenous material; nothing could be more uniquely American than the "real" (as opposed to minstrel and melodrama stereotypes) experiences of the African American. In the words of W.E.B. Du Bois, "the plight of the black man in America [is] the most dramatic stuff of the modern world."[2]

The material being produced for the commercial theatre was, with very few exceptions, being produced by Euro American playwrights and assessed by Euro American critics for a Euro American audience. In the African American com-munity the authenticity and veracity of much that white critics and audiences accepted was subject to question. African American critical voices had to be developed to provide critical balance. More significantly, African American crit-ics were needed to help shape and define the debate over the nature of a black theatre aesthetic, and to assist in the formation and development of a body of work by a tiny but growing cadre of African American playwrights. Drama, though the weakest, least developed area of African American arts during the 1920s, the Harlem Renaissance period, was considered important, not only as a cultural ambassador which would reveal less distorted and stereotypical views of the black community but also as a potential cultural unifier through the development of a national African American theatre, in a vein similar to that of Ireland's Abbey Theatre or the Moscow Art Theatre. An older generation of intellectual leadership, represented by W.E.B. Du Bois (1868–1963), Alain Locke (1886–1954), and James Weldon Johnson (1871–1938), paved the way for a younger generation of critics, such as Theophilus Lewis (b. 1891) and George S. Schuyler (1895–1977). The voices raised were by no means monolithic.

Du Bois, prodigious scholar, cofounder of the NAACP (National Association for the Advancement of Colored People) and founding editor of its journal, *The Crisis*, recognized the power of theatre to educate and proselytize. In 1913 he wrote and produced a pageant of African American history, *The Star of Ethiopia*, which was performed by hundreds and seen by thousands in New York, Washington, D.C., Philadelphia, and Los Angeles. He wrote theatre criticism for *The Crisis* and through the journal founded Krigwa (Crisis Guild of Writers and Artists). In 1925 Krigwa undertook sponsorship of a literary contest which included a playwriting competition; *Opportunity*, the Urban League's journal, instituted its own contest that same year. Though he encouraged contestants to "write about things as you know them"[3] without reservation as to subject or approach, Du Bois was deeply concerned with shaping political and social perspectives through the mass medium of theatre. His agenda was to attack and replace the images presented by the commercial theatre because to him, "all art is propaganda."[4] When he founded a Little Theatre company, the Krigwa Players, he composed a manifesto which declared:

> The plays of a real Negro theatre must be: 1. About us. That is, they must have plots which reveal Negro life as it is. 2. By us. That is, they must be written by Negro authors who understand from birth and continual association just what it means to be a Negro today. 3. For us. That is, the theatre must cater primarily to Negro audiences. . . . 4. Near us. The theatre must be in a Negro neighborhood near the mass of ordinary people.[5]

Du Bois felt that the African American could tell his or her own story better, but did not object to white playwrights' efforts if they were honest. He greatly respected Ridgely Torrence's characterizations in *Three Plays for a Negro Theatre*, produced on Broadway in 1917. He defended O'Neill's *Emperor Jones* to the black community for the dynamism of the character, though Brutus Jones was in many ways the stereotypical black brute. O'Neill was invited to serve as a judge for the Krigwa playwriting competition, which was open only to black authors. Du Bois objected to characterizations of blacks by whites which he felt denigrated or demeaned his race. He attacked *Porgy* and more cheaply sensational plays of the period such as *White Cargo* and *Congo* for placing sexually explicit or racy material in a black community because they would be censored if they did so in the context of a white community. Du Bois deplored *In Abraham's Bosom*, which won a Pulitzer Prize in 1926, as yet another example of the failure of white playwrights to view the black experience in America in terms other than defeatist.[6]

Du Bois viewed such writing as a form of propaganda and sought to counter negative propaganda with positive propaganda. In the introduction to an unpublished volume of his own plays, he wrote about the "taboos," the unwritten rules of dramaturgy when writing about African Americans, which he wanted to break:

1. Negro-American drama must be defeatist. . . . One sees this in Green's "Abraham's Bosom" and O'Neill's "Emperor Jones." 2. The characters of the drama must not simulate ordinary intelligent people. . . . This is illustrated in "Porgy" and in many of the Negro musical comedies. 3. Interracial love or marriage must not be recognized . . . it must be regarded as a tragedy . . . and there can be but one ending, suicide or disappearance. . . . This is illustrated in DuBose Heyward's "Brass Ankles" 6[sic] and Sheldon's "Nigger." Even personal devotion and friendship must be limited to the abject grovelling devotion of a servant to a white master, or the patronizing help of a white person for a Negro. 4. Even love-making among Negroes themselves must not be emphasized, except in caricature or farce. . . . 7. Mulattoes must be portrayed as . . . criminals or . . . carrying on a "war between the races" in their own souls.[7]

Alain Locke, like Du Bois, sought to shape a new direction for theatre by and about African Americans, and like Du Bois he did not exclude white playwrights from this process. The two differed sharply on the aesthetic framework to be used: while Du Bois favored the "problem play" which offered some direct insight into sociopolitical conditions, Locke favored development of the folk drama and rediscovery of connections to African roots.

Locke, the first African American Rhodes Scholar and a professor of philosophy at Howard University, edited a landmark volume which some critics view as the seminal work of the Harlem Renaissance, *The New Negro*, an anthology developed as an outgrowth of an edition of the journal, *Survey Graphic*, guest-edited by Locke. Published in 1925, it spoke of a change in the psychology of the African American which denoted a new self-assurance and sense of identity. No longer would the African American be simply on the defensive, attempting to prove his humanity; he would take his aesthetic destiny into his own hands and shape it in his true image. Locke brought a younger generation of writers forward to project more progressive images. Every area of arts and letters, including drama, was represented in *The New Negro*. Two essays, "The Drama of Negro Life" by Montgomery Gregory and "The Gift of Laughter" by Jessie Fauset, provided historical background on the African American in theatre and expressed the desire for establishment of a national Negro theatre. *Compromise*, a one-act folk drama by Willis Richardson, served as an example of writing for this theatre of folk expression. Richardson's one-act comedy, *The Chip Woman's Fortune*, had been the first nonmusical play of African American authorship to be produced on Broadway, in 1923.

In 1916 Locke had participated in the production of *Rachel* by Angelina Grimke, presented by the NAACP in Washington, D.C. This, too, was a landmark production which inspired further development of African American theatre by African Americans. The political content of the play, which told the story of a black woman who sacrificed her opportunity for marriage rather than risk bringing up children in the racially hostile environment of the United States, did not appeal to Locke, who believed, "Propaganda, pro-Negro as well as anti-Negro, has scotched the dramatic potentialities of the subject."[8] He broke away, and with Montgomery Gregory, a colleague at Howard, established a theatre program at Howard University and cofounded the Howard Players, a Little Theatre company, to perform the types of drama he favored: "The creative impulse is for the moment caught in this dilemma of choice between the drama of social analysis and the drama of expression and artistic interpretation. But despite the present lure of the problem play, it ought to be apparent that the real future of the Negro drama lies with the development of the folk play."[9]

In 1927 Locke and Gregory coedited an anthology, *Plays of Negro Life*, the first collection of its kind. Black and white playwrights were represented equally among the twenty one-act plays included. Among them were Eugene O'Neill, Paul Green, and Ridgely Torrence as well as leading young black playwrights Willis Richardson, Eulalie Spence, Frank Wilson, and Georgia Douglas Johnson. Locke regularly contributed dramatic criticism to *Opportunity*. His essays "The Negro and the American Stage" and "The Drama of Negro Life" were among the prolific output of writing which exposed his views to a general audience in such publications as *Theatre Arts Monthly*. White arts patrons sought out Locke as a matchmaker when looking for African American talent to support. He enjoyed extensive contacts with the European arts community, especially in France. While Du Bois's commitment to the arts was partially an outgrowth of his social and political activism, Locke's commitment was more purely aesthetic, though he firmly believed that the arts could and should serve as an avenue toward social justice through aesthetic appreciation. Locke carried a tremendous amount of weight as a critical force and was not hesitant to let the weight of that force be felt.

James Weldon Johnson appreciated the views of Du Bois and Locke but brought a more pragmatic sensibility to the discussion of the shaping of black arts. Though perhaps better known as the novelist who wrote *The Autobiography of an Ex-Colored Man*, or as a cultural historian through his book *Black Manhattan*, which includes a history of the African American in the New York theatre, or as an essayist, poet, social activist, and ambassador, Johnson was also a man of the theatre. In partnership with his brother, composer Rosamond Johnson, he wrote songs for the musical produced by Bob Cole, *The Shoofly Regiment* (1906) and *The Red Moon* (1908). These black-authored shows helped weaken the hold of the minstrel stereotype on Broadway. As a man who had tried to make a living in the theatre, Johnson articulated the problems artists faced when writing for an audience in a racially segregated nation. Johnson saw the problem as more connected with content than form. Just as years earlier, Du Bois had described the dilemma of the double consciousness (the awareness of one's true nature as an African American human being juxtaposed against the persona that must be adopted to survive a hostile power structure), Johnson described the dilemma of the double audience, the recognition by an artist that an attempt at honestly following his muse put him at risk:

If the Negro author selects white America as his audience he is bound to run up against . . . a whole row of hard-set stereotypes which are not easily broken up. . . . American Negroes as heroes form no part of white America's concept of the race. . . . In plain words, white America does not welcome seeing the Negro competing with the white man on what it considers the white man's own ground. . . . He has no more absolute freedom to speak as he pleases addressing black America than he has in addressing white America. . . . The colored people . . . are a segregated and antagonized minority in a very large nation, a minority unremittingly on the defensive . . . consequently, they have a strong feeling against exhibiting to the world anything but their best points. . . . It is an extremely difficult thing for the Negro author in the United States to address himself solely to either of these two audiences. . . . But it is impossible for a sane American Negro to write with total disregard for nine-tenths of the people of the United States. . . . Of course, the Negro author can try . . . putting black America in the orchestra, so to speak, and keeping white America in the gallery, but he is likely at any moment to find his audience shifting places on him, and sometimes without notice.[10]

The problem for the African American artist became whether to align himself or herself with the assimilationists, who believed in cultural integration, or with the nationalists, who supported the idea that there could be a sustaining, separate African American culture. To write for the commercial theatre as an assimilationist meant to write for a predominantly white audience. To write for a black audience meant very little chance to make a living; commercial outlets for legitimate theatre in the African American community were too few. The issues of what to write, how to write it, and whom to write for became the focus of intense debate.

Du Bois carried this debate through several issues of *The Crisis* in a series titled "The Negro in Art/How Shall He Be Portrayed/A Symposium." Questionnaires were sent to black and white artists, producers, and publishers; among the respondents were DuBose Heyward, Langston Hughes, Sinclair Lewis, Vachel Lindsay, and Sherwood Anderson. Replies fell into three general categories: that now that the African American was "in vogue," material should be exploited while it was hot; that black art should serve to correct stereotypes and uplift the race; and that black art should seek no obligation from the artists other than truthfulness.

Langston Hughes forwarded the cause of artistic freedom, as well as advocating the position that there exists an African American culture and a black aesthetic. Hughes gained recognition as a poet during the 1920s and wrote plays at that time, though his contributions as a playwright would not gain widespread recognition until 1935 with the Broadway production of *Mulatto*. Among the best and brightest of the New Negro writers, he joined in public debate against the conservative views of novelist and journalist George Schuyler.

Schuyler wrote and edited for *The Messenger*, and contributed literary and theatre reviews to the *Chicago Defender*, a nationally circulated African American newspaper. He wrote for all the major African American print publications, including *The Crisis* and *Opportunity*. His work was regularly seen in *The New Masses*, *Reader's Digest*, and *American Mercury* as well as in a number of other American, European, and African journals. His strong anticommunist views made him popular among all the leading conservative publications; he may have been the first African American to become an active member of the John Birch Society. His best-known novel is *Black No More* (1931), a satire on color consciousness and those who make a living from it.[11] His might be described as the most disparate of the black critical voices of the Harlem Renaissance.

Schuyler and Hughes took each other on in the pages of *The Nation*. In an article entitled "The Negro Art Hokum," Schuyler brushed aside the idea of a black aesthetic:

the Aframerican is merely a lampblacked Anglo-Saxon. . . . In the homes of the black and white Americans of the same cultural and economic level one finds similar furniture, literature, and conversation. How, then, can the black American be expected to produce art and literature dissimilar to that of the white American? . . . This nonsense is probably the last stand of the old myth palmed off by the Negrophobists for all these many years . . . that there are "fundamental, eternal, and inescapable differences" between white and black Americans.[12]

Hughes counterattacked with "The Negro Artist and the Racial Mountain," describing the metaphorical mountain of racism the black artist must climb over in order to discover himself and his people; that process includes taking the risk of alienating the present audience in hope of being understood by a future audience. But the African American artist must develop a sense of an African American aesthetic. If all he or she is taught is a white interpretation of beauty, that is all he or she will see. Hughes identified the material derived from spirituals, blues, jazz, modes of religious worship, and everyday life in African American communities in the North and South as distinctive enough to mold a black aesthetic, declaring, "We younger Negro artists who create now intend to express our individual selves without fear or shame. If white people are pleased we are glad. If not, it doesn't matter. We know we are beautiful. And ugly too. . . . If colored people are pleased we are glad. If they are not, their displeasure doesn't matter either. We build our temples for tomorrow . . . free within ourselves."[13]

No consensus was reached on a definition for African American drama in form or content. From this lack of consensus a heated sub-debate arose over the appropriate use of dialect; the dialect of the stage Negro had been so distorted that some playwrights were not sure it should be used at all, even in folk drama. Dialect was considered essential for folk drama but was attacked by a number of critics as retrogressive and subject to stereotypical interpretation.

Theophilus Lewis, the first African American critic of this period to focus solely on the theatre, cut through the confusion to provide logical and practical insights into the problems and to suggest some solutions. Lewis provided a regular column, "The Theater: The Souls of Black Folks," to *The Messenger*, the comprehensive journal published by the Brotherhood of Sleeping Car Porters, from 1923 through 1927. He covered every type of theatre from musical revues to vaudeville to legitimate drama to Little Theatre, from Harlem to Broadway. Unlike Romeo Doherty, who reviewed plays and sports events for the *Amsterdam News*, or William E. Clark, reviewer and arts editor for the *New York Age*, which were New York's African American newspapers, Lewis did much more than describe the merits or demerits of selected major productions. He attempted to raise the consciousness of his audience to the potential of African American theatre and drama. He advocated a national African American theatre and encouraged the efforts of those who were attempting to develop the artistic and producing infrastructure that could make this possible. He tackled aesthetic questions and came up with answers of his own.

Like Du Bois, for example, Lewis admired *The Emperor Jones* as a great dramatic work. Unlike Du Bois or Locke, he did not see the play as African American drama:

Negro drama . . . is . . . the body of plays written by Negro authors. The kind of life represented in the play is immaterial. The scene may be in Norway or Spain and the characters presumably natives of one or the other country; nevertheless it will be a Negro play if it is the product of a Negro's mind. *Hamlet* is not a Danish play nor is *The Merchant of Venice* an Italian play. Both are English plays. The *Phaedra* of Euripides is Greek, while the *Phaedra* of Racine is French. . . . To maintain that Negro drama consists merely of plays about Negro life, regardless of who writes them, is to alter the accepted meaning of terms.[14]

African American theatres had to be scaled to the abilities of African American communities to support them, and ownership and management of these theatres must be in African American hands. Lewis attached artistic freedom and integrity to economic autonomy; if, as he estimated, 50 percent of the theatres and 75 percent of the theatre patronage of African Americans were in white hands, the theatre would remain measured by white standards, catering to the lowest common denominator for maximum profit.[15]

Lewis challenged African American performers to refuse demeaning roles, and African American writers and theatre practitioners to study and perfect their craft. He exhorted the audience to demand a higher-quality product. In his columns he brought together the abstract debate of the intellectual leadership with the needs and desires of the mass of African American theatregoers from all strata of society. He predicted that the focus of the debate would shift, as class conflict would eventually overshadow racial conflict: "As the class cleavage between whites and whites becomes more pronounced the consequent friction is bound to either overshadow the race problem or absorb it. . . . The race problem, of course, cannot be solved; it can only be ameliorated. In which respect it is just like every other human problem."[16]

The national African American theatre Lewis advocated never came to pass. In his own assessment of the decade of the 1920s and African American theatre which appeared in the October 1930 issue of *Opportunity*, African American theatre educator and playwright Randolph Edmonds (1900–1986) wrote, "the conclusion is almost inescapable that the so-called Negro Renaissance has been almost a total failure in so far as the development of the drama is concerned."[17]

In Edmonds's view, the relatively recent development of the African American as a serious subject for drama in the commercial theatre, the lack of adequate training and performing facilities for African American playwrights and actors, and lack of mass audience support hindered the maturation of African American drama. White playwrights had popularized African American subject matter in the legitimate theatre but had not broken through to authentic portraits of African American life. Access to commercial Broadway had been granted to only four African American playwrights during this decade: Willis Richardson (*The Chip Woman's Fortune*, 1923), Garland Anderson (*Appearances*, 1925), Frank Wilson (*Meek Mose*, 1928), and Wallace Thurman (*Harlem*, 1929). Richardson's play ran for a very short time, and Edmonds cited a number of flaws in the others, though he found more merit in *Harlem*; the developing playwrights appeared to be too derivative of their white counterparts. Edmonds, too, advocated folk drama and the use of dialect (refuting James Weldon Johnson's statement that "dialect is an instrument with two stops, comedy and pathos"[18]) and cited *The Green Pastures* (1930) by white playwright Marc Connelly as a step in the right direction, toward the depiction of African American life as a reflection of universal human experience.

During this period of ferment all sides in the aesthetic debate would have agreed with the goal of finding the universal through the unique experience of the African American. There was no consensus on how that goal should be pursued, and too few opportunities to test and develop enough of the artists necessary to sustain a theatre of cultural nationalism or an avenue into the commercial mainstream for African American playwrights which might match the growth of opportunities for African American actors. Despite the difficulties, the African American critics of this period recognized the potential· for African American theatre as mass communication and made concrete contributions to its growth and progress, playing an active as well as a reflexive role in the struggle for greater truth in the depiction of African Americans on the stage.

NOTES

1. Jennie M. Waugh, "The Last Decade on Broadway," *The Drama* 20 (January 1930): 108.

2. W.E.B. Du Bois, Introduction, *Playthings of the Night*, unpublished manuscript, n. pag.

3. W.E.B. Du Bois, "Krigwa 1926," *The Crisis* 31 (1926): 115.

4. Leonard C. Archer, *Black Images in the American Theatre* (New York: Pageant-Poseidon, 1973) 65–66.

5. W.E.B. Du Bois, "Krigwa Players Little Negro Theatre," *The Crisis* 32 (1926): 134.

6. W.E.B. Du Bois, "In Abraham's Bosom," *The Crisis* 34 (1927): 12.

7. W.E.B. Du Bois, *Playthings of the Night*, n. pag.

8. Alain Locke, "The Drama of Negro Life," *Theatre Arts Monthly* 10 (1926): 701.

9. Locke, "The Drama of Negro Life" 703.

10. James Weldon Johnson, "The Dilemma of the Negro Artist," *American Mercury* 15 (December 1928): 479–481.

11. Arthur P. Davis, *From the Dark Tower: Afro-American Writers, 1900–1960* (Washington, DC: Howard University Press, 1981) 105.

12. George S. Schuyler, "The Negro Art Hokum," *The Nation* 122 (1926): 662.

13. Langston Hughes, "The Negro Artist and the Racial Mountain," *The Nation* 122 (1926): 693.

14. Theophilus Lewis, "Main Problems of the Negro Theater," *The Messenger* 9 (July 1927): 229.

15. Lewis, "Main Problems of the Negro Theater" 229.

16. Theophilus Lewis, "The Theater: The Souls of Black Folks," *The Messenger* 8 (April 1926): 116.

17. Randolph Edmonds, "Some Reflections on the Negro in American Drama," *Opportunity* 8 (October 1930): 303.

18. Edmonds, "Some Reflections" 304.

7

Garland Anderson and *Appearances*: The Playwright and His Play

Alan Kreizenbeck

Appearances, Garland Anderson's initial playwriting attempt, was the first full-length drama by an African American author to be produced on the Broadway stage. First presented in 1925, it was also one of the earliest legitimate productions in New York to use a racially mixed cast. Play and author, however, receive scant attention in American theatre history texts. Information about Anderson and *Appearances* has been published by Doris Abramson, James V. Hatch, and James Weldon Johnson.[1] But the nature of the volumes in which this information is published does not allow for a full picture of Anderson and his accomplishments. Further, the overtly religious motif of *Appearances* distracts from the racial attitudes and conflicts central to the play. The following pages provide a more nearly complete look at Anderson, as well as a new analysis of *Appearances*.

Garland Anderson's life story reads like a Horatio Alger novel, in which hard work, perseverance, belief in one's self, and luck combine to reward a hitherto unknown individual with fame and fortune. Anderson's story is based on presentation and perception: he presented himself to the press as a humble servant, desiring only to serve mankind; the press perceived him as the "right" kind of African American and presented him to the public as such with many column inches describing him and his quest. The public perceived in Anderson a personification of the national belief in self-realization through self-determination and presented him with the respect and rewards he sought. Anderson's circumstances as African American, poor, and undereducated intensified the public's interest in him and made his eventual success not just personal but societal and racial as well.

Most of the primary information available concerning Anderson comes from his own scrapbooks, now part of the Billy Rose Collection at the New York Public Library at Lincoln Center.[2] Most of the material in these scrapbooks is newspaper clippings about Anderson and his play. Most of these clippings are not annotated with publication or date. The source of the information in many of those clippings is Anderson himself: the record of much of Anderson's life is according to Anderson.

So, according to Anderson, he was born in Wichita, Kansas, in 1886, the fourth of twelve children. When he was eight, his family moved to Sacramento where his father had secured a job as a post-office janitor. Four years later Garland's mother died. This event deeply affected him: he ran away from home, hopped a freight train, and spent six months living among hoboes in Chicago. He returned to San Francisco but did not return to school. At the age of thirteen, equipped with a fourth grade education, Anderson joined the work force. He was first a newsboy, then a dining car waiter. In 1917 he found permanent employment as a bellhop and switchboard operator at the Braeburn Hotel Apartments.

Genteel and well-mannered, Anderson talked whenever he could with the hotel's guests, asking questions, discussing news and current events. He was—despite his limited formal education—a voracious reader. He became a believer in Couéism, also known as New Thought, a dogma which emphasized the power of the mind and the effects of positive thinking.[3] These beliefs sustained Anderson throughout his life and are the basis for *Appearances* and his later writings. Although Couéism's tenets seem naive and simplistic to many, American mythology supports Couéism's notions that belief in one's self and in one's own rightness can bring fulfillment.

One evening an elderly couple suggested to Anderson that he see a local production of Channing Pollock's *The Fool*. He attended the production, an event that changed the course of his life: "After seeing it the thought came to me that it would be wonderful if I too could write a drama in which I could give my message to the world. So I decided on a three act play. . . . For three months before I tackled it I kept telling myself 'you can do it, you can do it!' " (Anderson, scrapbooks).

Between hopping bags and answering the switchboard, Anderson wrote his play, using a pencil to put down lines and scenes on whatever scraps of paper were handy. He never had more than a few minutes between interruptions, but he applied positive-thinking techniques to use the disruptions constructively: "Whenever the switchboard would ring while I was writing I would say to myself, 'This is just a loving call coming just at the right time to refresh my thoughts in order that I might be able to write better'; and when someone would speak to me I would mentally say, 'This is a loving interruption coming at just the right time to prevent me from writing the wrong thing' " (Anderson, scrapbooks). This technique evidently worked. He finished the first draft of his play in three weeks.

Positive support for Anderson's efforts came from his typist, who told him that she had become engrossed in the play and that it had helped solve a difficult problem in her life. In interview after interview, Anderson would say, "I only want to serve" (Anderson, scrapbooks). Armed with proof from the typist that his play could indeed serve humanity, Anderson took *Appearances* to George Warren, drama critic for the *San Francisco Chronicle*. Warren told him that the script contained some excellent ideas but suggested a rewrite. Anderson followed that advice, submitting a second version to the actor-manager Richard Bennett, who was appearing in San Francisco. Bennett assured Anderson that his play could be successful on Broadway but that he was unable to produce or perform in it himself. This may have been Bennett's polite way of extricating himself from the situation, but Anderson seems to have believed Bennett totally, taking his remarks as further proof of *Appearances*' appeal.

Anderson was, however, at a loss as to what to do next. He gave the script to another newspaperman. Not influential in theatrical circles himself, he had a cousin who was—Al Jolson. When Jolson was next in town, the newsman showed him the play. Jolson liked it and, although he too was unable to produce or star in it, as a gesture of his support he offered to pay Anderson's way to New York so that he might try to convince a Broadway producer of the play's potential.

Greatly flattered, Anderson took a leave of absence from the hotel and departed for Manhattan. He arrived in November 1924 and took up residence at the Harlem Y.M.C.A. He spent the next several months attempting to attract a producer. The *Amsterdam News*—the city's most influential African American newspaper—became aware of Anderson and published several articles about him, his beliefs, and his background. "White" newspapers picked up the story and published similar articles, most picturing Anderson as a personification of the American quest for recognition and fulfillment, only in blackface. Anderson instigated many of these stories by visiting newspaper offices, introducing himself to appropriate reporters, and offering them the opportunity for an interview. It is important to note that there seems to have been little or no cynicism indulged in on either side of the desk: Anderson believed in his play and the reporters believed in Anderson. All this free publicity, however, did not convince any producers to back *Appearances.*

Discouraged by his lack of success (or as discouraged as he ever seemed to get), Anderson devised a plan to create national attention. He took the train to Washington, D.C., where he persisted until he was allowed to personally present a copy of the script to President Calvin Coolidge. The President reportedly promised to give the script a careful reading and wished Anderson every success. Governor Al Smith of New York later received a similar visit, made a similar promise, and provided *Appearances* with even more publicity. The reported endorsements of America's two most famous politicians (one from each party) still failed to attract a producer.

In April of 1925 *Appearances* was still unstaged. Undeterred, Anderson invited all the city's well-known theatrical personalities and politicians to a public reading. It took place on 5 April in the Waldorf Astoria Hotel ballroom. Anderson's rapport with the press resulted in extensive publicity. "That name Al Smith on the invitations brought them in," Anderson recounted to the *San Francisco News* of 11 September 1935. Whether or not Smith's name actually did appear is unknown, but over 600 persons attended, including the Governor, John Hylan (mayor of New York), Heywood Broun, David Belasco, Richard Bennett, and Channing Pollock. Richard B. Harrison, later famous as "De Lawd" in *Green Pastures*, performed the reading, and according to the *Herald Tribune*, "changed his voice at times to suit the characterization" (Anderson, scrapbooks). Response to the play was positive: one unidentified newspaper reports, "They [the audience] were favorably impressed, often interrupting Harrison with applause. Some of them wept at the more touching portrayals" (Anderson, scrapbooks). Anderson—wearing his bellhop's uniform—sat next to Harrison on the stage; at the end of the reading he took up a collection for the play's production. Receipts amounted to $140 cash and several pledges. Harrison also performed a second reading on 21 April at the Manhattan Opera House. Reports of this presentation also indicate a responsive audience, but no mention is made of prominent guests or funds collected.

Anderson's efforts were finally rewarded in June when Lester W. Sagar, manager of the Central Theatre on Forty-fourth Street, offered to produce the play. He had been associated with the Shubert brothers on several productions; *Appearances* was to be his first venture as an independent producer. He received an option to purchase half the show for $15,000, while Anderson retained separate rights for presentations on the West Coast. Sagar hired John Hayden to direct.

The sale of his play accomplished, Anderson returned to his bellhop-receptionist job in San Francisco. He could not have stayed away from work much longer as he provided the sole support for an eight-year-old son (no mention of a wife has been discovered), his brother's widow, and her four children. He planned to remain at the Braeburn until late August, then return to New York to supervise rehearsals. On the way to San Francisco, Anderson stopped in Chicago, gave a reading of his play at the Blackstone Hotel, and received an enthusiastic response.

While he was in San Francisco, Anderson managed to sell half interest in West Coast production rights for another $15,000. This sale was accomplished after two public readings, one given on 9 July at the Knights of Columbus Hall featuring Anderson's niece Tabitha, "a colored elocutionist of some note" according to one newspaper (Anderson, scrapbooks). The second, broadcast over radio station KFCR, featured Tabitha, the City of Paris Players, and Anderson himself reading the leading role. The purchasers, Fergus and H. S. Wilkinson, planned to present the play in San Francisco before it opened in New York. They later decided to first observe the Broadway rehearsals.

The playwright (and the Wilkinsons) received a well-publicized send-off from the people of San Francisco for the trip east. The mayor wrote Anderson a letter of introduction to his New York counterpart, which was printed in several San Francisco papers (Anderson, scrapbooks). When Anderson arrived in Manhattan he was greeted by His Honor on the steps of City Hall. Hylan managed to use the event for a little politicking: "This colored man bears a letter from Mayor Rolph of San Francisco, who, like myself, has preserved the five cent fare to the city" (Anderson, scrapbooks).

Rehearsals began on a potentially destructive note when the two actresses—Myrtle Tannerhill and Nedda Harrington—hired to play the female leads quit the production after discovering that African American performers were included in the cast. Sagar, contrary to the custom, had not hired white actors for the African American parts but had filled them instead with principals from the Lafayette Stock Company. In an interview concerning her decision, one of the actresses "emphasized the fact that her decision must not be construed as indicative of race prejudice, but said the production of the play called for so close an association with the other players that she felt she could not be happy under the circumstances" (Anderson, scrapbooks). Luckily, replacements —Hazele Burgess and Daisy Atherton—were quickly found so that no real harm was done. The two walk-outs created more free publicity for the production through the notice that their actions generated.

The play premiered on 13 October 1925 at the Frolic, which was situated atop the New Amsterdam Theatre. The opening night audience gave the performers a standing ovation and would not leave the theatre until Anderson answered their call for "author." John Forbes, writing for the *Morning Telegraph*,

reported that "Mr. Anderson made a modest speech, in which he said in effect
that if a man desires to do a good thing earnestly enough, he will succeed, even
though a bellhop. Mr. Anderson had a nice address, appeared very happy at the
reception of his play, and regretted he could not express in words the feeling of
gratitude in his heart. He appeared sincere" (Anderson, scrapbooks).

Appearances is divided into a prologue, three acts, and an epilogue.[4] The
prologue takes place in a San Francisco hotel lobby, where a retired judge
(Thornton) and an active one (Robinson) are discussing a case tried by the latter
earlier in the day. They ask Carl, the "colored" bellhop, his opinion of the verdict. He tells them of a dream he had the night before which included a trial
remarkably similar to the one being discussed. Carl's dream constitutes the
play, and as he begins to relate it, the curtain opens on act 1.

It is set in the same hotel lobby. The hotel's owner, Mr. Thompson, has
been unfaithful to his wife. She has discovered his deceit and now Thompson is
asking Carl what he should do. Their exchange presents Anderson's philosophy
in a context preoccupied with race; it exemplifies much of the play's dialogue:

> THOMPSON. I've heard you talk about these ideas you have and I've seen
> some of them work. Now what would you do if you were in my place?
> Forget your color, what would you do?
> CARL. (*looks at book*) This little book says, first put myself right, sir, and
> everything else would be all right. (100)

Rufus enters and interrupts the discussion. The audience knew his race by
his name, an example of Anderson's awareness and use of white stereotyping of
African Americans. Rufus is an uneducated "field negro" who provides most of
the play's comedy. Anderson will later reveal another side to his character, but
the audience's first impression harkens back to the minstrel show, an impression
that Anderson reinforces in an exchange that occurs when Thompson offers
Rufus a job at $18 a week. Rufus says he didn't hear him. Thompson, in a
louder voice, offers him $15, to which Rufus replies, "I heard you the first time,
boss" (101). Rufus is also the minstrel Malaprop, fracturing the English language in a variety of ways: "Oh, which reminds me of a story, if I may exude";
"I suttinly avail myself of your professional proclivities"; and "I gives yuh my
firmest condemnations" (102).

Ella enters. Although African American and a maid at the hotel, she is the
antithesis of Rufus, as different in the audience's mind as Harvard was from
Harlem. Ella is well-spoken and educated; in fact she is attending law school at
night. Her character is an early clue that Anderson will not always satisfy white-
audience preconceptions of either gender or race. But *Appearances* is not about
Ella: she is Carl's fiancée and does little in the play but exist as proof of his
seriousness and high ideals.

Anderson continues an entrance-exit pattern as a way to introduce the play's
other characters. Efficient but unimaginative, this technique betrays Anderson's
lack of writing experience and is probably one of the structural weaknesses referred to in the play's reviews. Ella exits, Kellard enters. He is a he-man rancher
whose land contains valuable mineral deposits. Louise, Judge Thornton's
daughter, enters. She meets Kellard, they are instantly smitten. She exits to the
street; Kellard, saying he has to "mail a letter," follows her.

Wilson enters. He is the District Attorney and the play's villain. More important to the play's conflict is his overt and—until much later in the play—unchallenged racism. His first line exposes his prejudice: (to Carl and Rufus) "What is this? A colored convention?" (102). Wilson wants to marry Louise and believes that Carl is influencing her against him. Carl refuses Wilson's offer of $500 to convince Louise to accept his proposal. An angry Wilson accuses Carl of being a "slick nigger," and suggests that the "big thing he is after is money." Carl's response is Anderson speaking, explicating a strong belief in his own self-worth while acknowledging that he lives in a society that degrades him. Anderson allows Carl to tell a white man that he is wrong, but the telling is restrained:

> CARL. You call me a "slick nigger" and say these things I work so hard to believe in are "bunk." You're wrong, Mr. Wilson. You're wrong when you say I'm slick, wrong when you call my ideas "bunk." Mr. Wilson, I'll admit that I'm just a negro servant, a good servant to everyone, even to you. (103)

Carl and Rufus exit; Louise and Kellard return together to an angry and jealous Wilson, who berates them. A commotion is heard offstage. A white woman, Elsie, is helped on stage. She accuses Carl and Rufus of attacking her. The curtain falls on Carl's line, "I've done nothing wrong and have nothing to fear" (109).

Act 2 is Carl's trial. Critics of the time thought it provided most of the play's drama, particularly after a first act that was mostly exposition. Judge Robinson is presiding. Carl opts to defend himself while Judge Thornton comes out of retirement to defend Rufus. Wilson is the prosecuting attorney; Elsie is his first witness. She testifies that Carl grabbed her and tried to force himself on her, and that Rufus helped prevent her escape. A policeman testifies that he saved Carl from an angry mob that came to Elsie's defense. Two members of that mob then take the stand to verify Elsie's story: Saunders, a house painter who has some comic business with the pronunciation of his name, and Matthews, an extremely slow talker who also provides some comic moments. Both men are white and so must be believed when testifying against an African American, but Anderson emphasizes both characters' buffoonery, negating the value of their testimony.

Carl then takes the stand. He has no witnesses; the truth will be his defense: "I firmly believe that when a man tells the truth, the whole truth and nothing but the truth, knowing in his heart that it will be reacted to as the truth, no other result possibly can follow. I am speaking now simply to tell the truth" (113). He tells the court that he met Elsie on the street and that she demanded money from him, threatening to cry rape if he didn't give it to her. Events very similar to this happened to Anderson himself. He told an unidentified newspaper reporter the following:

One day a white woman stopped me in a lonely corridor and said, "You owe me ten dollars." "I don't owe you ten dollars," I said. "Maybe you don't," she replied, "but I'm going to say you do, and unless you hand it over I'll scream and tell 'em you attacked me. You know whose word the police will take." I knew . . . I'd never seen the woman before, but I couldn't do anything else but pay. (Anderson, scrapbooks)

Carl steps down and Kellard testifies that it appeared to him that Carl was attempting to escape from the woman's clutches, not vice versa. Now Rufus speaks. His testimony is predictably humorous but offers two chilling glimpses of American racism. In the first, Rufus recalls how he was nearly lynched once before:

I was workin' for a lady back home and she 'cused me of stealin' a ring, so they takes and locks me in the smoke house till the Constable can come. So I digs myself out and gets away an' into a swamp and hides myself. In the middle of the night the bay-ing of the dogs wakes me up and I knows they got the scent by the way they bays, and I starts travellin', but 'taint no use, so I climbs a big old stump and soon the dogs is all round me, then the white folks come and they want to string me up, but the Constable wouldn't let them; and they drags me back to the house, when we gets there, the lady she finds her ring where she lost it, and tell the folks I didn't steal it at all. (118)

The second episode struck much closer to home for the urban audience. It took place just before the alleged attack. Rufus states that he had been sent from the hotel to purchase some ice cream, but "I knows these places around here don't sell ice cream to no colored folks, so I goes way down South, take me ten minutes on the car and I go to Carlins drug store. That's the colored drug store your Honor" (117). When Wilson points out to him that such discrimination is against the law, Rufus replies that some stores will serve him, but "they put some flavor on that ice cream that just spoils it for eatin'." Wilson calls this observation "preposterous," and, as Abramson points out, Anderson uses humor to take the edge off the story by having Rufus respond, "Is that so sir? I never hears with what they calls it before. It sure taste worse than it sounds" (119).[5] Anderson's frequent use of humor to deflate tension is another structural pattern in *Appearances*; the tension he deflates frequently arises from racial rather than personal conflicts.

Throughout the trial, in fact, race is never far from anyone's mind. Ander-son's recognition of racial prejudice in the following exchange between the two judges is as close as he comes in the play to naming and condemning the atti-tudes exhibited in varying degrees by nearly every white character in the play. Judge Robinson has questioned why Judge Thornton (now Rufus's lawyer) wanted Rufus to recount the "ring" story:

> JUDGE THORNTON. Only that it shows the blind hatred that seems to in-flame certain types of white minds where a Negro is concerned; and will explain to the jury why some of the testimony may have been in-fluenced by this hatred.
> JUDGE ROBINSON. You wouldn't wish to infer that the *Court* has been in-fluenced by that, Judge?
> JUDGE THORNTON (*to bench*). No, Your Honor, but the *jury* have to decide this case on *evidence* perhaps influenced by this prejudice. (118)

Wilson's closing argument attempts to exploit this very prejudice:

The law says there must be one law for white and the same law for the Black, and I subscribe to the law, but there is something that the law cannot control and that is the honor of a white woman when attacked by a Black man . . . [guilty is] the only verdict you, as men, can bring in, for by it you will prove your humanity; by it you will prove your protection of you own homes, your daughters, your wives, your sweethearts. (120–121)

Just as the jury is about to begin deliberations, a message is passed to Judge Robinson. It states that Elsie is a Negress—not white—and that Wilson forced her to entrap Carl. Abramson is again astute with the observation that by making Elsie black, it satisfies "that element of the audience which might worry about a white woman being portrayed as an immoral character in a play about a highly moral Negro."[6]

A mistrial is declared, and Carl and Rufus are released. It is revealed that Mrs. Thompson (the hotel manager's estranged wife) was compelled by some "irresistible force" to write the note that freed them. The second act curtain drops on a happy Carl, a dazed Rufus, and a fuming Mr. Wilson.

Act 3 returns to the hotel lobby. Wilson has successfully blamed the hapless Elsie for everything; she has been escorted out of town. Mrs. Thompson has disappeared. A new character is introduced, "Mr. A. A. Andrews," Wilson's business partner. Andrews attempts to convince Kellard to sell his property; the two exit discussing a possible deal. Elsie sneaks into the lobby and hands Carl a letter. From Mrs. Thompson, it defends Elsie as a victim of Wilson's treachery and reveals that the two (Elsie and Wilson) cohabited for a time in Oakland. Wilson's sexual relationship with an African American woman clarifies his villainy, particularly for the mostly white, 1920s audience.

Carl confronts Wilson with this information just as Andrews enters to announce that he has convinced Kellard to sell his land for much less than it is actually worth. Wilson's gloating over his financial chicanery is cut short as Kellard enters to reveal that "A. A. Andrews" is actually his brother and that they have been working together to expose Wilson's dirty dealings. The brothers leave to fetch the sheriff, telling Rufus to guard Wilson; the two are alone on the stage.

In the short scene that follows, Anderson, through this reversal of the accepted dominant-subservient social relationship, exposes the rage behind the minstrel mask, revealing emotions to the white audience that they may have imagined but probably preferred not to think about. Rufus drops the guise of the fun-loving, good-humored, not-very-bright dupe to express his anger at Wilson in a confrontation that is once again as motivated by race as it is by personality. Wilson tries to get to the telephone and Rufus threatens him with bodily harm:

WILSON. You wouldn't dare to strike a white man.
RUFUS. Ain't never did it yet, outside the ring, but the Boss man told me to watch that phone.
WILSON (*starts for phone*). Get out of my way.
RUFUS (*stops him*). Mr. Wilson, if you like your face don't start nothing, because if you does you ain't going to recognize you' own self for months and months.
WILSON (*sits*). You damn orang-outang you!
RUFUS. What's that you called me?

WILSON. An orang-outang.

RUFUS. I don't know what that is, but if you don't take it back I'se going to lam you one for luck. Now is I what you said, or isn't I? Answer yes or no.

WILSON. No.

RUFUS. What? What you say?

WILSON. No, I mean—yes.

RUFUS. What you mean—No, I mean yes.

WILSON. You stay in your place!

RUFUS. One of the rules of the prize ring is . . . never hit a man when he's down . . . and you're safe while you're setting. . . . But don't rise, white boy . . . don't rise. (125)

Anderson again diffuses the confrontation by writing a laugh line later in the scene as Rufus misspells the word "eat." But the laughter is distant enough from the tensions of the previous exchange for Rufus's anger to have an undiluted impact.

Before the police can arrive, Thompson returns. In a last-ditch effort for revenge, Wilson insinuates that Carl is having an affair with Mrs. Thompson, offering as proof a letter she has sent to Carl. What the letter implies so angers Thompson that he physically attacks Carl, choking him and throwing him to the floor. Only Ella's intervention saves his life. When she explains that Mrs. Thompson's true intention was to inform Carl that she was returning to her husband, Thompson rushes upstairs to see her. To the dying strains of Rufus singing "a spiritual—an old convict song," Carl tells Ella that he is leaving white society to go "back among our own people. For I realize now how much we need them, and they need us" (126–127).

This decision comes as a surprise. It has not been foreshadowed, and it is not consistent with the openly autobiographical content of the rest of the play. Carl has endured Wilson's overt racism, an accusation of rape, a near-lynching by a white mob, a trial in which his race presupposed guilt, and now mistrust and violence from a white person who had previously shown him some respect. Perhaps the racism implicit in Thompson's actions is simply the last straw. Carl provides no explanation for his decision, possibly because an explanation would seriously compromise the positive Christian message that Anderson wanted his play to deliver.

Anderson denied that his play had any social relevance in a quote that speaks volumes regarding his treatment of race relations in the play: "My play doesn't touch upon the race question at all. There is a Negro bellboy who is the central character, but he is always polite and courteous, remembers his position and speaks only when spoken to."[7] Throughout his adult life Anderson strove to become and finally was recognized as a genteel Christian gentleman—but he lived most of that adult life in a society which saw only an African American bellhop. Anderson's beliefs taught him that he was as good as the next man, yet he was quite aware that it would be judicious to keep that opinion to himself if that next man were white. This duality is exhibited throughout *Appearances*. Anderson was writing a play about what he knew, providing the audience with a factual picture of how the races related to one another in his world. He is also writing his play for a primarily white audience. His solution was to walk a thin line between telling the truth and telling the truth in such a way that would not make his intended audience feel uncomfortable, immoral, or guilty. Carl will defend himself but retain the servant's demeanor; he will advise the white characters, but only when they seek him out; he will be privy to their secrets but never become their intimate; and he will leave white society but never tell his reasons.[8]

In the play's original version—the one presented at the public readings—Carl performs an act of faith healing and at the play's end is rewarded with a position managing a restaurant. It is easy to see why the faith healing event was deleted from the final draft—the play is already permeated with religiosity. As to the new job, for Carl to accept the restaurant position implies that the white world has the power and the right to reward him for his good behavior. That their "reward" is Carl's servitude with a grander title is a diminution that was probably not lost on many African Americans who read or heard this early draft. But Carl's decision in the play's produced version—to reject the position and "go back among our own people"—would not be consistent with the attitudes expressed throughout the play or consistent with Anderson's own life. A possible explanation for this change is that, while Anderson was in New York, he came into contact with what would have been for him new ideas about being African American in white society, particularly the concept of fully integrated equality as set forth by W.E.B. Du Bois. His ideas may have affected Anderson enough to change the play's ending. Although he may not have been aware of it, Anderson was actually having it both ways on a major issue facing African Americans in the 1920s. When he rewrites the play so that Carl rejects the implied powers of white society and its "rewards," Anderson is siding with those African Americans who supported Du Bois's relatively new ideas; and when Carl decides to leave to work among his own people, he is siding with those who supported the more traditional "separate but equal" doctrine championed by Booker T. Washington. Ella's response to Carl's plan, in which she compares him to Frederick Douglass and Washington, would seem to indicate the philosophy Anderson really admired (127). And while it is Washington's philosophy that is implicit in Carl's final decision, it could also be considered a rejection of white social attitudes more akin to Du Bois's position if the rewritten ending of the play's earlier version is kept in mind. Either ending would satisfy the expectations of the play's mostly white audience: the first would allow them to feel that justice had been done, the second would provide a safe alternative to the more socially disruptive ideas of Du Bois. The new ending is disturbing because it seems so out of character for Anderson and for the clearly autobiographical hero of his play. The playwright does seem to travel in a large circle to achieve a closure that he might have reached more directly; what is offered here is a possible explanation for an important change in the script.

A policeman arrives to take Wilson to jail; Louise and Kellard embrace; the Thompsons are reunited. The lights begin to dim, and in a Pirandellian sequence, the characters in the dream (who, like Thornton and Robinson, are all real people) appear and demand to know if they are flesh and blood or figments of Carl's imagination. He assures them they are actual people:

> CARL. And as my dream came to an end, I could hear Mr. Kellard say, "Wait a minute! You mean to say I'm a dream?" And then Miss Thornton said, "Am I engaged to marry him?" Then Mr. Thompson spoke—all I

could hear was "Real—Real"—Then I knew my dream had ended in a
wonderful reality, for they were dreams, and now they were real people.
And I thank God my dream has come true. (129)

The play's premiere was reviewed by all the major New York papers.[9] Most
critics noted the audience's enthusiasm but were unimpressed by the production.
It is clear from the reviews that *Appearances* was not a critical success while at
the same time it is hard to escape the feeling that it would have been impossible
for the newspapers to publish an unflinchingly damning critique. The publicly
recorded support Anderson had solicited from the political and theatrical establishment, the rags-to-riches romance that surrounded the production, and the
critics' desire to prove their right-mindedness in racial matters (condescending
though it was) compelled the writing of reviews that strained to be kind.[10] It
seems clear that the press did not want to be responsible for destroying what it
had helped create, what one newspaper described as the "Garland Anderson fairy
tale come true." The *Herald Tribune* grappled with the problem in its review:

The new play . . . is a strange potpourri of not ineffective melodrama and Pollyannish
preaching that is made worthy of respect, if not whole hearted admiration by the
transparent sincerity of the author. . . . Written by a white playwright, these addresses
to the audience would have been unbearable, but in the hands of a Negro actor and
writer they breathe a profound truth and disarming spirit of belief. (Anderson, scrapbooks)

The condescending racism of the above review was more blatant in the *New
York Morning Telegraph*: "[The character Rufus] fell in with the American idea
of the Negro. He talked like a negro, acted like a negro, and made you laugh as
negroes do make you laugh in everyday life. He liked gin and ice cream" (Anderson, scrapbooks). The review from the *New York Sun* attempted to excuse
Anderson, blaming acting and directing that were "below par" and explaining
that "no author with his dogged earnestness and meager knowledge of the techniques of his craft could write a thoroughly effective play." But the review ends
with the frank admission: "If the circumstances surrounding the play had been
less romantic, the reviewer is well aware the above remarks might have been a
great deal sharper" (Anderson, scrapbooks).

Burdened with such lukewarm reviews, the first week's gross for *Appearances* amounted to less than $2,000. Extra advertising was purchased in the next
week's newspapers, but it did little good. At the end of the third week Sagar
announced that he was closing the production.

Anderson refused to give up, but he had to raise $30,000 to keep the play
alive. The press once again sensed a good story—several ran prominent articles
describing his latest difficulties. The *Amsterdam News* continued to be Anderson's major champion. It reported that Belasco and Jolson each gave him
$1,000 and convinced several others to do the same. The paper also started a
campaign of its own, encouraging its readers to support Anderson's cause; once
a week it published a list of contributors. One unidentified publication reported
that a large corporation—"one of the most widely known firms in Greater New
York"—was willing to pledge $20,000 if Anderson could raise $10,000 on his
own (Anderson, scrapbooks). But before this could happen, help came from a
totally unexpected source. Three white businessmen from Dallas pledged the

entire $30,000, asking nothing in return for their investment save that the pro-
duction continue.[11] Despite the publicity that this story generated, ticket sales
did not improve. *Appearances* finally closed in mid-January 1926.

Anderson was saddened and disappointed, but all was not lost. He had
made many valuable contacts in New York's theatrical and political circles, but
more important, he still owned one-half interest in West Coast production
rights. He was quick to turn this potential into reality. On 9 April 1927, amid
the same bellhop-makes-good newspaper stories that preceded its New York
premiere, *Appearances* opened in Los Angeles, where it was reported that *that*
city's socially prominent first night audience gave the play a standing ovation.
Their enthusiasm was moderately infectious: the play enjoyed a five-week run.

Shortly afterward several Los Angeles newspapers reported that Anderson
was attempting to sell the film rights to his play (Anderson, scrapbooks). One
tabloid erroneously reported that they had been sold to Universal; another stated
that Anderson would produce the film himself, backed by local African American financing "so as to keep this wonderful production within the hands of the
race" (Anderson, scrapbooks). While it is possible that some film companies
were interested in the play, it seems probable that most were waiting to see how
Cecil B. De Mille's predominantly African American production of "Porgy" did
at the box office, particularly in the heavy movie-going South.[12] Although conservative socially, the stage of this time was far ahead of the screen in tackling
sensitive issues. Film director Lois Weber, recently fired from "Uncle Tom's
Cabin," summed up Hollywood's attitude toward Broadway's relative liberal-
ism, stating, "There is no reason for the decadence of the stage being reflected in
motion pictures."[13] Similar sentiments from producers and studio moguls might
be another factor that kept *Appearances* from ever being filmed.

On 19 March 1928, Anderson and his play returned to their hometown,
opening in San Francisco's Community Theatre. Civic pride contributed to
heavy advance ticket sales that were credited with saving the historical show
place from the wrecker's ball. The theatre's management spurred sales on by
offering half-price tickets to attorneys and to anyone employed in the hotel industry.

It was also announced that members of the audience would be selected to
portray the jurors in the trial scene. The response by would-be Thespians was so
great that the scene was restaged so that the entire audience became jury and
courtroom spectators. The play received further free publicity with the story that
one of the actresses in the cast was the daughter of a local millionaire who dis-
owned her because of her role in the play. It was reported that this was not because the millionaire was opposed to the racially mixed cast but because he was
opposed to the stage in general (Anderson, scrapbooks).

The play closed in San Francisco on 9 June. An extensive tour began almost immediately and included dates in Oakland, Seattle, Vancouver, and Minneapolis, among other cities. Harry B. Mills, the critic in Seattle, described the
play as a Christian Science lecture but also said it was "decidedly unusual and
interesting"; in Vancouver, the critic's reaction was printed on the editorial page:
"Young people who want to succeed in life should visit the Empress Theatre
today or tomorrow and see . . . *Appearances* . . . to enjoy the comedy . . . is
just like going to the bank and drawing money in the form of inspiration and
courage" (Anderson, scrapbooks). The production then traveled to Chicago,

where it was received with more favorable reviews and a press corps predictably as interested in Anderson as they were in his play. Yet another millionaire was involved in the Chicago production with yet another daughter in the cast. But this millionaire was supportive, actually investing a substantial amount in the production. Advance ticket sales were heavy in all locations, notably so in Chicago, where they were strong enough to guarantee a profitable run. The critic of the *Chicago Whip* wrote the most positive review the play received in the paper's 29 December 1928 edition: "*Appearances* should be compelled by law . . . to remain in Chicago until every citizen has seen it. It is educational, marvelous, great, unbelievable."

Buoyed by the tour's success—and, as Anderson saw it, the success of his message—the playwright decided to try New York once more. *Appearances* opened for the second time on 1 April 1929 at the Hudson Theatre with C. Michel Picard producing. A new cast was hired, except Doe Doe Green, who repeated his role as "Rufus." Green had appeared in all the road productions and—after Los Angeles—was the only African American in the cast.

Reviews for the first production had tried to be kind. Critics commenting on the revival were not so forgiving. Most took extensive notice of the play's structural faults. The *Herald Tribune* performed a notable about-face. It had praised the play in 1925 for its "profound truth and disarming spirit of belief." In 1929 it acidly commented that "the revival of the production at the Hudson stamps it again as naive and pointless" (Anderson, scrapbooks). Sympathetic reviews failed to save the first production; negative ones helped close the second. *Appearances* lasted only twenty-three performances.

A legal dispute further marred the revival. Several newspapers reported that one John Locke claimed to have rewritten the play and to have introduced some original material. Locke asked for 2 percent of the play's gross receipts; Anderson refused. Both men agreed to submit their differences to the Author's League of America for arbitration (Anderson, scrapbooks). The League's decision is not recorded, but Anderson continued to be known as the play's author while articles about Locke no longer appeared.

Other stories reported that Anderson had completed a second script, a collaboration with Tom Overton (stage name: Doe Doe Green) entitled *The Prison Farm*. It was reported that one reader for a prominent Broadway producer thought "there are several reasons why this play should be an outstanding success," but Ella Weiler, who held a similar position at a Hollywood film studio, had a different opinion. Her report is dated 28 July 1929: "Absolutely useless. It is written very badly. The dialogue is stilted and muddled. The construction is even worse. The characters are dead" (Anderson, scrapbooks). Needless to say, *The Prison Farm* never became a movie, and although Anderson told several newspapers that Belasco was interested in the script, a stage version was never produced.

Despite *Appearances*' second failure on Broadway, Anderson still believed in the play and its message. Audiences and critics outside New York had responded enthusiastically. So like all evangelists, he went searching for more converts; and like many American theatrical entrepreneurs before him, he looked to England. *Appearances* opened in London on 11 March 1930, Anderson's unique personal history again garnering extensive preshow publicity. The reviews were generally better than the last ones from New York although London critics found Carl to be priggish and the plot poorly constructed. The London response was best exemplified by the *Sunday Graphic* of 16 March, which called the play "ingenuous" and appealing, "owing to its sincerity."

After a run of several weeks, the production left London for performances in other English cities, Wales, Scotland, Brussels, and Paris, a tour lasting for twenty weeks. It is interesting to note that although Anderson was the first African American playwright to be produced in most of the production's European stops, very little mention of that fact appears in the newspapers from those locations.

Doe Doe Green was still with the show and was also by far the play's most popular performer. He continued to be the only African American in the cast. Promoters took advantage of his popularity, stressing in their advertisements the aspects of Green's role which they believed the audience would consider typical of African American behavior. The advertisements often consisted of a cartoonish drawing of a minstrel-style "blackface" and a quote from one of Doe Doe's speeches, usually one of his malapropisms (Anderson, scrapbooks).

There were no millionaire's daughters or racially motivated walkouts in the London cast, but there was a well-publicized story concerning one of its actresses, Ann Herriot. After Herriot was crippled in an automobile accident some years earlier, doctors told her she would never walk again. She turned to faith healing, miraculously grew new tissue, and regained the use of her legs. She met Anderson at a religious service, told him her story, and got a part in the play. None of the Herriot stories contain any collaborating evidence—from a doctor or a hospital, for example—demonstrating how the press continued to be infatuated with stories about or connected to Anderson.

Anderson remained in London while *Appearances* was on tour. He was in demand as a public speaker, especially from religious groups. He gave a series of "tea talks" at the Mayfair Hotel, discussing topics such as "Mastering Your Environment," "Seeking and Finding," and "Why Prayers Are Answered." He later traveled to Paris, Vienna, and Berlin, spreading his message of prayer and positive thought.

Anderson became the first African American member of P.E.N. (International Association of Poets, Playwrights, Editors, Essayists, and Novelists) and had his portrait painted by A. Christie. He wrote a well-received book of inspirational thoughts titled *Uncommon Sense*, which led to a BBC program, "The Voice of Uncommon Sense," on which Anderson answered letters about personal problems sent in by listeners. He also found time to open a combination snack bar–nightclub—"Andy's Nu Snack"—which specialized in malted milks.

Anderson returned to the United States in 1935 for a lecture tour, designed to "bring the people out of their depression" (Anderson, scrapbooks). Beginning at Town Hall, New York City, on 20 May, Anderson traveled for two years, visiting Canada, Hawaii, and every state in the Union except those in the Deep South. While in Seattle, Anderson became a minister for the Center of Constructive Thinking.[14] And at an unspecified location he married his secretary, Doris Sequirra, the daughter of a prominent London physician. Only the most liberal considered racially mixed marriages acceptable. Upon the couple's return to England in 1937, Sequirra wrote a book entitled *Nigger Lover*, which chronicled her experiences among the intolerant.

Back in London, Anderson continued lecturing, writing, and managing his business interests. He purportedly finished a new play, also entitled *Uncommon Sense*, but was unable to interest producers in London or New York. He suffered a heart attack while speaking in a London church in 1939. He was immediately flown back to the United States, where he died on 31 May at the age of fifty-three.

It must have seemed remarkable to the 1925 American public that an African American bellhop could write a Broadway play. It must have seemed equally remarkable to 1930s Londoners that they would be receiving personal advice over the radio from this same man. But this uniqueness was also reassuring as it reaffirmed the truth of the American Dream in times that were making belief in that dream increasingly difficult. Anderson presented himself as an honest, humble, and religious person whose only real interest was serving those around him—the perfect "darky" for the white audience. He was not "uppity," he was not threatening; his reward was that he became an English gentleman. And although he would seem the perfect role model for African Americans who found solace in the self-sacrificing tenets of Christianity, African Americans of that time did not buy many tickets to Broadway plays. Those who did were probably offended by the play's passive attitude toward the racism of some of its characters and by the social naiveté of Carl's belief in the powers of positive thought. This may have been Anderson's reality, but it was not theirs. After Carl announces that he is returning to his "own people," Ella responds, "Oh, I'm so proud of you. You're going up and up—and will take your place along with Frederick Douglass and Booker T. Washington" (126–127). Given the popularity of the concepts of integrated and equal put forth by such leaders as W.E.B. Du Bois, Carl's move back to his "own people" must have seemed a surrender and his admiration of "separate but equal" proponents as Booker T. Washington outdated. For whatever reasons, Anderson never became a leader or a role model in the African American community. His place in African American history is poignantly noted at the conclusion of Hatch's introduction to *Appearances* in *Black Theatre U.S.A.*: "A newspaper in Regina, Canada reported on one of Mr. Anderson's lectures (in 1936), that 'He is the first Negro since Booker T. Washington to tour the country speaking to white people only. Seldom, he admitted, does a Negro ever appear to hear him. "They are not interested," he said rather sadly' "(97).

NOTES

1. Doris Abramson, *Negro Playwrights in the American Theatre 1925–1959* (New York: Columbia University Press, 1969) 27–32; James V. Hatch and Ted Shine, eds., *Black Theater USA: Plays by African Americans 1847 to Today*, rev. and exp. ed. (New York: The Free Press, 1996) 95–97; James Weldon Johnson, *Black Manhattan* (New York: Antheneum, 1969) 203–205. The Hatch and Shine book contains the only published version of the play (97–129). The only other copy of *Appearances* is on microfilm at the main branch of the New York Public Library. References to the play, *Appearances*, will be cited in the text using the Hatch and Shine edition.

2. Subsequent references to these scrapbooks will be cited in the text.

3. Émile Coué (1857–1926) was a French psychotherapist who lectured in America on autosuggestion. New Thought is similar to Christian Science, a denomination with which Anderson is closely identified.

4. The original cast included Lionel Monagas as Carl, Doe Doe Green as Rufus, Joseph Sweeney as Mr. Wilson, Edward Keane as Mr. Thompson, Mildred Wall as Elsie, and Evelyn Mason as Ella.

5. Abramson, *Negro Playwrights* 30–31

6. Ibid. 31.

7. *San Francisco Chronicle*, 15 July 1925.

8. Abramson writes that Anderson "was as brave as he dared to be" (40). It is hard to argue with her on this point, but it is hoped that this chapter shows that Anderson was braver and more aware of social issues than she supposes.

9. The following publications printed reviews: *The Drama Calendar*; *Billboard*; *New York Sun*; *New York Herald Tribune*; *New York Evening World*; *New York Graphic*; *New York Star*; *Brooklyn Standard Union*; *Wall Street Journal*; *New York Morning Telegraph*; *New York Times*; *New York American*; and *Woman's Wear*. All are found in Anderson scrapbooks.

10. A good example of this is the review from the *New York Evening World*: "There is much naive pomposity about the piece and a tendency to interrupt its action with long speeches furthering its frankly partisan propaganda. But the driving sincerity of its purpose gave it an impetus that many more polished works lack."

11. The men were James S. Strader, H. W. McQuinn, and Jack Hodgson.

12. This despite the fact that both the Micheaux and the Lincoln film companies had produced films with African American themes and casts that had played well to white audiences in the South—*Troopers of Troop K* (Lincoln) and *Homesteaders* (Micheaux).

13. Qtd. in a column by George Perry, dated 2 September 1927. Publication not known. In the Anderson scrapbooks.

14. Abramson, *Negro Playwrights* 27.

8

The First Serious Dramas on Broadway by African American Playwrights

Jeanne-Marie A. Miller

Although blacks had been writing serious, that is, nonmusical plays in the United States at least since the 1820s when Mr. Brown's *King Shotaway* was produced by the African Grove Theatre and Company in New York City in 1823, it was 100 years later when a serious play by an African American was produced on Broadway, the primary center of theatre in this country. In 1923 Willis Richardson's *The Chip Woman's Fortune* became the first serious play by a black writer to be commercially produced on Broadway. *The Chip Woman's Fortune* was followed by Garland Anderson's *Appearances* (1925), Frank Wilson's *Meek Mose* (1928), and Wallace Thurman and William Jourdan Rapp's *Harlem* (1929). These black-authored plays were produced during a time when New York theatre was enjoying an unprecedented prosperity for most of the decade. In 1927–1928, for example, 280 productions were presented on Broadway, of which 200 were new plays.[1] This golden era in Broadway theatre coincided with the New Negro Renaissance, the decade-long flowering of black art and culture primarily in Harlem.

On 7 May 1923, at the Frazee Theatre in New York City, Chicago's Ethiopian Art Players added new lines to American theatre history. The group presented the first nonmusical drama by a black American on Broadway. *The Chip Woman's Fortune*, a one-act play by Willis Richardson, was a curtain raiser that appeared in repertory with Oscar Wilde's *Salome* and an original interpretation, a jazz version, of Shakespeare's *The Comedy of Errors*.

The Chip Woman's Fortune is set in a sparsely furnished room in the home of a poor black family in an unnamed city. The central dramatic conflict is between Silas Green, who has been "furloughed" without pay from his job as a store porter as punishment for not paying a debt, and Aunt Nancy, the old chip woman who lives rent free with the Green family. Silas must settle his debt before he can return to work. Aunt Nancy occupies her days by moving about the streets picking up chips of wood and lumps of coal or searching through trash cans for whatever truck she can find. She has nursed Silas's ill wife Liza, who attributes her improvement to the old woman's care and the folk medicine Aunt Nancy concocts from herbs. She also gives the family some of the wood and coal she has collected to warm their home. On the streets people have given the chip woman money, which is believed to be buried in the Greens' backyard.

Every time Silas goes out there, Aunt Nancy mysteriously appears. It is fifty dollars of this money that Silas needs in order to pay for the Victrola that is threatened to be repossessed this day. Aunt Nancy, however, is keeping the money to help her soon-to-be-released son Jim, who was imprisoned after beating an unfaithful woman whom he loved and a boyfriend who was mishandling her. Because a strong bond exists between this mother and her son, Aunt Nancy forgives Jim of his crime. Further, maternal love outweighs her feelings of indebtedness to the Green family. The men who come to seize the unpaid-for phonograph are followed moments later by Jim, who relieves Silas of his troubles by giving him his money as well as half of the money his mother has saved. The Victrola is pushed back into place, and the conflict is happily resolved. Before Jim and Aunt Nancy leave, the old woman promises Liza that she will return and look after her every day. Silas prepares to return to work.[2]

The Chip Woman's Fortune, a comedy about an incident in the life of this poor black family, is straightforward and uncomplicated. The characters are the folk whose daily struggles often involve eking out just enough on which to survive. Here the man of the family, without deep bitterness, utters a weary complaint about living from hand to mouth, and his wife holds fast to her God and his teachings. One rests assured that even if they do not always triumph over, they at least will not succumb to forces that can render one helpless. Although hinted that racism might have been at the core of Silas's temporary dismissal from work, the drama does not dwell on this point. The dramatic struggle is over retaining the single luxury item in the home—a phonograph—and salvaging Silas's job. In this drama both the language, which is black dialect, and the characters, who are ordinary black people, are realistic. Even Jim, who is the rescuer, is not idealized. Continuity is implied as a love interest might develop between Jim and Emma, Silas and Liza's eighteen-year-old daughter. This deceptively simple story, in addition to showing how the characters bind together and give undergirding aid to one another in their skimpy battle of life, also suggests, deep down, a lowly people's underlying strength and determination to go on.

One New York critic described this one-acter as trifling and at times amusing,[3] and another referred to it as "an honest, well played little comedy."[4] Heywood Broun found the drama excellent. "The quality of the performance and the plot itself," wrote Broun, "is somewhat akin to something of Lady Gregory's as done by the Abbey Theatre. The dialogue is rich and authentic and the story has the virtue of utmost simplicity." The play he found convincing with "a not infrequent beauty arising from the shrewd collection and combination of the commonplace."[5] While dismissing *Salome* as a dull play, Alexander Woollcott wrote the following:

If all the rejoicing must be confined to this curtain raiser [*The Chip Woman's Fortune*] it is because it is the stuff of which a true negro [*sic*] theater will one day take form to the permanent enrichment of the American stage. Those who groan at the mulatto "Salome" do so because there are so many players who can play "Salome" and so few who can give such plays as "The Chip Woman's Fortune."[6]

During the second week of the Ethiopian Art Theatre[7] on Broadway, *The Comedy of Errors* replaced *Salome*, and *The Chip Woman's Fortune* was retained. The critics who returned to view these plays for the most part favored Richardson's drama over Shakespeare's. Some black writers have suggested that white critics expressed racial prejudice when they wrote negative reviews of *Salome* and *The Comedy of Errors* with blacks performing in traditional white roles.[8] It seems that reviewers overlooked the significance of Richardson's *The Chip Woman's Fortune* as the first serious drama by an African American to be produced on Broadway.

The Ethiopian Art Theatre closed on Broadway at the end of its second week. Although none of Richardson's dramatic work was presented on Broadway again, this playwright became popular with black college, community, and other amateur theatre groups, especially during the 1920s.

The first full-length serious drama by an African American playwright to be produced on Broadway is Garland Anderson's *Appearances*, which opened at the Frolic Theatre on 13 October 1925. It is essentially a moralistic drama, a message play. Like the play's hero Carl, Garland Anderson was a San Francisco bellhop and switchboard operator, who held fast to the metaphysical belief that with the proper faith, one can accomplish anything. It was this faith that drove Anderson to write a play despite his limited education and lack of experience in playmaking; it was his tenacity that resulted in his work being produced at all. He was inspired to write *Appearances*, originally entitled *Judge Not According to Appearances*, after seeing Channing Pollock's play *The Fool*. In getting his play produced, Anderson enlisted the aid of such people as Al Jolson, the famous entertainer.[9]

Appearances begins with a prologue that provides the framework for the play. In the lobby of Hotel Mount Shasta, a small residential hotel in San Francisco, California, Judge Robinson and Judge Thornton discuss a case that Judge Robinson tried, in which the defendant, by all appearances, was guilty. Judge Thornton tells Judge Robinson about a dream that Carl, the black bell boy, revealed to him, in which there was a trial scene similar to the one they are discussing. Carl's philosophy is brought into focus: that a man can do anything he believes he can if his purpose is right. Carl reasons that if he "with color, lack of education, lack of money and all against him can work his dream out in real life, it will prove that other people with greater advantage can naturally do greater things" (2).[10] Judge Thornton asks Carl to tell Judge Robinson his dream. This scene leads into act 1 as Carl relates his dream. The play is the dream, and Carl's voice is that of the playwright.

Framed by Jack Wilson, a villainous white man who is also a district attorney, Carl is accused of the attempted rape of a white woman. Louise Thornton, Wilson's fiancée, is postponing their wedding because she is influenced by her inner voice that reflects Carl's philosophy. This action results in Wilson becoming Carl's enemy. In addition, Wilson is trying to sell a selenium mine illegally. In the second act, a courtroom scene, Carl serves as his own attorney because he believes that the truth needs no defense. He is exonerated when it is revealed that Elsie Benton falsely accused him and was forced by Wilson to trap Carl. A woman with a sordid past, she is revealed to be not white, but rather a light-skinned African American. Freed, Carl will marry his sweetheart, a law student, and together they will return to their people and help them.

Of particular interest in *Appearances* is the manner in which the playwright uses the comic porter, Rufus George Washington Jones, first as a minstrel figure or traditional stage "darky" and then as a vehicle for the articulation of strange truths about the African American experience. When offering his congratulations to the hero and his fiancée on their engagement, Rufus uses the mutilated language long associated with the black stage buffoon: "I gives yuh my firmest condemnations. I gives 'em for both of you each" (13). One of the obvious purposes of this character is comic relief. When Rufus testifies in court, nervousness prevents his remembering his full name, the legal terminology is confusing to him, and his account of what occurred on the night of the alleged attempted rape is, at best, wandering. But he does make clear the distance he had to travel to find a store that would give proper service to an African American. Under questioning, he clarifies his statement: "Well, they will serve you, sir, but they put some flavor on that ice-cream that just spoils it for eatin', sir" (31). When he heard the crowd, summoned by the woman's screams, mention dogs, he became terrified because of an earlier traumatic experience. Back home, he tells the court, he was accused once of stealing a ring from his employer, and after escaping from a smoke house in which he had been confined, he was pursued by a mob of dogs. He narrowly escaped lynching. Meanwhile the woman found the ring where she had lost it and gave Rufus two dollars for his troubles. He took the money, for it was the first time he had ever had a "whole two dollars" in his life. And this time he ran away from the scene with Carl and the woman because he was frightened.

> WILSON. I said, if you are innocent, why did you run?
> RUFUS. Because you're innocent ain't goin' ter do yer no good if you're
>   hanging from a telegram pole. (33)

While delighting audiences with his outlandish lines and exaggerated behavior, Rufus makes some pertinent statements about racial prejudice in America.[11]

   Appearances has merits along with its blemishes. The courtroom scene has some theatrical effectiveness. The drama, however, is weakened by the oversimplification of the first and final acts where the white villain is pitted against the pure, uncomplicated black hero. The revelation, too, that the woman with the infamous past is really a light-skinned African American and not white damages the credibility of the story and seems an attempt on the part of the playwright not to offend the sensibilities of the largely white middle-class Broadway audience. And propaganda intrudes when the hero preaches his gospel of optimism, where the message overrides literary merit.

   While many white critics found the play amateurish, they did not find it completely ineffective. A critic writing for the *Sun* referred to the flashes of crude genius in *Appearances* but felt the playwright had not yet arrived.[12] Some black critics interpreted *Appearances* as an anti-lynching play. William Pickens, a black reviewer, wrote about a treatment of race in the play that had been overlooked or underplayed by the critics occupied with the universality of the philosophical message. Pickens stated that in comparison with such works as Eugene O'Neill's *The Emperor Jones* and *All God's Chillun Got Wings* and Paul Green's *In Abraham's Bosom*, also produced during the 1920s, *Appearances* is a play in which the black character "is the genuine hero and 'triumphs.'" Carl is not sacrificed. "We do not mean that every heroic Negro soul, in real life, must triumph, but neither do they all fail. And what we mean is, that Garland Anderson is almost the only recent playwright who has had the courage to risk his success on showing the heroic, superior souled Negro who does not fail."[13]

Appearances closed after twenty-three performances. It opened again on 1 April 1929 at Broadway's Hudson Theatre for twenty-four performances. In 1930 it was produced in London at the Royalty Theatre. *Appearances* remains the only play by Garland Anderson ever produced.

The script is not extant for Frank Wilson's *Meek Mose*, which opened on Broadway at the Princess Theatre on 6 February 1928 for twenty-three performances. Wilson was a talented actor who played such roles as Abraham in Paul Green's *In Abraham's Bosom* as well as the title role in DuBose and Dorothy Heyward's *Porgy*. His plays were produced by Little Theatre companies, namely, the Acme Players, Ethiopian Art Theatre, Players' Guild, and the Lafayette Players. *Meek Mose* was to be the inaugural production of Lester Walton's Negro Theatre Company, but unfortunately it was the company's only production.

Meek Mose is set in Mexia, Texas. There is a dramatic conflict between two groups of African Americans: those who follow Mose, the spiritual leader who adheres to the biblical teaching, "Blessed are the meek, for they shall inherit the earth," and the militant opposition, led by Enos, who challenges the authority of the whites. The problem that gives rise to the action stems from a white group's desire to build a cotton gin on the land now occupied by blacks and to relocate them to an undesirable area called the Gut. Mose, in keeping with his nature and the encouragement of Mr. Harmon, his white employer, moves with his followers to the new location. Some of those who follow Mose to the Gut, a marshland, suffer ill effects such as sickness and death, and Mose is blamed for their hardships. When seemingly the depths of despair have been reached, there is a reversal in Mose's fortune. Oil is discovered on the land with the help of Mr. Harmon. Misplaced papers are found, and the drama ends on a happy note. Thus the meek, having trusted in God, triumph over the doubting black folk as well as over the white dispossessors and inherit at least this portion of the earth, which first causes anguish and now promises wealth. Spirituals are interspersed throughout the drama.

Meek Mose appears to have had a dual purpose: to dramatize a social problem and to entertain with its low comedy. White greed has driven the blacks from their land. Discovering oil on the new land does not eradicate the injustice behind the blacks' having to move to their undesirable location in the first place, an uprooting which seemed not to trouble the whites' conscience. In the drama, however, passivity is rewarded. Throughout *Meek Mose* the desire of the playwright to be inoffensive to Broadway audiences has taken precedence over that of stirring consciences about social problems, a safe method that results in a weak play. Solecistic language, sometimes used with comedic emphasis, is a part of the folk speech. Caught between its dual aims, *Meek Mose* did not appear to amuse whites, and it offended many blacks.

The play met with the disapproval of most critics. "A mess of oversweet theatrical marmalade," wrote Percy Hammond for the *New York Herald Tribune*. "The effort was pathetic in its anxiety to be like one of those old Winchell Smith–John Golden confections," he continued, "and it used nearly every familiar device to make itself a saleable 'show' "—a mob or two, the "lost papers" found, oil struck on the hero's property, and a double marriage at the end.[14] Life in this drama was depicted in shop-worn theatre terms. This critic found the spirituals sung by the choir to be the real assets of the production.

Brooks Atkinson saw the characters in the play not as real people, but only as exaggerations.[15] Another first-night reviewer described *Meek Mose* as a simple, straightway story of blacks in Mexia, Texas. Wilson's drama differed from others of its type in that there were less bitterness and more mirth, and missing were "the tragic spirit and despairing note" dominating other black plays.[16] Alexander Woollcott made the following observations:

> The portents of a dozen seasons past have foreshadowed that inevitable and welcome day when this city will have a theatre for plays of Negro life written by Negro playwrights for Negro players.
> A feeble and faltering step in that direction was taken last night at the Princess Theatre when a scant audience attended the first performance of a play called "Meek Mose."[17]

Lucien H. White of the *New York Age* wrote that the actors in *Meek Mose* were superior to the play.[18] Though he did not commend the play, Romeo L. Dougherty of the *Amsterdam News* believed it was "a very important step in the right direction."[19] Randolph Edmonds, a black scholar, critic, and playwright, later wrote in *Opportunity*: "The bowing and scraping of the meek old man failed to excite a large number of Harlemites, and did not contain enough force or melodrama to satisfy the satiated Broadway theatre-goers."[20]

Wilson revised *Meek Mose*, which was successfully produced as *Brother Mose* in 1934 by the works division of the Department of Public Welfare in New York City and later by the Federal Theatre Project. On 4 February 1936, his *Walk Together Chillun* was the inaugural production of the Negro Theatre Unit of the Federal Theatre Project at the Lafayette Theatre. While Wilson did not return to Broadway as a playwright, he did so as an outstanding actor.

Harlem by Wallace Thurman, a member of the New Negro Renaissance literati, and William Jourdan Rapp, a white writer, opened on 20 February 1929 at the Apollo Theatre on Forty-second Street and closed on 11 May 1929 at the Times Square Theatre.[21] It ran for ninety-three performances. In October 1929 the play returned to Broadway at the Eltinge Theatre and closed at the end of its second week.

Harlem, an action melodrama which takes place in New York's famous black community, focuses on the Williams family, recent transplants from the South in search of that fabled Promised Land in the North. This elusive land brings more misery than joy to the family. Here the American blacks meet the West Indians, who, because they will work for less wages, are unfair competition in the labor market. Here the honest hard workers contrast with the Harlem racketeers and their easy money; here the God-fearing are juxtaposed with those drawn to the swirling life of urban sin. Into the window of the Williamses' railroad flat during the first of the three acts pour the familiar cacophonic sounds of the city: a man swearing at a woman, the deep tones of a blues singer from a nearby phonograph, the frying of food, and the grating sound of a pulley line from which dried laundry is taken. This Harlem is shabby, poor, crowded, lonely, dirty, and cold in the winter. The action centers on Cordelia Williams, an overmatured young woman not yet eighteen years old, selfish, lazy, sensuous, and sullen. It is she who has accepted best the wicked side of the new life in the North, but it is her brother Jasper, the idealist, the strongest character, who dominates his family and has brought them to this urban center so that they can improve their lot. The parents do not share his belief. The mother pours out to him the sorrow and disappointment of her hegira to Harlem, and the father concurs. Jasper, however, clings fast to his dream. To soften the expensive burden of living, Basil Venerable, a West Indian, is one of several boarders living with the Williams family. Ambitious to become a lawyer, he complicates his life by falling in love with Cordelia, whom he wishes to marry. He adds to the problems of the family because, he, too, has difficulty making ends meet. The parents, however, encourage his pursuit of their wayward daughter, for he, except for his consuming passion for her, is steady and decent.

Cordelia, a rebellious youth and an anti-heroine, refuses to accept, as she sees it, the prescribed life for a black woman—that of a washerwoman or maid. She says at one point that she wants to go on the stage. Desperation informs her life, a desperation to not have a life like those caught in the whirlpool of misery around her.

The first act of the play is mainly exposition and leads into the "house rent" party on which the family depends for the additional money it brings. At the party the men of the Harlem underworld meet with the hardworking laborers. Here one hears the hot, live music of the piano player and witnesses the passionate dancing, the eating of pigs' feet, and the drinking of corn liquor, which are sold to the paying guests. Cordelia, the center of the activity, immediately causes a clash between Roy Crowe, a gambler whom she momentarily favors, and Basil. She goes off with Roy to his apartment, leaving behind an angry Basil.

The remainder of the drama involves the melodramatic gangland murders. Kid Vamp, a former prize fighter and now one of Harlem's reigning racketeers, murders Roy, who doublecrosses him. Basil, searching for Cordelia in Roy's apartment, is framed by the Kid for Roy's murder. The Kid, in turn, is killed by opposing white mobsters. At the play's end, the Williams family begins to fall apart visibly as Cordelia leaves the home with still another man. She exclaims before departing that she will make the whole world look up at her. The mother asks God to save her daughter's soul as jazz music rises to a crescendo from a nearby party (Thurman and Rapp).

Harlem, then, dramatizes a fragment of black life in New York City during the 1920s. The transplanted black family struggles ineffectually for its share of a decent life in a large, unsympathetic metropolis—struggles against the odds of poor education and low wages. Blacks from other parts of the world come together in this black community, represented in *Harlem* by Basil, the West Indian, and blacks from America's South. At times there is intraracial prejudice, fundamentally stemming from economic rivalry in the job market. While house-rent parties provide entertainment for Harlem's black population, they, above all else, supply the additional and needed revenue from the sale of liquor and food. Playing the illegal numbers game gives hope to those who remember someone who once won some exorbitant sum of money. Racketeers, black and white, prey on the victims and use this black community also for the convenience of their white customers who escape there to indulge their sins. Tension among the characters is omnipresent, but is triggered by the licentious Cordelia, around whom the action swirls. The characters themselves are painted with broad strokes—the shameless Cordelia; the idealistic Jasper; the emotional lover, Basil; the prayerful mother; the helpless, defeated father; the coarse gangsters; and the like. Subtle character shadings are missing. While *Harlem* reflects the times in which it was written and produced, there is an overemphasis on or a foregrounding of the sensuous and sensational: the orgiastic dancing, gambling, and violence. The focus is on surface realities; the spiritual is left largely untouched or underdeveloped. Even though the Thurman and Rapp play concentrates on the murky side of Harlem life, the stress on sensationalism distorts this picture, and the distortion interferes with the creation of a viable work of dramatic art. Tugging at the seams of the play are the frustrated battles of the Williams family in an alien land, battles dramatic in themselves but lost in the superficial glare of the plot.[22]

While *Harlem* was indeed a controversial play, of the plays by African Americans produced on Broadway during the 1920s, it had the longest run and received the most favorable criticism. One of the most controversial points affecting black critics themselves was that members of the black press were not invited to the opening of this play; neither did they receive advance publicity. According to the *New York Age*, when an inquiry was made as to why, the reply was that *Harlem* was primarily for "white consumption" and that eventually some advertising would be given to the black press.[23]

When William E. Clark of the *New York Age* reviewed the play, he wrote the following:

> If you go to the theatre for entertainment, and do not expect a "message" from every dramatic play you see, you'll like "Harlem," for it is a colorful and entertaining melodrama, which in many respects is true to life, even though it shows but one side of Negro life in that section of New York which one of the cast described as a "refuge for the Negro. . . ."
> On the whole, Wallace Thurman and William Jourdan Rapp, the authors, have treated some of the foibles of New York Negroes in a sympathetic manner, instead of burlesqueing them as they might have done.[24]

Brooks Atkinson believed that *Harlem* did not represent the entire black microcosm. The nostalgia of the newly migrated southern family, however, was "the germ of an illuminating dramatic idea," but that idea was lost in the emphasis on entertainment.[25] Arthur Ruhl wrote that *Harlem*

> looked at strictly from the standpoint of Negro drama . . . represented promise rather than fulfillment. . . .
> It was composed of two different strains, and of these what might be described as the white or Broadway element overlaid the black. It was the many bits of authentic Negro life and Harlem color that made it humanly novel and interesting, but comparatively routine racketeering melodrama—good of its kind—which made it move as a play.[26]

Harlem was the only Broadway-produced work of Thurman, who died in 1934 of tuberculosis. Langston Hughes, the famous African American writer and a contemporary of Thurman, wrote that Thurman was not made happy by any of his work. Although distorted for box office purposes, *Harlem*, according to Hughes, was a compelling study of the impact of that community on a black family newly arrived from the South.[27] Unlike *The Chip Woman's Fortune* and *Meek Mose*, *Harlem* was not invited to be performed in the community from which it took its title.

While these four plays by Richardson, Anderson, Wilson, and Thurman were not brilliant triumphs of playwriting, they were not works of little significance. These playwrights were pioneers who brought their plays to Broadway audiences during a time when racial prejudice was raging in the land and was reflected in the theatre.[28] During the 1920s African American playwrights on Broadway had to appeal to two different audiences—one white and the other black—and each with different expectations. Sometimes plots were manipulated and covert ways were used in recognizing the problems of blacks. Gaps and silences were present, with some of the information about blacks pushed to the margins of these plays. At times goals had to be achieved through subversion. Nevertheless, these plays gave some insight into where African Americans stood and how they felt during this golden period of Broadway theatre. While overshadowed by the popularity of Eugene O'Neill's *The Emperor Jones*, the recognition given Paul Green's *In Abraham's Bosom*, and the interest in DuBose and Dorothy Heyward's *Porgy*, all plays about black life by white playwrights, *The Chip Woman's Fortune*, *Appearances*, *Meek Mose*, and *Harlem* added to the canon of black-authored drama. They were a foreshadowing of things to come.

NOTES

1. Barnard Hewitt, *Theatre U.S.A., 1668–1957* (New York: McGraw-Hill, 1959) 381–382.

2. Willis Richardson, *The Chip Woman's Fortune* in *Black Drama in America: An Anthology*, ed. Darwin T. Turner (New York: Fawcett 1971) 27–47.

3. "Ethiopians Act 'Salome': Art Theatre Gives a Performance Not Entirely Art," *New York Times* 8 March 1923, New York Public Library, Theatre Collection, Lincoln Center Library and Museum for the Performing Arts, Collection of Newspaper Clippings of Dramatic Criticism, 1922–1923.

4. Percy Hammond, "The Theatres," *New York Tribune* 8 May 1923, New York Public Library, Theatre Collection, Lincoln Center Library and Museum for the Performing Arts, Collection of Newspaper Clippings of Dramatic Criticism, 1922–1923.

5. Heywood Broun, "At the Frazee Theatre," *World* 9 May 1923, New York Public Library, Theatre Collection, Lincoln Center Library and Museum for the Performing Arts, Collection of Newspaper Clippings of Dramatic Criticism, 1922–1923.

6. Alexander Woollcott, "Shouts and Murmurs," *New York Herald* 9 May 1923: 12.

7. This is the name of the group when it appeared on Broadway.

8. Abram L. Harris, "The Ethiopian Art Players and the Nordic Complex," *Messenger* 5 (1923): 774–775, 777.

9. Garland Anderson, "How I Became a Playwright," *Anthology of the American Negro in the Theatre: A Critical Approach*, ed. Lindsay Patterson (New York: Publishers Co., 1969) 85–86.

10. Garland Anderson, *Appearances*, New York Public Library, Theatre Collection, Film Reproduction. Page references appear in the text.

11. See James Weldon Johnson, *Black Manhattan* (New York: Atheneum, 1969) 202–205; Doris E. Abramson, *Negro Playwrights in the American Theatre,*

1925–1959 (New York: Columbia University Press, 1969) 27–32, 39–40; James V. Hatch and Ted Shine, eds., *Black Theater USA: Plays by African Americans 1847 to Today*, rev. and exp. ed. (New York: The Free Press, 1996) 95–97; and Alan Kreizenbeck, "Garland Anderson and *Appearances*: The Playwright and His Play," *Journal of American Drama and Theatre* 6 (Spring/Fall 1994): 28–48.

12. "The Frolic Reopens," *New York Sun* 14 October 1925, New York Public Library, Theatre Collection, Lincoln Center Library and Museum for the Performing Arts, Collection of Newspaper Clippings of Dramatic Criticism, 1925–1926.

13. William Pickens, "Book Chat," *Norfolk Journal and Guide* 2 June 1928, New York Public Library, Schomburg Collection, Garland Anderson Scrapbook.

14. Percy Hammond, "The Theatres," *New York Herald Tribune* 7 February 1928, New York Public Library, Theatre Collection, Lincoln Center Library and Museum for the Performing Arts, Collection of Newspaper Clippings of Dramatic Criticism, 1927–1928.

15. Brooks Atkinson, "Mayor at Opening Night of Negro Theatre," *New York Times* 7 February 1928, New York Public Library, Theatre Collection, Lincoln Center Library and Museum for the Performing Arts, Collection of Newspaper Clippings of Dramatic Criticism, 1927–1928.

16. "'Meek Mose,' Negro Life Play, Brought to Uptown House," New York Public Library, Theatre Collection, Lincoln Center Library and Museum for the Performing Arts, Collection of Newspaper Clippings of Dramatic Criticism, 1927–1928.

17. Alexander Woollcott, "A Negro Play in 39th Street," *World* 7 February 1928, New York Public Library, Theatre Collection, Lincoln Center Library and Museum for the Performing Arts, Collection of Newspaper Clippings of Dramatic Criticism, 1927–1928.

18. Lucien H. White, "In the Realm of Music," *New York Age* 18 February 1928: 7.

19. Romeo L. Dougherty, "'Meek Mose' at the Princess," *Amsterdam News* 8 February 1928: 9.

20. Randolph Edmonds, "Some Reflections on the Negro in American Drama," *Opportunity* 8 (October 1930): 304.

21. Wallace Thurman and William Jourdan Rapp, *Black Belt: A Melodrama of Negro Life in Harlem in Three Acts,* Yale University Library, James Weldon Johnson Collection, ts.

22. See Abramson, *Negro Playwrights* 32–39, 40–43; Johnson, *Black Manhattan* 217; and Freda Scott Giles, "Glitter, Glitz, and Race: The Production of *Harlem*," *Journal of American Drama and Theatre* 7 (Fall 1995): 1–12.

23. "Negroes Not Wanted as Spectators of Play, 'Harlem,' Says Producer," *New York Age* 2 March 1929: 1.

24. William E. Clark, "'Harlem' Is Entertaining Melodrama of One Phase of Negro Life in New York City," *New York Age* 23 March 1929: 6.

25. Brooks Atkinson, "Up 'Harlem' Way," *New York Times* 3 March 1929, New York Public Library, Theatre Collection, Lincoln Center Library and Museum for the Performing Arts, Collection of Newspaper Clippings of Dramatic Criticism, 1928–1929.

26. Arthur Ruhl, "'Harlem' Negro Melodrama of Racketeer Sort," *New York Herald Tribune* 21 February 1929, New York Public Library, Theatre Collection, Lincoln Center Library and Museum for the Performing Arts, *Harlem* Clippings File.

27. Langston Hughes, *The Big Sea* (New York: Hill and Wang, 1963) 235.

28. Of these four playwrights, only Willis Richardson did not originally write his play for Broadway production.

REFERENCES

Bond, Frederick W. *The Negro and the Drama*. Washington, DC: Associated Publishers, 1940.

Brown, Sterling. *Negro Poetry and Drama*. Washington, DC: Associates in Negro Folk Education, 1937. New York: Atheneum, 1969.

Flanagan, Hallie. *Arena*. New York: Duell, Sloan, and Pearce, 1940.

Hay, Samuel A. *African American Theatre: A Historical and Critical Analysis*. Cambridge: Cambridge University Press, 1994.

Hewitt, Barnard. *History of the Theatre from 1800 to the Present*. New York: Random House, 1970.

Hill, Errol, ed. *The Theater of Black Americans*. 2 vols. Englewood Cliffs, NJ: Prentice-Hall, 1980.

Huggins, Nathan Irvin. *Harlem Renaissance*. New York: Oxford University Press, 1971.

Isaacs, Edith J. R. *The Negro in the American Theatre*. New York: Theatre Arts, 1947.

Johnson, James Weldon. *Black Manhattan*. New York: Alfred A. Knopf, 1930. New York: Atheneum, 1969.

Mitchell, Loften. *Black Drama: The Story of the American Negro in the Theatre*. New York: Hawthorn Books, 1967.

Quinn, Arthur Hobson. *A History of the American Drama: From the Beginnings to the Civil War*. New York: Appleton-Century-Crofts, 1943.

———. *A History of the American Drama: From the Civil War to the Present Day*. New York: Appleton-Century-Crofts, 1936.

Sanders, Leslie Catherine. *The Development of Black Theater in America: From Shadows to Selves*. Baton Rouge: Louisiana State University Press, 1988.

Woll, Allen. *Dictionary of the Black Theatre: Broadway, Off-Broadway, and Selected Harlem Theatre*. Westport, CT: Greenwood Press, 1983.

———. *Black Musical Theatre: From Coontown to Dreamgirls*. Baton Rouge: Louisiana State University Press, 1989.

9

Theatre and Community:
The Significance of Howard University's
1920s Drama Program

Scott Zaluda

The date is 7 April 1923, the first performance by the Howard University Players of Thelma Myrtle Duncan's one-act play, *The Death Dance*, subtitled "An
African Play."[1] *The Death Dance* is a "folk drama" about purging corrupted
power. Driven by the impending execution of her lover, an intoxicating woman
instigates the political demise of her lover's judge, a corrupt tribal medicine
man. The chorus or community dances a condemning death dance initially
around the hero-lover, finally around the medicine man. Although at first the
community's will seems to be controlled by the powerful medicine man, the
community itself becomes the play's most imperious force, turning as one
against whomever is currently bound and gagged. Whether it was intended or
not, a critique of community lies under the surface of Duncan's play.

Duncan had written her folk play as a student in Howard English professor
Montgomery Gregory's classes in "Dramatic Technique." When *The Death
Dance* was produced, Howard University's drama curriculum was a little over
two years old. In 1920 Gregory along with his colleague from the philosophy
department, Alain Leroy Locke, formed the Department of Dramatic Art and
Public Speaking and a performance group, the Howard Players, around courses
in playwriting and production. According to the 1919–1920 Howard University
catalogue, for the first-level course in "Dramatic Art," attention was to be "directed to Negro folklore and history as materials for dramatic composition."
During the second level, students were to be given "practical training in the production of dramas and pageants," with emphasis "placed upon community
drama."[2]

Howard's student performance group, the Howard Players, has been examined in the context of the development of an African American theatre. But
Howard's early drama program should also be linked to a national movement of
this era, that is, community drama, as theorized and enacted in the 19-teens by
such figures as W.E.B. Du Bois and Percy Mackaye. Although community
drama is popularly associated with its little, local theatres, one phenomenon of
community drama, the pageant, was mounted, in some cases, in stadiums by
hundreds of performers. Du Bois's celebrated allegorical pageant of black his-

tory, *The Star of Ethiopia*, was enacted by members of local communities before 6,000 spectators in a Washington, D.C. stadium in 1915. That was one
year before Percy Mackaye's *Caliban: By the Yellow Sands*, an allegory which
celebrated an American national unity as processed through Christian and
Shakespearean imagery, was mounted before 15,000 spectators in New York's
City College stadium, its cast reportedly representing the ethnic and racial diversity of New York City.[3]

Ever its ardent priest, Percy Mackaye characterized community drama as a
"ritual of democratic religion," to be observed in "temples of the communal
imagination."[4] One of Mackaye's goals was to force dramatic art out of the
bourgeois stagnation within which commercial theatre was, in his view, mired.
But, more importantly, he believed the stage to be the greatest hope for social
progress. Out of cultural difference and social competitiveness, his eclectic spec-
tacles were designed to synthesize an American "International Mind," forged by
a "mentality of cooperation."[5] "The harmonizing of nations within nations—of
communities within communities"[6] did not imply for Mackaye, as it would
have for the nativistic social conservatives of the day, "less nationality in our
culture, but more civilized culture in our nationalism."[7]

Notably, this particular vision of social progress saw cultures being harmonized and "civilized" by means of certain "art inheritances of drama," Shakespeare's *Tempest* blended with "the simplicity of Christ's social message."[8]
Within the haze of Mackaye's mystifying language for community drama, his
liturgies of democratic religion were therefore only able to offer a unified picture
of what a social historian has recently called the "complex and mixed experience" of American culture and community by processing that culture through an
Anglo Saxon iconology.[9]

But when we juxtapose Mackaye and Du Bois's contemporary pageants, the
community drama movement becomes especially interesting for the contrasting
allegories of culture which informed its diverse *communities*. From its beginnings, competing narratives were already destabilizing one foundational ideal
upon which the theatrical temples of Mackaye's democratic religion seemed to
be built: the ideal, that is, of a harmonized, singular *national* community.

Nevertheless, Mackaye's aphorism, *more culture in our nationalism*, or a
variation, *more difference in our community*, might have been printed across the
covers of either his own or Du Bois's pageant programs, or used as philosophical frame for curriculum proposals offered by multidisciplinary faculty who, in
the early twenties, were attempting to start up an "experimental laboratory" in
drama at Howard University. African American transformations of community
drama were often justified, in fact, as reactions against mainstream anxiety about
the proliferation of different cultures in our nationalism. To realize more culture
in our nationalism, more inclusiveness in our communitarianism, African
Americans created theatres and dramatic narratives intended to complicate the
nation's view of its "native" homogeneity and, significantly, to subvert and
erase some of that imaginary monoculture's stereotypes—legacies of another,
persistent, theatrical movement, minstrelsy.

In 1921, after Howard's new Department of Dramatic Art and Public Speaking was absorbed by the English department, a third-level course was set up so
that student compositions from the second-level course could be "revised and
plays of a more advanced type" written. Moreover, the Howard Players would

now act as an "experimental laboratory of Negro drama" by staging trial performances of "the meritorious dramas in the Dramatic Workshop preliminary to the public presentation. These courses," the 1919–1920 catalogue stated, were intended "to develop the dramatic literature for a Negro Theater."[10]

Based upon Harvard professor George Pierce Baker's celebrated "47 Workshop," Howard's new curriculum has the distinction of being one of the first credit-bearing drama programs offered by an American university. The program's development coincided with efforts by African American faculty from across the disciplines to make the university into a center for a distinctly African American academic inquiry and discourse, one that could be woven into traditional western cultural study. New textbooks for literary study produced by members of Howard's English department in this period emphasized African American contributions to American literature. Symposiums sponsored by the history department attempted to give legitimacy as a field to African history. Meanwhile, Howard's sociologists published widely and developed new curricula in order to undo the damage that racist myth-making had done to academic perceptions of society and culture. Pivotal for all of these curricular initiatives at Howard was a fight by some faculty, students, and alumni for black administrative control, which culminated in 1926 with the appointment of Howard's first nonwhite president.[11]

Like his colleagues in history, sociology, philosophy, and English, Montgomery Gregory believed that academic remedies were needed to address the "unfortunate" history and social status of blacks in America. Indeed, many who taught at and administered historically black colleges and universities believed they had a special mission to lead the way toward defeating the "evil of the racial situation in this country," notably through speaking and writing, musical and stage performance. "Our only salvation," Gregory wrote in setting out his vision of a Howard drama program, "lies in self-expression." And because the "Negro has been denied access to the aesthetic and artistic life of America," he said, "we must evolve a drama of our own."[12]

Gregory and Locke's project at once both reinforced and contested the rhetoric of the community drama movement. Their theatrical enterprise was intended, first, to establish "a common ground where the architect, the painter, the musician, the dancer, the actor, and the social worker shall construct plays that shall be things of beauty." Indeed, drama at Howard, Gregory said, was to carry out its brand of cultural work by democratizing the theatre, that is, by making it "the property of all the people." Through the community drama movement, Gregory said, "where all the artistic and social agencies of the community cooperate in the production of plays or pageants for the people," drama realizes its potential as an "agency for the moral, social, and spiritual well being of the nation."[13] The significance of the Howard Players was, Locke would insist, "if anything, more national than racial."[14]

Kelly Miller, a Howard dean, professor of sociology, and Negro press columnist, in a 1925 article on Howard that appeared in Locke's anthology, *The New Negro*, found it necessary to remind readers that the Negro college existed because history had constituted African Americans as a "community far more separate and distinct in needs, aims, and aspirations than any other racial or sectarian element in our national life."[15] Howard would have to function, in part, as a site for African Americans to comprehend the meaning of their particular cul-

tural identity and circumstances through fostering and developing "special studies of race history" and race relations.[16] Given Locke and Gregory's nationalistic
and pluralistic aims, their enterprise was necessarily a struggle against the pluralistic ideals of community pageantry such as Mackaye's, where diversity is
processed through a particular, hegemonic iconology. Indeed, they presented the
Howard Players as the foundation for a "National Negro Theater."

The term "National Negro Theater" occurs commonly in letters Gregory
wrote during the early twenties, seeking support for his program. A letter Gregory wrote on 20 January 1921 to Eugene O'Neill is typical: "Our ultimate aim
and dream is the establishment of a National Negro Theater which shall give
true expression to the life of the race."[17] In his reply of 25 January, O'Neill expressed enthusiastic support for Gregory's goals and gave permission for the
Howard Players to stage *Emperor Jones*. Indeed, by working with the plays of
O'Neill and other prominent white playwrights who wrote about Black experience, Gregory and Locke may have believed their embryonic Negro theatre could
more easily reach beyond Negro audiences. They hoped that the small productions put up by Howard faculty and students would evolve into a theatre for
communities well beyond the red-lined boundaries enclosing African Americans
during the period.

During an interview Gregory gave in 1921 to Kenneth Macgowan, theatre
critic for the *New York Globe*, he explained that ultimately a national Negro
theatre would not establish its theatres in African American districts, "for that
would tend to prevent the white community from seeing their art." Drama was a
"wonderful opportunity," Gregory told Macgowan, for the Negro to "win a better understanding in the community."[18] *The* community, Gregory appears to
acknowledge here, means the white community.

A national Negro theatre's major objective was to reconfigure *the* community—and thereby the nation—first of all by revising the language and symbols
constituting its ideologies of race. Despite the decline of white minstrelsy at the
close of the nineteenth century, many African Americans of the early twentieth
century remained much concerned that minstrelsy and its signs had come to
shape the white world's sense of African America. "Minstrel nonsense," Houston Baker has said, "marred" the lives of African Americans "during thirty un-
easy years from emancipation to the dawn of a new century."[19] Even in 1925,
Gregory lamented, "the average play of Negro life . . . whether employing white
or black actors, reeks with this pernicious influence."[20]

In his introduction to *The New Negro*, which heralded a Harlem-based cultural renaissance, Alain Locke wrote that because the old Negro's "shadow self
has been more real to him than his personality," he continued to require a "reorientation of view."[21] Restating the theme in the same collection, Kelly Miller
depicted Howard University's mission as "calculated to put a new front on the
whole scheme of racial life and aspiration."[22]

For Howard's theatre program, the new front's theatrical forms were "folk"
and "native" drama. In his own *New Negro* contribution Gregory wrote that "the
only avenue of genuine achievement in American drama for the Negro lies in the
development of the rich veins of folk-tradition of the past and in the portrayal of
the authentic life of the Negro masses of to-day."[23] When Locke and Gregory
together published another anthology in the late 1920s, *Plays of Negro Life*,
they gave as their subtitle "A Source Book of Native American Drama." As

Kathy Perkins has pointed out, the term native drama signified a dramatic genre which gave more depth to black experience than had minstrel nonsense or earlier plays by white authors.[24] The purpose of the native dramas created at Howard was to deeply examine the meanings of black identity and experience in America and in the world. In addition, the universal idea of the American *native* was being recast to encompass richer black meanings and experience. Eugene O'Neill justified his sympathy with Gregory's project by his belief that "the gifts the Negro can and will bring to our native drama are invaluable ones."[25]

Inspired partly by Irish folk theatre, African American "folk plays" such as Thelma Duncan's *The Death Dance* concentrated on black experience without, as Perkins has said, emphasizing "the oppressive issues blacks faced daily and racial tensions."[26] Folk plays "were a part of black pride," writes James V. Hatch, "a black pride stimulated into consciousness largely by Marcus Garvey's Universal Negro Improvement Association." Folk plays sought "the real Afro-American—a being whom whites had no way of knowing"—instead of the exotic.[27]

Locke and Gregory believed that the "most promising path" in the "quest of modern American realism" was the folk play rather than the currently dominant "problem play"[28] with its tendency toward "moralistic allegories of melodramatic protests as dramatic correctives and antidotes for race prejudice."[29] Gregory had had the idea for the Howard Players, in fact, in reaction to the NAACP-sponsored production of Angelina Grimke's propagandist "race play," *Rachel*. The Howard Players were founded, Gregory wrote late in the 1920s, to promote a "purely artistic approach and folk-drama idea."[30]

By 1923 the Howard Players were beginning to stage works created by students in Gregory's classes. Besides Thelma Duncan's folk plays, other homegrown works included *The Yellow Tree* by DeReath Irene Byrd Busey, *The Desert Sun* by Lucille Banks, and *The Bird Child* by Lucy White. *The Bird Child*, a one-act "native drama," examines haunting entanglements resulting from southern miscegenation.[31] *Mortgaged* by Willis Richardson, already an established playwright when the Players were formed, was written for the Players and staged in 1924.[32] Locke and Gregory had attempted two years earlier to produce this conflict of morals among "uplifted" middle-class blacks, but were blocked by Howard president J. Stanley Durkee. Only after Richardson had become nationally recognized when his play, *The Chip Woman's Fortune*, was shown on Broadway, were the Players able to present the earlier play. In 1924, Howard audiences also viewed a production of Jean Toomer's expressionistic folk play, *Balo*, also written for the Howard Players.[33] *Balo* is a sketch of poor black farmers in Georgia who end their exhausting workday with a kind of mystical revelation through the singing of spirituals. Here the folk and native themes are indistinguishable. Encounters with poor white neighbors and the repressed unhappiness of the black mother make this play a rich exploration not only of folk ways but of the complex psychological subtleties of segregated southern society.

Indeed, the "purely artistic approach" Gregory claimed for the Players and his theatre curriculum, a reaction to what he viewed as the propagandist "race play," almost sounds like an evasion of each production's deep political significance. Moreover, in terms of the politics of 1920s American theatre, Gregory and Locke's program was generating an "authentic" Negro drama at a time of great commercial interest in Negro literary materials both on Broadway and in publishing houses but continuing prejudices against Negroes themselves developing such a literature.[34]

Nellie McKay points out that all the major theorists of an "authentic" African American theatre in this era had in common the desire to correct the "disastrous" consequences of minstrelsy. However, not everyone agreed on what an authentic African American drama comprised.[35] The questions of who created and who viewed such a drama were paramount for one theorist of drama of the age, W.E.B. Du Bois. For Du Bois, who continued to organize his own community theatre enterprises throughout the twenties, any real folk-play movement had to comprise plays "About us . . . By us . . . For us . . . Near us."[36]

It is interesting that few members of the Howard Players' advisory board were black. Along with Gregory and Locke, the African American novelist, teacher, and NAACP leader James Weldon Johnson served on the board, joined there by, among others, Eugene O'Neill, Ridgely Torrence, Kenneth Macgowan, Robert Benchley, and Samuel Eliot, the president of Smith College. (Although he attended productions and corresponded with Gregory, Du Bois himself was not on the Players' advisory board.) While Du Bois was creating his little theatre in a Harlem basement free from institutional pressures, Gregory and Locke were creating their theatre in the context of a Congressionally sponsored institution's complicated racial politics. During a period of administrative resistance at Howard to the taint of exceptionalism, the Howard Players' stability may have been buffered early on by the tacit approval of this predominantly white board of advisors as well as by the staging of productions by white playwrights.

Late in the twenties two major anthologies of drama took stock of how the decade had so far defined an American Negro theatre. As they had done in organizing the Howard Players, Locke and Gregory's *Plays of Negro Life: A Source Book of Native American Drama* combined works *about* African or African American subjects *by* both white and African American authors, thereby reflecting an era in which largely unknown African American playwrights competed with little success against the white playwrights like O'Neill and Torrence who were achieving widespread success in exploiting Negro themes. Several of the works included in the sourcebook, by black and white writers, had been staged by the Howard Players, suggesting once again the representative importance they ascribed to their efforts.

The other anthology of this period was Willis Richardson's 1930 collection of plays exclusively by African American authors, *Plays and Pageants from the Life of the Negro*, coedited by Carter G. Woodson. In addition to several of his own plays, Richardson includes works by Thelma Duncan and May Miller, another student of Gregory's and the daughter of Howard dean Kelly Miller. Indeed, one consequence of theatrical workshops and programs at Howard was that the new native drama was being written by women. Other women who had studied under Gregory include Zora Neale Hurston, Georgia Douglas Johnson, Shirley Graham, and Eulalie Spence.[37] Perkins credits the Howard program with being a "major catalyst behind the promotion and recognition of plays by early black women writers."[38] Through plays and performances, the work of complicating the meanings of culture and community often turned during the 1920s upon the meaning of being an African American woman.

In 1926, the Howard Board of Trustees would appoint the university's first African American president, Mordechai Johnson, who for over thirty years would prove to have a keen enough understanding of the politics of "race consciousness" to enable Howard to become the major center for the study of African and African American culture that various faculty members had fought for almost since the turn of the century.

But two years before Mordechai Johnson's appointment, both Locke and Gregory were fired by Howard's last white president, J. Stanley Durkee. Gregory and Locke were both deeply involved with efforts to diversify the curriculum, within forums other than their experimental theatre laboratory; Locke especially, an important scholar and anthologist, served as a faculty leader in several contests against the administration's positions and tactics.

Nevertheless, although both men were gone a year before Durkee's own resignation, the drama programs they created had been among the most sustainable initiatives to reorient university culture. A program intended "to develop the dramatic literature for a Negro Theater" did not in fact receive as much resistance as did, for instance, Professor William Leo Hansberry's groundbreaking courses in African history. Possibly this was because theatre remained a fringe discipline, indeed, after the program's first year, a group of electives within the English curriculum, while history carried weight as a sanctified academic discipline. Certainly, the Howard Players also garnered some official support because Gregory's publicity efforts had been remarkably successful and because he had attracted the public support of prominent white public figures such as Eugene O'Neill and Samuel Eliot. Nevertheless, during this notably transformative period in Howard's history, all those who worked to make the curriculum more inclusive did so within an atmosphere of anxiety over whether the college, its faculty, and its students were equal to their white counterparts. Efforts to reach conciliation between racial exceptionalism and the dominance of a white culture and curriculum typically encountered a great deal of resistance, as clearly evidenced by the firing of Gregory and Locke.

Publicity for and interest in the Howard Players weakened significantly after Gregory left Howard to become superintendent of state-segregated "colored schools" in Atlantic City, New Jersey. Soon after Mordechai Johnson became president, Locke would return to Howard, and in 1929 would write a letter trying to persuade Gregory to return also. "How do you stand on the proposition?" Locke asked. "I have either a dream or a mirage of our Negro Theater rising again from its ashes."[39] But Gregory remained in Atlantic City with a better salary to support his family and far away, he wrote to Locke, from the "mess" at Howard.[40]

In addition to the loss of Gregory's energy and his fundraising activities, Alain Locke's phoenix might have become somewhat overweighted by the rhetoric through which it articulated its social visions, that is, the rhetoric of community which was a commandment of the religion of democracy throughout the Progressive era. The language that Percy Mackaye had used to justify community drama, a language of pluralism whereby the magic of theatre work transforms conflicts of class and culture, is echoed in Gregory and Locke's writings to promote their own community theatre activities. But the rewards and influences of the original Howard workshops and productions were undoubtedly more personal and local than societal and national. Gregory and Locke's Howard Players might never have won any widespread better understanding in the nation of African American experience, let alone transformed the meaning of *the* community, but the theatre they gave birth to would be the root of an important and successful academic drama program that, to this day, continues to train, support, and launch playwrights, directors, actors, and others for careers in the theatre—among them, the contemporary playwright August Wilson.

The word *community* itself, used frequently in Gregory's letters and articles, and the assumptions or desires it carried of unified individual experience and culture, was a term that elicited considerable dialogue and disagreement within this period. Some years after the Howard Players were created, in 1931, the historian Carter Woodson—who in 1917 had created and taught Howard's first courses in African American history and in 1928 had coedited a collection of plays by African American writers—wrote a column in the *New York Age* about the difficulties of delimiting a "Negro community." The terms for delimitation were problematic, Woodson said, because they had been articulated historically by outsiders and because African Americans were, in Woodson's words, "influenced socially and economically in various directions."[41] Woodson was reacting to the same gestures of white racism that had inspired the dream of a national Negro theatre, that identification of the other, the minority, as undelimited, as univocal. But he was also trying to persuade his African American readers to take stock of the social complexity of their varied experience. Indeed, Woodson's critique echoes the criticisms of the single-minded, oppressive community implied within Thelma Duncan's play, *The Death Dance.* Reorientation, a catchword for black intellectuals of the 1920s—or, as Kelly Miller called it, putting a "new front on the whole scheme of racial life and aspiration"—should not mean replacing one set of abhorred limitations, such as those imposed by minstrelsy, with a "new front" that would itself delineate an African American identity and community as having less rather than more cultural diversity.

Howard's own community was decidedly middle-class and well-educated, and can be said to have represented the complex and mixed experience of African America no more than Alain Locke's construct of a Harlem-based renaissance articulated all geographies and iconographies of African American culture. The Howard Players emerged from particular *communities*, entered into some resonant dialogues among African American *theatres*, and developed within a complex and mixed experience of African American and American identity.

Finally, then, rather than their published visions, it is within the productions themselves that the Howard Players' important cultural legacy may be found. For within a contentious national discourse on culture and society, the Howard Players, alongside other theatre groups of the 1920s, effected social progress through writing and performing allegories of culture that were in clear contrast to a range of cultural articulations attempting to put a claim on meanings for black identity, community, and nation.

NOTES

1. Thelma Duncan, "The Death Dance," in *Plays of Negro Life: A Source Book of Native American Drama*, ed. A. Locke and M. Gregory (New York: Harper, 1927) 323–331.

2. *Howard University Catalogues* (Washington, D.C.: Trustees of Howard University, 1920, 1921).

3. My account of *Caliban* is drawn from both Percy Mackaye, *Community Drama: Its Motive and Method of Neighborliness, An Interpretation* (Boston and

New York: Houghton Mifflin, 1917) and Louise Burleigh, *The Community Theatre in Theory and Practice* (Boston: Little, Brown, 1917) 37–40.

4. Mackaye, *Community Drama* 11.

5. Ibid. 13.

6. Ibid. 29.

7. Ibid. 67.

8. Ibid. 47.

9. Richard Sennett, "The Identity Myth," *New York Times* 30 January 1994: Op-Ed page.

10. *Howard University Catalogues*; Montgomery Gregory, "A Chronology of Negro Theater," in *Plays of Negro Life* 416.

11. Elsewhere, I have more extensively reviewed some of the curricular struggles marking Howard's part in what Raymond Wolters terms the "black college rebellions of the 1920s." See Scott Zaluda, "Black Colleges and the Culture of Reform: Alternative Perceptions and Practices in the Teaching of Writing at Howard University," Modern Language Association Convention, December 1994. See also Rawmond Wolters, *The New Negro on Campus: Black College Rebellions of the 1920s* (Princeton: Princeton University Press, 1975).

12. Montgomery Gregory, "Drama at Howard University: A Vision." *Howard University Record* 14 (June 1920): 440–441.

13. Gregory, "A Vision" 440.

14. Alain Locke, "Introduction," *Plays of Negro Life*.

15. Kelly Miller, "Howard: The National Negro University," in *The New Negro: An Interpretation*, ed. Alain Locke (1925; New York: Athenaeum, 1992) 312.

16. Miller, "Howard" 320.

17. Montgomery Gregory, "Montgomery Gregory Folders—Correspondence," Moorland-Spingarn Research Institute, Howard University.

18. Qtd. in Kathy A. Perkins, "Introduction," *Black Female Playwrights: An Anthology of Plays Before 1950*, ed. Kathy A. Perkins (Bloomington: Indiana University Press, 1989) 6.

19. Houston Baker, *Modernism and the Harlem Renaissance* (Chicago: University of Chicago Press, 1987) 36.

20. Montgomery Gregory, "The Drama of Negro Life," in *The New Negro: An Interpretation* 155.

21. Alain Locke, "The New Negro," in *The New Negro: An Interpretation* 4.

22. Miller, "Howard" 320.

23. Gregory, "The Drama of Negro Life" 159.

24. Perkins, "Introduction" 3.

25. Gregory Folders.

26. Perkins, "Introduction" 3.

27. James V. Hatch, "Introduction," *Black Theater, USA: Forty-Five Plays by Black Americans, 1847–1974*, ed. James V. Hatch (New York: Free Press, Macmillan, 1974) 209–210.

28. Locke, "Introduction," *Plays of Negro Life*.

29. Qtd. in Nellie McKay, "Black Theater and Drama in the 1920s: Years of Growing Pains," *The Massachusetts Review* 28 (Winter 1987): 621.

30. Gregory, "A Chronology of Negro Theater" 414.

31. Lucy White, "The Bird Child," in *Plays of Negro Life* 255–267.

32. Willis Richardson, "Mortgaged," in *The New Negro Renaissance: An Anthology*, ed. Michael W. Peplow and Arthur P. Davis (New York: Holt Rinehart Winston, 1975) 103–117.

33. Jean Toomer, "Balo," in *Black Theater, USA* 218–224.

34. Harold Cruse, *The Crisis of the Negro Intellectual* (New York: Morrow, 1967) 35.

35. McKay, "Black Theater and Drama in the 1920s" 617.

36. W.E.B. Du Bois, "Krigwa Players Little Negro Theatre: The Story of a Little Theatre Movement," *The Crisis* 32 (July 1926): 134.

37. Perkins, "Introduction" 7–8.

38. Ibid. 3.

39. Alain Locke, "Alain Locke Folders—Correspondence," Moorland-Spingarn Research Institute, Howard University.

40. Locke Folders.

41. Carter G. Woodson, "Comments on Negro Education; Finding the Negro Community and Working in It," *New York Age* 21 November 1931: 9.

10

"To Doubt Is Fatal":
Eva Le Gallienne and the Civic
Repertory Theatre, 1926–1932

Estelle Aden

"To doubt is fatal." This credo of Eva Le Gallienne was initially an off-hand remark to a newspaper columnist in Boston.[1] The actress had just completed performances of Gerhart Hauptmann's *Hannele's Himmelfahrt* (The Assumption of Hannele). During the run of the play she had taken over the direction of the production from John D. Williams. The year was 1924. It was to take two more years from that date until the Civic Repertory Theatre would open its first season with eight plays in repertory at the Fourteenth Street Theatre.

PITFALLS OF THE REPERTORY SYSTEM

Several theatres continued to flirt with the repertory system as late as the 1920s, and a definition of what repertory theatre is would define the goals that Eva Le Gallienne was working toward:

These are institutions with permanent companies that give a variety of plays each week. The most popular productions are given quite often. Those less popular find their audiences at less frequent performances: they do not have to compete for long runs night after night. . . . The important point is that the repertory theatre keeps the best plays alive for years, and makes possible an acting company that gains by long practice together.

Long runs in New York killed the repertory companies of a hundred years ago; our stock companies with their weekly changes of bill, died when the films lured away the audiences that had supported them and the touring system. . . . In 1925–26 the Theatre Guild tried a modified repertory system with productions alternating weekly at two theatres.[2]

When the Neighborhood Playhouse opened in 1915 at 466 Grand Street the theatre company, under the direction of Alice and Irene Lewisohn, had already had nearly ten years of experience at the Henry Street Settlement. Though the company decided to produce plays in repertory, by 1926-1927 Alice Lewisohn Crowley explains the problems that the repertory system imposed:

Repertory was unquestionably failing, not only . . . at the box office but at the core, because of our lack of conviction in repertory as a form. We had from the beginning been committed heart and soul to unexplored fields, as well as to synthesizing the media of expression. Repertory had been undertaken as a concession to circumstances rather than an urge, and commitment to its forms was a contradiction to our essential values.[3]

The Theatre Guild, founded in 1918, had a strong sense of the position it would fulfill. In the introduction to an anthology of plays presented by the Theatre Guild, the directors of the Guild note that it "was founded . . . without a theatre, without a play, without an actor and without a scrap of scenery. Its sole artistic asset was an idea."[4] Only later, in 1926-1927, did the Theatre Guild seek to retain "at least the nucleus of a permanent acting company," and Waldau points to both the visit of the Moscow Art Theatre's studio group the previous season and the example of Le Gallienne's success with the Civic Repertory Theatre as the motives behind this alteration of policy.[5]

The Civic Repertory under the direction and inspiration of Eva Le Gallienne would have the fervor for and commitment to repertory that set it apart from other theatres of its time. Making the theatre available to its audiences was paramount. To this end, the ticket prices were kept low. Revivals of great plays were part of the repertory plan. No scenery was discarded. Her vision for the Civic Theatre was to lift it from the slough of commercialism to the ideal city on the hill.

"The Galleries and Balconies Sell out First—the People Want Theatre"[6]

Eva Le Gallienne was convinced that there was a public ready and eager for quality theatre at a minimal price. The theatre would thrive as the public thrived. The cardinal requirement had to be low prices which ranged from thirty-five cents to a dollar fifty. Those prices would enable working people to enjoy a season of masterworks. New plays would alternate with the classics from time to time. Even when raising the ticket price seemed the only way to secure the survival of the Civic Repertory, Le Gallienne refused. Raising the ticket price would disenfranchise the public for which the Civic Repertory Theatre was intended. "One of America's greatest needs is to build up the theatre. . . . The theatre is yet far away from its loftiest possibilities. To restore or to attain these the actor must take his vow to God as does the priest. . . . Of the stage and its condition today we might use the words of Christ of the ancient temple. 'This was a house of prayer and ye have made it a den of thieves.'"[7]

Her dedication was one that could benefit all who were involved. The audience was not considered a source of income but rather a "witness." That implies a communion between the players and those who take in the play as an experience. The foci of the Civic Repertory were the audience, the actor, the classics, and the renewed accessibility of those productions that were favorites. It was to be a kind of library where fine plays could be renewed season after season.[8]

It was clear why Eve Le Gallienne was convinced that this was a viable plan. She came from a European tradition. The theatre comprised an important part of the community's cultural life in countless towns and cities across Europe. Why not in New York City?

They have also, as a matter of course people's repertory theatres, permanent institutions that are an integral part of the life of the communities, "libraries of living plays" that enable the pubic to become familiar with and enjoy the finest dramatic work of all periods and all countries, classic and modern, national and international, played by the best acting talent, and at *popular prices*. In many lands such theatres are objects of national pride and it is an honor for actors to be members of these companies.[9]

ABOUT EVA Le GALLIENNE
AND THE CIVIC REPERTORY THEATRE

At twenty-seven years of age Eva Le Gallienne was a Broadway star. The level of her art as an actress had been fully appreciated. Such eminent critics as Alexander Woollcott and Brooks Atkinson had given her glowing reviews. Having made a great success in the Theatre Guild production of *Liliom* (Molnar), her stature as an artist was secure. "She was not poetic . . . she was poetry," as one *New York Times* critic wrote.[10] She was in great demand and played many roles, but one of her major complaints was the "extended run." She was bored by the repetition of a role for an extended period of time and was searching for an answer to that problem in terms of the actress as a creative artist. Her decision was to leave the Shubert Organization: "I turned my back on Broadway because it had nothing to give me but money and I had nothing to give it."[11]

Le Gallienne turned to repertory to play roles of substance in plays of substance which Broadway was not going to consider producing. There was an audience for Ibsen, Shakespeare, and Molière, and the Civic Repertory proved it at its Fourteenth Street Theatre and on tours across the country. She was certain that great plays would create audiences. Another feature of repertory that attracted her was the growth and development of an artistic company involved in developing these masterworks for stage presentation. Artists are not instant products. Their development requires experience, talent, training, and nurturing: "There is no fatal haste. . . . They grow facile and flexible. I like a quiet actor, one who does not give out a great deal in conversation, one who sets and lets the world go by, listening."[12]

The location of the theatre was another daring risk that Le Gallienne took. The Civic Repertory was housed in a theatre built in 1866 on Fourteenth Street. It had not been in use since 1911. Consequently, it needed extensive renovation. "From 1911 to 1926, it remained dark for all practical purposes except for an occasional engagement by a stock or opera company. In 1926, it was rejuvenated as the Civic Repertory Theatre under the management of Eva Le Gallienne and achieved the only solid fame of its long career. After six seasons, the Civic Repertory relinquished the theatre and in 1938, it was razed."[13]

Le Gallienne chose it because the playing space was well designed. Another important asset, which most modern theatres do not have, was ample storage space for scenery. The Fourteenth Street Theatre also had good rehearsal facilities. The auditorium seated eleven hundred. The floor above was a huge costume department running the entire depth of the building. The third floor was a

library for students and business offices. The fifth floor of the theatre building
was to become Le Gallienne's apartment. She was performing and working
around the clock. She recounts her schedule in her autobiography, *With a Quiet
Heart.*

Each morning at nine o'clock Santelli arrived and we fenced for half an hour. I then
had breakfast. After that I gradually descended from one floor to the next, stopping
on the way at various departments that needed my attention, until at noon I found
myself at the stage level, ready for the daily rehearsal. We rehearsed every day from
noon to five or five thirty, either on the current new production or on some of the old
ones that needed tuning up. Immediately, after rehearsals I had dinner, and then slept
for an hour before going down to play. After the performance, I usually had a few
people up to supper for informal conferences—actors, authors or scenic designers.
These sessions usually lasted til around 2 A.M.[14]

Her duties were manifold. She was directing the productions, acting in
them, administering the theatre, fund raising, translating Ibsen texts, and super-
vising the planning for the future projects. In response to a highly successful
production at the Civic Repertory Theatre of *Three Sisters* (Chekhov) Alexander
Woollcott observed: "As a General she leads her generation in the theatre. All
our players sigh ostentatiously for the great plays. Miss Le Gallienne merely
acts in them."[15] This was the second play of the inaugural season. In order, the
eight plays that opened the 1926–1927 season were: Benavente's *Saturday
Night*, Chekhov's *The Three Sisters*, Ibsen's *The Master Builder* and *John
Gabriel Borkman*, Goldoni's *La Locandiera*, Shakespeare's *Twelfth Night*,
Glaspell's *The Inheritors*, and Sierra's *The Cradle Song*.

Two of plays were not well received: *Saturday Night* and *The Inheritors*.
The final production, *Cradle Song*, was a solid hit. "Virtually all the fifty-six
performances in the spring of 1927 were sold out."[16]

The first season was enormously ambitious. The schedule of productions
lasted twenty-eight weeks. Though the actors were paid less than their Broadway colleagues, the security of working throughout the season compensated for
the financial loss. Some of the players that season were: Egon Brecher, Sayre
Crawley, Beatrice de Neergaard, Josephine Hutchinson, Paul Leyssac, Harold
Moulton, Leona Roberts, and Beatrice Terry. Stage stars who joined the Civic
Repertory Company included Jacob Ben-Ami, Merle Maddern, Alla Nazimova,
and Joseph Schildkraut. Nevertheless, the Civic Repertory was an ensemble
company. The consistency of rehearsal practice and performance preparation was
an important element in the company. Eva Le Gallienne directed the entire first
season. The only two productions not under her direction during six years of
repertory playing were *Camille* (Dumas, *fils*) in the 1931 season, directed by
Constance Collier, and *Martine* adapted by Arnold Moss in the same season.
Martine was directed by Robert F. Ross.[17] The company was strong and the
performances were of a high caliber. Eva Le Gallienne had leading roles in
many of the plays and she also played supporting roles. In the 1929–1930 season she cast Merle Madden in the role of Irina opposite Jacob Ben-Ami as
Trigorin in Chekhov's *The Sea Gull*. She directed the production and played
Masha. "The critics were enthusiastic, applauding the orchestrated, ensemble
acting as well as the truthful and sincere characterizations. Eva's portrayal of

Masha was rated by many as her greatest achievement in years. . . . The performance ended with a five-minute standing ovation."[18]

Le Gallienne started a school for young apprentices. There was no tuition but there were strenuous auditions. New talent was being developed. The training included voice, dancing, fencing, text analysis, and daily constant rehearsal. There were also lectures on make-up and student workshop productions. Members of the Apprentice Group were J. Edward Bromberg, John Garfield, Robert Lewis, Burgess Meredith, Arnold Moss, May Sarton, and Richard Waring, among others.

All of this activity had to be funded. Otto Kahn, a leading philanthropist, invested $18,000 in the Civic Repertory Theatre initially. Ward Morehouse states, "everyone in the theatre automatically turned to him when the need for funds became urgent."[19] Mrs. Edward Bok (later Mrs. Efrem Zimbalist) of Philadelphia provided scholarship funds for the best four apprentices to remain for a second year. Other people who contributed to the Civic Repertory were Adolph Lewisohn, Ralph Pulitzer, and John Davison Rockefeller, Jr. In addition to strenuous fund raising activities, a membership drive was initiated toward the end of the first season. One dollar was the fee, and there were 3,000 members by the end of the year. It was organized by Mrs. Anna Faller. At the end of the second season the membership had risen to 50,000.[20] The weekly revenue did not cover expenses. The attendance was excellent: 79 percent of capacity during the first season and 95 percent during the second season, but "the economic situation, with excellent attendance could not meet expenses. An annual subsidy of $80,000 to $100,000 was necessary for new productions."[21] There were ominous financial signs because of the Depression. There were cutbacks.

In the second season (1927–1928) five plays were offered in repertory. Although *Hedda Gabler* was a sell-out, the others were not popular with audiences. The season closed with this play. All of Ibsen's plays were huge successes for Eva Le Gallienne. She could fill a theatre at 10:30 in the morning for an Ibsen play.

Le Gallienne reminisces in an article, "Ibsen, the Shy Giant," about the overwhelming success she had in her productions of Ibsen.

Everywhere they met with enthusiastic response and these two Ibsen plays, *The Master Builder* and *John Gabriel Borkman* proved to be the cornerstone of the Civic Repertory which I started in 1926. Early in 1928 *Hedda Gabler* was added to our list of plays, which included works by Shakespeare, Chekhov, Moliere, Goldoni, Sierra and others. The Civic Repertory celebrated the centenary of Ibsen's birth March 28, 1928 by giving a morning performance (10:30 A.M.) of *The Master Builder*, a matinee of *Hedda Gabler*, followed by *John Gabriel Borkman* that same evening, proving that the old Civic was a repertory in fact not just in name.[22]

But, as Schanke has observed, "no theatre group was committed to Eva's ideals—to provide the best in theatre at the lowest possible rate and to present plays in repertory. The Actors' Theatre, Walter Hampden's Theatre and the Theatre Guild espoused the same intent but fell short. They charged regular prices for tickets and arranged for long runs with their hits."[23] Added to these three salient factors are the charisma, intelligence, and talent of this young woman who through her strength as an actress, director, and producer was the spearhead for the Civic Repertory.

In the 1928 season *Peter Pan* (Barrie) was produced. Le Gallienne was in the title role. It was a resounding success. She decided that it should be revived at every holiday season. Year after year it ran during Thanksgiving, Christmas, and Easter, "when everyone old and young is a child again."[24] Her portrayal, vigorous and energetic, was mercurial in contrast to Maude Adams's sentimental portrayal of 1905. She "flew through the air with the greatest of ease." "We learned a great deal at the Civic and I suppose we were ten years ahead of our time. I made a great many mistakes that I would not now repeat. . . . We drew people who really loved the theatre to those Fourteenth Street plays. . . . We never had enough capacity at the Civic. *Peter Pan* and *Romeo and Juliet* went wonderfully but *The Cherry Orchard* was probably the best."[25]

The economics of the time were worsening. The Great Depression was affecting the entire country. Raising the ticket prices was not an option for Le Gallienne. The Civic Repertory was filling the house but not paying the expenses. Many efforts, plans, and appeals were made, but not enough money was generated. "We are doing what few theatres in New York are doing, playing to capacity houses. We are now in the eighteenth week of the most successful season we have ever had."[26] This was part of a form letter. She did not give up. The response netted less than was needed to meet the weekly payroll for the staff of 115 people. The financial debt of $94,000 was a reality and reality finished the Civic Repertory. All of Le Gallienne's appeals to Actors Equity, the actors' union, to allow performances on Sunday were refused. The box office receipts showed that midweek attendance was not as strong as those on the weekend. Two performances on Sunday would have made a big difference. When the ban was lifted against Sunday performance, it was too late for the Civic Repertory Theatre.

In that final season of 1932, on 12 December, the production of *Alice in Wonderland* opened. The credits represent the quality of the undertaking. Scenery and costumes were designed by Irene Sharaff. The music was composed by Richard Addinsell. The puppets, masks, and marionettes were crafted by Remo Bufano. Sharaff, Addinsell, and Bufano were outstanding creative artists in their artistic fields. The script was adapted by Eva Le Gallienne and Florida Friebus using Lewis Carroll's original text. In the foreword to the acting scripts used in the 1947 production at the American Repertory Theatre Le Gallienne writes: "It is not without trepidation that I started work on my first 'Alice' production at the Civic Repertory Theatre. I realized that the word 'faithful' must be the keynote for any such venture if it were to find favor with an audience. . . . I felt a deep and solemn responsibility to Carroll, Tenniel, and the public."[27]

The production was a huge success but the financial plight of the company could not be overcome. The theatre was closed and she moved the production to Broadway. It was a short-term measure in a desperate attempt to raise money. The move to the New Amsterdam did not raise enough money.

Alla Nazimova was engaged to repeat her success in the Civic Repertory production of *The Cherry Orchard* (1928). The reviews were glowing but financially the production ended with a debt of $22,000. At this point in time, the theatre was sublet and a national tour of *Romeo and Juliet* and *Alice in Wonderland* was undertaken for the 1933–1934 season. They played in New Haven,

Boston, Providence, Springfield, Baltimore, Washington, D.C., Philadelphia, Pittsburgh, Cincinnati, Columbus, Louisville, Indianapolis, and Chicago. The net loss amounted to $19,000 a week. The box office receipts covered the running expenses but not the original production costs. Brooks Atkinson summed the situation up: "Between 1926 and 1933, Eva Le Gallienne managed her repertory in her theatre in 14th Street. But she had to abandon it when, during the depression, her sponsors were no longer able to meet the annual deficit. A valiant theatre institution that provided the public with a series of classics was too expensive to operate after seven admirable seasons."[28]

Nothing could have had more finality than this small news item published on 3 May 1938 in the *Daily News*: "'Theatre Fire:' A fire at the Old Civic Repertory former home of Eva Le Gallienne group and the Theatre Union was extinguished yesterday. The old playhouse is being demolished and the wreckers continue without difficulty."[29]

Born on 11 January 1899, Eva Le Gallienne died on 3 June 1991. She was ninety-two years old. The theatre was her life for seventy-six years.

NOTES

1. Untitled newspaper clipping, Boston, 1924, in Billy Rose Theatre Collection, New York Public Library for the Performing Arts.

2. Kenneth Macgowan and William Melnitz, *The Living Stage: A History of the World Theatre* (Englewood Cliffs, NJ: Prentice-Hall, 1955) 503–504.

3. Alice Lewisohn Crowley, *The Neighborhood Playhouse* (New York: Theatre Arts Books, 1959) 234.

4. *Theatre Guild Anthology*, "Introduction," by the Board of Directors (New York: Random House, 1936) ix.

5. Roy S. Waldau, *Vintage Years of the Theatre Guild, 1928–1939* (Cleveland and London: Press of Case Western Reserve University, 1972) 28.

6. Untitled newspaper clipping, Boston, 1924.

7. Eva Le Gallienne, in a speech at Yale University, 14 December 1925, qtd. in Robert A. Schanke, *Shattered Applause: The Lives of Eva Le Gallienne* (Carbondale and Edwardsville: Southern Illinois University Press, 1992) 69.

8. Mollie B. Steinberg, *The History of the Fourteenth Street Theatre* (New York: Dial Press, 1931). Table composed by Harold Moulton: 103.

9. Eva Le Gallienne, *With a Quiet Heart: An Autobiography* (New York: Viking, 1953) 74.

10. *New York Times*, 20 April 1921.

11. Eva Le Gallienne, address at Old South Hall, Boston, 18 December 1928, qtd. in Steinberg 91.

12. Eva Le Gallienne, "Temptations, Tribulations, and Triumphs," *Theatre Magazine* 1927.

13. Mary Henderson, *The City and the Theatre* (Clifton, NJ: James T. White and Company, 1973) 140.

14. Le Gallienne, *Quiet Heart* 54–55.

15. Alexander Woollcott, *New York World* 27 October 1926.

16. Schanke, *Shattered Applause* 73.

17. Ibid. App. B.

18. Ibid. 83.

19. Ward Morehouse, *Matinee Tomorrow* (New York: McGraw-Hill, 1949) 215.

20. Steinberg, *History* 91.

21. Jack Poggi, *Theatre in America: The Impact of Economic Forces 1870–1962* (Ithaca, NY: Cornell University Press, 1968) 140.

22. Eva Le Gallienne, "Ibsen, the Shy Giant," *Saturday Review* (1971): 26.

23. Schanke, *Shattered Applause* 69.

24. Eva Le Gallienne, "Sir James Barrie, Peter Pan and I," *Theatre Magazine* 49 (January 1929).

25. Eva Le Gallienne, qtd. in Ward Morehouse, *Matinee Tomorrow* 215.

26. Schanke, *Shattered Applause* 102.

27. Eva Le Gallienne, "Foreword" in acting script, *Alice in Wonderland* (New York: Samuel French, 1947) n. pag.

28. Brooks Atkinson, *Broadway* (New York: Macmillan, 1970) 219–220.

29. *Daily News*: 3 May 1938.

11

Sophie Treadwell's Play *Machinal*: Strategies of Reception and Interpretation

Kornelia Tancheva

Writing about Sophie Treadwell, one of the early feminist playwrights in the American theatre, is not an easy task. For all her prolific work over a span of sixty years,[1] the critical attention she has received is not overwhelming.[2] Despite Treadwell's relative unpopularity with scholars today, however, those few (feminist) critics who actually know her work and consider it worthy of critical attention never fail to praise it lavishly, especially as far as her expressionistic play *Machinal* is concerned.[3]

Machinal premiered at the Plymouth Theatre in New York on 7 September 1928 and ran for ninety-one performances.[4] It tells the fragmented life story of Helen Jones, a young woman who is first seen working in an inhumanely stifling office dominated by the presence of machines; she is desperately and unsuccessfully trying to escape an environment that reduces everyone else to a mere extension of a machine. For the lack of a better alternative, she almost forces herself into believing that marriage to her leering, repulsive boss would constitute the easiest escape route out of misery and drudgery into some financial security for herself and her mother. After all, this is the way of the world ("All women get married, don't they?").[5] A kaleidoscopic texture presents a string of scenes designed to illustrate the stages of her life: the honeymoon, with her husband's smug complacency and her animal-like terror; the unwanted motherhood, with the doctor's spiteful indifference and her piercing pain; the prohibited quest for pleasure in the speakeasy with little scenes of seduction, desertion, punishment, resignation, and some (imaginary) hope for human understanding between the Young Woman and the Man; the intimacy of the Lover's bedroom, suggesting a faint possibility for happiness, yet overwhelmingly haunted by the Lover's "Quien sabe?" (223); the insufferably suffocating domestic scene, with the failure to communicate on any level whatsoever; the courtroom, with the law machine effectively at work, objective and inhuman, administering justice to all, that is, a death sentence for Helen Jones who murdered her husband; and finally, the machine that never fails, the nothingness of the electric chair, cutting off the Young Woman's final plea for somebody out there.

In the light of *Machinal*'s later appreciation and appropriation within a feminist discourse of women's resistance, it is intriguing to note that the original production was successful both with mainstream (Broadway) audiences and mainstream (New York) critics.[6] To explain this curious development, a number of possibilities present themselves. First, one can assume that mainstream audiences' and critics' sensibilities of the 1920s and modern feminist interpretations curiously converge at some point. Second, *Machinal*'s popular success in the 1920s and its feminist interpretations today may be taken as an illustration of diachronic cultural relativism and the impossibility of fixed meaning; that is, the mainstream endorsement in the past and the antimainstream appropriation in the present are purely coincidental and have no bearing on any "textual evidence." Since the latter possibility can serve only to preclude discussion, this chapter examines the former at greater length.

As arbitrary as historical parallels might be, it is not inconceivable that distinct historical periods share common if not identical concerns and consequently that intellectual climates overlap at various points. Such parallels between the 1920s' socially acceptable and condoned semiotization of gender and our present-day feminist debates on the construction of gender, however, seem somewhat unwarranted. For one, there is the difference of positioning within the larger cultural context, that is, a difference of "mainstream" versus "marginal." What is more, there is also a profound conceptual clash. An exhaustive consideration of the 1920s in terms of pro- and antifeminist issues and discourses will greatly overstep the limited boundaries of this essay, so this chapter will only point to a few characteristic trends that are clearly at variance with a post-1960s feminist cultural milieu.[7]

After the decades of the women's suffrage movement culminated in the adoption of the Nineteenth Amendment in 1920, there was a swing back of the pendulum: the battle had been won and a respite was due.[8] Whether or not the backlash was anything more than representational is certainly open to debate, yet as far as culturally produced images went, a clear metamorphosis of the challenging figure of the New Woman into the neurotic housewife had been effectively accomplished.[9] A reconfiguration of women's place in society was begun that had to somehow reconcile traditional ideas of the private sphere with the very public political stand of the earlier decades, advocated by a radical feminist movement. One of the channels through which this was accomplished was the popular discourse on marriage, which sought to present it as the venue of *true* equality and independence. On the one hand, the idea of the *companionate marriage* was reinforced.[10] On the other, the discourse on marriage was successfully intertwined with the one on technological progress and mechanization of household labor which allowed for an increase of women's leisure time and thus represented marriage as a desirable goal for young women.[11] If that was the mainstream cultural attitude—largely antiwoman by feminist standards—then *Machinal*'s mainstream success cannot be considered tangential to its modern feminist stature.[12]

Now, since mainstream success in the 1920s can hardly be reconciled with a strong subversive feminist message,[13] it might be argued that *Machinal* has no bearing on contemporary feminist concerns and was only later reinterpreted along such lines. Unfortunately (or maybe fortunately), the complacency of this claim is instantly exposed when Treadwell's own involvement in the earlier stages of the women's movement (she not only espoused feminist ideas, but took an active part in the women's suffrage marches as well), or her introductory notes to the play, insisting that it is an Everywoman's story (173) are taken into account. Granted this is external evidence, granted authorial intentions no longer count, there still remains the uneasiness of reconciling such a conflict. The claim collapses entirely, however, when the play itself is explored as much as possible on its own terms. It is so strongly immersed in the discussion of gender roles and gender interaction as to render such a claim virtually void.

If none of these possibilities will sufficiently stand on its own, then a third explanation must be sought. On the basis of the critical reviews that appeared after the original production of *Machinal* (unfortunately no audience surveys are available), we can reasonably assume that its success was due to the choice of the interpretative framework within which it was inserted. The interpretative choices made by the critics attempting to come to terms with what might be seen as a potentially very unsettling and upsetting text that appeared to subvert the very foundations of the culture that produced it reveal the mechanisms of reconfiguration *Machinal* was subjected to. The ultimate result was its unproblematic inclusion in a more traditional (i.e., already conventionalized) horizon of expectations.[14]

The first line of critical interpretation that contributed most to toning down whatever subversion could be perceived in *Machinal* was the critics' preoccupation with the theatrical realization of the production and its importance within the work of Arthur Hopkins, the director, and Robert E. Jones, the set designer. Much of the praise was lavished on Hopkins, Jones, and the leading actors, Zita Johann (the Young Woman), George Stillwell (the Husband), and Clark Gable (the Lover). Even some of the headlines suggested the focus of attention: "Zita Johann Gets Ovation in 'Machinal' " (*WWD*), "*Machinal*, a Tragedy in Fine Stage Clothing, with Sudden Glory for Zita Johann" (*NYS*), "Elaborate Drama and New Lighting Seen at Plymouth" (*NYA*). Hopkins's production was alternatively immensely skillful (*NYT* 16 September), unfailingly effective (*NYEJ*), superintelligent (*NYA*); Jones's suggestive backgrounds were vividly alive and splendidly lighted (*NYT* 16 September), illuminated by his fine imagination and his superb taste (*V*); Zita Johann's performance was superb (*NYA*), thrilling, warm, honest, heartbreaking, true, vivid (*NYEJ*), the most sensational aspect of the evening (*WWD*), conveying simplicity, power, delicacy, and understanding that "charms, thrills, and impresses" (*TM*); her voice was singularly beautiful (*TAM*); the other members of the cast were admirable, excellent (*NYEJ*), splendidly competent (*TM*). This list can go on forever.

Second, and closely related to the first, there was a unanimous concentration on the style of the piece as one of its greatest achievements, which allowed for its comparative positioning within the already established expressionism on the American stage.[15] Treadwell's style inspired such great approval for its unsurpassed beauty and splendor that superlatives were typical: "There is a fine fluency in the writing of the scenes. Miss Treadwell has stripped them down to bare bones of drama, and flung them across the play in a swift staccato movement, which gives it *unique power and terrific momentum*" (*NYEJ*, emphasis added). Even those critics who were not particularly happy with the drama itself made sure to comment positively on the production: "The evening is primarily Mr. Jones's, secondarily Miss Johann's, Mr. Hopkins's, then Miss Treadwell's," insisted David Carb in *Vogue*;[16] or found a single redeeming quality in the rhythm or the setting, as did Gilbert Seldes in the *Dial*.

Third, there emerged an exclusive concern with the antimechanization message of the play facilitating its unproblematic incorporation within the register of another universal discourse, that on technological progress and its effect on human interaction.[17] The play's interpretation as a powerful representation of antimechanization and dehumanization obscures all other interpretative possibilities: "probably it is the story of Ruth Snyder; which doesn't matter, since beyond that 'Machinal' is the piteous, terror-laden tale of human revolt against the engine" (*NYEJ*); "'Machinal' is less murder play than . . . study of character," the character of the Young Woman, who only asks for "rest and peace, clean air, quiet, freedom from the endless pressure of bodies, pity and understanding," but can never find them in this "shrill and clattering metropolis to which the French title refers" (*NYT* 16 September); it displays a "treacherous chorus of machinery" (*NYEJ*), the "breathless pace of a woman fleeing from one treadmill to another, the din of machines always in her ears, the iron rain of noise beating her down until she dies at last in the embrace of a grim machine of wires and wailing agony" (*NYEJ*). The Young Woman is a "human fly caught in the web of the spider, Life, thwarted and frustrated at every turn, squelched by the insuperable Will of the Great Machine" (*WWD*), a "child and victim of the Machine Age . . . fed into the greedy maw of the machine" (*TM*).

A typical interpretation in which the discourse on mechanization was privileged at the expense of that on gender interrelations is to be found in the *New York Sun* review: "It is no one man who hacks out the destiny of . . . Mrs. Jones. It is the Machine Age, and the Machine Age's wanton son, the City."[18]

Finally, the Young Woman and her actions were particularized by stressing the "real-life" basis of the play, that is, the Snyder-Gray murder case trial.[19] The link between the play and the Snyder-Gray case was explicit in the reviews in *Women's Wear Daily* ("definite memories of a recent infamous New York murder case"), the *New York Sun* ("seized upon the Snyder-Gray case," "founded on an all too recent and painful actuality"), the *New York Evening Journal* ("Snyder Case Suggested in a Magnificent Tragedy"), and the *New York American* ("Drama Founded on Ruth Snyder's Life Is Not for Morose"), among others. One reviewer referred to Helen Jones as "Mrs. Snyder's dramatic alias" (*NYS*), another saw the play as "obviously founded on the life story of Ruth Snyder" and its end paralleling "the end of Ruth Snyder's mean, pitiful life" (*NYA*), while yet another even recounted some rumors that Zita Johann's costume was identical to the one worn by Mrs. Snyder at her trial (*NYHT*).

To summarize the reviews of the original 1928 production of *Machinal*, one finds that most of them were exclusively concerned with matters of style, complimenting Treadwell for the unemotional yet convincing rendering of the story of a sensational murder that did not drown it in the maudlin idiom of melodrama as well as with the superb staging of the piece. Those of the reviews that went beyond these concerns clearly conceptualized it as partaking of a serious public debate, that on the disadvantages and advantages of a mechanized civilization. Yet its relevance to "feminist" anxieties was totally silenced, and in no way did the interpretation envision a construction of a female subjectivity either in the characters or in the audience. Despite some individual differences, the overall trend among critics was to avoid interpreting *Machinal* as referring to a broader social context determined and defined by patriarchal structures; rather, they construed it as a representation of an individual woman's predicament in a society in which the agents and venues of oppression did not discriminate on the basis of gender. The parallel with the Snyder-Gray case was used to obscure a potentially dangerous possibility, that is, that Helen Jones was indeed Everywoman in the contemporary context. Instead, by alluding to an all too familiar murder trial, sensationalized by the press, the critical interpretations particularized and disciplined the play. (On another level, of course this also allowed for the inclusion of *Machinal* within the host of murder plays popular at the time.) At least one significant difference was glossed over, namely, that in the actual case, both the woman and her lover were convicted and executed for the murder of the husband, while in the play Treadwell chose to have the Lover instrumental in convicting the Young Woman. (He sends an affidavit supplying the murder motive from Mexico, where he is at the time.)

In other words, the argument in this chapter is that *Machinal* was successfully interpreted within a mainstream cultural discourse precisely because it was universalized along the first three lines, and particularized along the fourth.

The concern hereafter will be a possible explanation for such a development beside the obvious ideological assumptions of the critics and the overall cultural and intellectual climate in which the play appeared where certain discourses were both available and popularly familiar. This chapter attempts to show that *Machinal*'s relatively unimpeded inclusion within the discourse of technological progress at the expense of a "feminist" one was facilitated, among other things, by its ambiguity as far as an indictment of the "patriarchal" institution of marriage was concerned. In other words, an analysis of the structure of the play, the speech patterns, and the resolution of the conflict can destabilize its appropriation by a consistent feminist critique, for it clearly leaves open the possibility for a *companionate marriage*, that is, a marriage of mutual love and understanding which Helen Jones did not obtain but could possibly have succeeded in obtaining—a view that a middle-class mainstream audience could easily endorse and identify with. The argument could be made that her ending up on the electric chair was as much her fault and bad luck as it might have been the fault of a socially construed practice.

In the first place, she started with the "wrong" premises, she married exclusively for financial security and provision, knowingly entering into a physically and romantically repulsive union.[20] Since other characters are also aware of the choices available to the Young Woman or their possible repercussions,[21] her decision can also be interpreted as being of her own making and not entirely the result of social pressure. The choice of interpreting Helen as bringing disaster onto herself is left open for an audience immersed in the discourse of the *companionate marriage* and the openly admitted significance of sexual compatibility for a privately and publicly successful marriage.

The scenes that further enhance a perception of the "false" premises on which Helen Jones married and, hence, could never succeed in convincing herself that she could learn to reconcile the conflicting longings for financial security and romantic love are the ones with the Lover. The explanation that he has of what is wrong with Helen is: "1ST MAN. You just haven't met the right guy—that's all—a girl like you—you got to meet the right guy" (217), suggesting that, if it had been somebody else, it might have been different—"Quien sabe?"

In other words, given the proper conditions, would it not be possible to transpose the Young Woman's inadaptability from a representative to an idiosyncratic level? Is she any woman, as Treadwell maintains in her notes (173), or is her character an isolated case study, that is, is there something wrong with the synchronic conceptualization of the institution of marriage, as many of the scenes will seem to argue, or is it a particular marriage arrangement that did not work out? Should one wonder at the critics' insistence on the Snyder-Gray connection, then, instead of recognizing a pattern of particularization launched by the ambiguous stand within the text itself?

The Lover is certainly not "the right guy" for the Young Woman, as the conflict resolution demonstrates. Let us go one step further, however, and see what interpretative possibilities are delineated in their brief encounter through a comparative analysis of the Young Woman's speech patterns. In the office scene, she is as caught in the mechanical pattern of linguistic and behavioral repetition as her co-workers, but in contrast to them she is not able to make the logical connections between the stretches of words that they seem to blurt out almost involuntarily. They repeat and shorten their phrases for reasons of clarity and efficiency, but never fail to hold on to a link of contiguity, while the Young Woman's speech pattern is broken to the point where it does not exhibit any trace of logical consistency. Instead, it hinges on similarity and allusion.[22]

The similarity/contiguity distinction becomes all the more relevant when considered in terms of artistic versus scientific/technological conceptualization. Contiguity is usually associated with progress logically pursued and attained by metonymically coping with reality, attempting to describe a part, or an effect, and infer the whole, or the cause. Similarity, on the other hand, metaphorically transcends the human ability to master reality logically for it strives at a totality of explanation and retreats into itself when baffled by its own frailty.[23]

Probably the first and only time when the Young Woman is able to contiguously describe a situation, instead of metaphorically allude to it, is in episode 6, "Intimate." When she is with her Lover, her sentences are complete and even the actual metaphors are explicated. Similarly, the only instance of a possible logical planning of her life comes, curiously enough, again in the scenes with the Lover. Curiously, since, in a way, she conforms to contiguity and machine-like precision when she is supposed to be escaping the mundane logic of everyday existence. Why should the Lover, of all characters, include Helen Jones in the abhorrent reality of mechanization and dehumanization? (The instance discussed here is merely preliminary to his ultimate betrayal, to be sure.) Is it not because he is not "the right guy" within the acceptable social behavior and mores of the times? Maybe. "Quien sabe?"

It is precisely this textual uncertainty in the representation of male-female relations and the institution of marriage, with all the entailing issues of economic, romantic, or sexual references, that must have played a vital part in ensuring the success of *Machinal*. Whether, however, the play's ambiguous stance and its deep entanglement in the contradictory ideas of women's place in society were deliberately ignored or genuinely not recognized at the time of its production is not to be settled from our historical distance and anachronistic perspective.

NOTES

1. Treadwell wrote about forty plays, most of which were repeatedly revised and reworked, as well as novels, newspaper reports, and short stories; yet only a few of her pieces have ever been published: three novels—*Lusita* (New York: Jonathan Cape and Harrison Smith, 1931), *Hope for a Harvest* (New York: Samuel French, 1942), and *One Fierce Hour and Sweet* (New York: Appleton-Century-Crofts, 1959); and two plays—*Hope for a Harvest*, based on the novel, as well as *Machinal* (in *Twenty Five Best Plays of the Modern American Theatre: The Early Series*, ed. John Gassner [New York: Crown, 1949] 494–529; and *Plays by American Women 1900–1930*, ed. Judith Barlow [New York: Applause, 1985] 171–255).

The rest of Treadwell's manuscripts are in the Special Collection at the University of Arizona Library at Tucson.

2. There exist two unpublished dissertations, one by Louise Heck-Rabi, "Sophie Treadwell: Subjects and Structures in 20th-Century American Drama" (Wayne State University, 1976), in which she argues that Treadwell's work functions as a link between an earlier generation of successful women playwrights in America and a post–World War II one. Another, by Nancy E. Wynn, "Sophie Treadwell: The Career of a Twentieth-Century American Feminist Playwright" (City University of New York, 1982), positions Treadwell as a successful feminist playwright. A few essays complete the picture: Louise Heck-Rabi, "Sophie Treadwell: An Agent For Change," in *Women in American Theatre*, ed. Helen Krich Chinoy and Linda Walsh Jenkins (New York: Theatre Communications Group, 1981) 157–162 on Treadwell's innovative play, *For Saxophone*; Jennifer Parent, "Arthur Hopkins's Production of Sophie Treadwell's 'Machinal,'" *The Drama Review* 26.1 (1982): 87–100; Barbara L. Bywaters, "Marriage, Madness and Murder in Sophie Treadwell's 'Machinal,' " *Modern American Drama: The Female Canon*, ed. June Schleuter (Associated University Press, 1990) 97–110, who discusses *Machinal* in terms of its subversion of dominant patriarchal structures and strictures by seeking to give a voice to women's struggle against oppression and submission; and finally, Ginger Strand, "Treadwell's Neologism: 'Machinal,'" *Theatre Journal* 44 (1992): 163–175, where *Machinal* is seen as opposing the master narrative of patriarchy by telling the story of a woman's experience.

Treadwell and/or *Machinal* are also mentioned in a few reference books; yet, as a whole, it appears that her work has largely been neglected.

3. In her own time she seems to have been fairly well-known in theatrical circles, though certainly not a raving success with critics and spectators. Only seven of her plays were produced on Broadway, *Gringo* (12 December 1922), *Oh Nightingale* (15 April 1925), *Machinal* (7 September 1928), *Ladies Leave* (1 October 1929), *Lone Valley* (3 March 1933), *Plumes in the Dust* (12 November 1936), and *Hope for a Harvest* (26 November 1941), and of these only *Machinal* was an unqualified success. It should be noted that those of her plays that were produced outside New York did fairly well but somehow could not make it once they came to New York.

4. It was also produced abroad, in London and Paris in 1931 as *The Life Machine*, and in Moscow in 1932–1933 as *Mrs. Jones*. It was revived at the Gate Theatre in New York in 1960, and off-Broadway in 1990.

5. Treadwell, *Machinal*, in Barlow, *Plays by American Women* 190. All subsequent references are to the same edition and will be incorporated in the text in parentheses.

6. Critical reviews on *Machinal* appeared as follows: Kelsey Allen, "Zita Johann Gets Ovation in 'Machinal,' " *Women's Wear Daily* (*WWD*) 19 September 1928: 5; John Anderson, " 'Machinal' Opens at the Plymouth. Snyder Case Suggested in a Magnificent Tragedy," *New York Evening Journal* (*NYEJ*) 8 September 1928: 10;

Brooks Atkinson, "The Play: A Tragedy of Submission," *New York Times* (*NYT*) 8 September 1928, sec. 10: 3 and Brooks Atkinson, "Against the City Clatter," *New York Times* (*NYT*) 16 September 1928, sec. 9: 1; Robert Benchley, "The Theatre. High Lights," *Life* (*L*) (92) 28 September 1928: 17; David Carb, "Seen on the Stage. 'Machinal,' " *Vogue* (*V*) 27 October 1928: 72–74, 108; Pierre de Rohan, " 'Machinal' Ugly But Great Play. Drama Founded on Ruth Snyder's Life Is Not for Morose," *New York American* (*NYA*) 8 September 1928, sec. 2: 15; Gilbert Gabriel, "Last Night. 'Machinal,' A Tragedy in Fine Stage Clothing, with Sudden Glory for Zita Johann," *New York Sun* (*NYS*) 8 September 1928, sec. 5: 1–2; Percy Hammond, "The Theatres. 'Machinal,' A Good, Grim and Deftly New-Fangled Story of Why and How a Lady Killed Her Husband," *New York Herald Tribune* (*NYHT*) 8 September 1928: 6 and Percy Hammond, "The Theatres. Bold But Not Too Bold," (*NYHT*) 16 September 1928, sec. 7: 1; Percy Hutchinson, "As the Theatre Practices the Art of Homicide. Considering the Murder Theme in Three of the Season's Plays," (*NYT*) 25 November 1928, sec. 10: 1, 3; Joseph Wood Krutch, "Drama. Behaviorism and Drama," *Nation* (*N*) 26 September 1928: 302; Robert Littell, "Chiefly About *Machinal*. Broadway in Review," *Theatre Arts Monthly* (*TAM*) (November 1928): 774–783; George Jean Nathan, "The Theatre. A Pretentious Zero," *American Mercury* (*AM*) 59.15 (November 1928): 376–377; Arthur Ruhl, "Off Stage and On," (*NYHT*) 14 September 1928: 18; Gilbert Seldes, "The Theatre," *Dial* (*D*) 85.5 (November 1928); Stark Young, "Joy on the Mountains," *New Republic* (*NR*) 56 (31 October 1928): 299–300; and "The Editor Goes to the Play. 'Machinal,' " *Theatre Magazine* (*TM*) 48 (November 1928): 46–47, among others. Its critical acclaim was practically unmitigated. The sole entirely scathing review was George Jean Nathan's "A Pretentious Zero," which attacked Treadwell's concept, subject, and style, as well as Hopkins's "producing chicane" and Robert E. Jones's setting and lighting. Subsequent references to these reviews are included in the text, using the abbreviations in parentheses as listed above.

7. Here, I am certainly not assuming that either of the periods was or is in any way univocal and unambiguous as far as gender roles and gender socialization go, since all historical periods exhibit contradictory trends in terms of issues they deem constitutive of their self-representation and identity-construction. Yet it also seems that in the struggle between opposing cultural discourses, certain tendencies prevail at certain points of time owing to their position of relatively greater power.

8. For a further elaboration on this point, see Rayna Rapp and Ellen Ross, "The Twenties Backlash: Compulsory Heterosexuality, the Consumer Family and the Waning of Feminism," *Class, Race, Sex: The Dynamics of Control*, ed. Amy Swerdlow and Hanna Lessinger (Boston: G. K. Hall, 1983) 52–61.

9. Bywaters, "Marriage, Madness and Murder" 9. Other scholars suggest that even earlier, the stage representations of women characters, for example, hardly did any justice to the complex issues involved in the women's rights movement. See, for instance, Larry D. Clark, "Female Characters on the New York Stage in the Year of Suffrage: Enter Advocacy Quietly, Stage Left," *Theatre History Studies* 7 (1986): 51–61. For an interesting study of the representations of women in contemporary film see Leslie Fishbein, "The Demise of the Cult of True Womanhood in Early American Film, 1900–1930," *The Journal of Popular Film and Television* 12.2 (1984): 66–72.

10. On the companionate marriage and the New Woman see Christina S. Simmons, *Marriage in the Modern Manner: Sexual Radicalism and Reform in America 1914–1941* (Ann Arbor: UMI, 1982), esp. ch. 3.

11. I have done an extensive study of advertisements in popular magazines of the twenties (*The Ladies' Home Journal* 1920–1927, *The Saturday Evening Post* 1920–1927, and *Current Opinion* 1920–1925), which indicates that the independ-

ence-within-marriage message was delivered in a number of ways, all of which took great pains to avoid overt emphasis on women's financial independence within marriage, but instead, semiotized what I call the-easy-and-quick-way-to-do-your-housework concept, through a number of signs: formal dress while engaged in cleaning, washing, and so on, images of women buying household appliances, rather than actually using them at home, women playing bridge, having parties, driving cars to parties, or going shopping in their now doubled spare time provided by technological innovations. Household work was no longer a drudgery, the happily proclaimed slogan of the times ran. No doubt, these images were geared toward a specific audience, (lower) middle-class (white) women, and if a similar study is conducted on publications designed for other social groups, the findings might be considerably different. The rationale behind my choice is that (lower) middle-class audiences prevailed in the mainstream theatre at the time as well.

12. Besides the larger cultural context, the evidence of the critical reviews, which I examine in the following, unequivocally suggests that the subversion of patriarchal oppression was not among the interpretative lines along which *Machinal* was construed.

13. In this respect, a significant contrast might be traced out between *Machinal* and Susan Glaspell's feminist play *Trifles*. Both texts were concerned with women killing their husbands, both were based on actual murder cases, and both enjoyed successful productions; the striking difference being the venues chosen for their presentation—*Machinal* on Broadway, while *Trifles* as part of the Provincetown Players' agenda of creating a theatrical enterprise in opposition to mainstream theatre.

14. This is, of course, a reference to Jauss's *Rezeptionsasthetik*, which along with a very broad concept of cultural materialism and new historicism provide the theoretical underpinnings of my project. See respectively Hans R. Jauss, *Toward an Aesthetic of Reception* (Brighton: Harvester Press, 1982), Raymond Williams, *Problems in Materialism and Culture: Selected Essays* (London: Verso and New Left Books, 1980), and Stephen Greenblatt, "Towards a Poetics of Culture," *Southern Review* 20 (1987): 3–15.

15. Here I have in mind plays like *The Emperor Jones* and *The Adding Machine*, to which *Machinal* was invariably compared.

16. "Seen On the Stage. 'Machinal,'" *Vogue* 108.

17. Hence, I think, the ubiquitous parallels with *The Adding Machine*.

18. Gilbert W. Gabriel, "Last Night's First Night. 'Machinal,' a Tragedy in Fine Stage Clothing, with Sudden Glory for Zita Johann," *New York Sun* 8 September 1928, sec. 5: 2.

19. On the connections between *Machinal* and the Snyder-Gray case see Strand. For further information on the trial itself see Edmund Wilson, *The American Earthquake: Documentary of the Twenties and Thirties* (Garden City, NY: Doubleday, 1958).

20. YOUNG WOMAN: You ought to be in love, oughtn't you, Ma?(. . .) When he puts a hand on me, my blood turns cold. But your blood oughtn't to turn cold, ought it?(. . .) I've always thought I'd find somebody—somebody young—and—attractive —(. . .) that I'd love—(192).

21. Even the Telephone Girl knows women should not be repulsed and disgusted by their future husbands, but the key scene is the mother-daughter one because it suggests other options available to Helen Jones. When she clutches the straw of "all women get married, don't they," her mother repeatedly cuts her short with an explicitly forceful "nonsense" (173). Admittedly, she does so only while

assuming that Helen wants to marry some unreliable boy, rather than the vice president of a company, yet the fact remains that not all women marry.

22. The prime example of the metaphorical quality of her speech and thought process is her monologue in the hospital after she has given birth to her child. Her feelings are poured out in images of stairs to heaven, a vixen crawling under the bed and eight puppies, "drowned—drowned in blood" (205).

On similarity and contiguity see Roman Jakobson, *Selected Writings*, vol. 2, *Word and Language* (Paris, The Hague: Mouton, 1971).

23. Consider, for instance, the contrast in the ways the Young Woman and the Husband read newspapers in episode 7:

> HUSBAND. Record production.
> YOUNG WOMAN. Girl turns on gas.
> HUSBAND. Sale hits a million—
> YOUNG WOMAN. Woman leaves all for love—
> HUSBAND. Market trend steady—
> YOUNG WOMAN. Young wife disappears. (227)

He is fully within the machine age of logical description: if A, then B, then C (record production leads to million sales, which stabilize the market), while she is again alluding in a multiplicity of similar ways to her own metaphorized dreams and anxieties. The three headlines she reads aloud stand for her own dissatisfaction in an exactly identical relation of metaphoric substitution. They do not logically proceed from one another; in fact, the second and the third might very well refer to the same story in the newspaper.

12

Sophie Treadwell's Summer with Boleslavsky and Lectures for the American Laboratory Theatre

Jerry Dickey

Ten days after the Moscow Art Theatre (MAT) gave the opening performance of its first American tour in January 1923, Richard Boleslavsky began a series of public lectures at New York's Princess Theatre. Boleslavsky, who had been known as "Stanislavsky's pet" during his tenure as director of the MAT's First Studio,[1] had been in America for only three months. With Stanislavsky's blessing and the translation assistance of Michel Barroy, Boleslavsky lectured on sixteen topics pertaining to the MAT's aesthetics and practices, and offered the first details to American theatre artists about Stanislavsky's famous acting "system."[2] Morris Gest, producer of the MAT American tour, organized the Princess Theatre lectures and provided sufficient publicity to attract a number of theatre notables, including the playwright Sophie Treadwell.[3] Boleslavsky's talks signal a dramatic turning point in the development of Treadwell's theatrical career, for within the next two years she would complete an intensive summer of actor training with Boleslavsky, return to acting on the stage after a five-year hiatus, offer lectures to Boleslavsky's American Laboratory Theatre, and make the first of several attempts to alleviate her dissatisfaction with commercial theatre practices by becoming her own producer.

At first glance, it may appear that Treadwell's attendance at Boleslavsky's lectures indicates little more than curiosity on her part. After all, her career as a playwright finally seemed to be taking off. She had closed her first Broadway play, *Gringo*, a scant three weeks before Boleslavsky's initial lecture, and she had recently optioned a play on Edgar Allan Poe to Guthrie McClintic. Yet Treadwell remained unsettled with the mixed critical response to *Gringo*, and she only optioned the Poe play to McClintic in a desperate attempt to prod into action John Barrymore, who had written to her two years previously stating his intent to act in her play but had subsequently failed to follow through with any written contract. Furthermore, from the moment she attempted to market her work as a beginning playwright under the sponsorship of Helena Modjeska, Treadwell encountered conflict with theatre managers and agents regarding the revision of her scripts.[4] Undoubtedly, Treadwell sensed early in 1923 that in order to succeed as a commercial playwright, she needed to develop a mastery of technique which would allow her a degree of confidence and self-sufficiency regarding her work. She may have concluded that the same lack of technique which plagued her early efforts as an actress throughout the previous decade might ultimately bring about her demise as a playwright, as well. As she later noted: "All the emotional intensity in the world may be concentrated into the writing of [a] play, but curiously enough nothing whatever of this comes out of it. . . . Why doesn't the emotion come out as it went in, strong, intense, sincere? The answer is very simple. Because the writer doesn't know how to write a play. I speak here with great authority. I've written so many plays like this."[5] Most likely, Treadwell attended Boleslavsky's lectures hoping she could adapt specific techniques used by the acclaimed MAT to her own development as a playwright.

Boleslavsky fueled Treadwell's interest with his thoughts on the desired physical and emotional conditions for theatrical success, as well as his summaries of the psychic concentration required for actors in "living" their parts. When Boleslavsky followed up his lectures with the plan of spending a summer with a small group of actors working to implement these theories, Treadwell eagerly sought and gained entry into this select group.[6] Having failed to pursue her acting interests since 1918, Treadwell left Boleslavsky's lectures with the realization of "the necessity of entering again into this life [of acting] so that I could come once more in touch with its reality."[7]

Boleslavsky organized the summer training sessions for sixteen actors under the aegis of the Neighborhood Playhouse. Working in a country estate outside Pleasantville, New York, Boleslavsky alternated the group's activities between studio exercises and rehearsals for Shaw's *The Shewing-Up of Blanco Posnet* and Yeats's *The Player Queen*, plays intended for presentation in the fall under the aegis of the Neighborhood Playhouse. Typed notes in Treadwell's papers reveal that Boleslavsky provided the group with orientation to key principles of Stanislavsky's system, including sensory awareness, affective memory, physical and intellectual development, and textual study, including the discovery of the spine of a play and unit analysis.[8] Alexander Koiransky, former Russian drama critic, designer, and interpreter and guide during Stanislavsky's tour, assisted in the instruction by offering classes in scenery and costumes.[9] The variety of instruction provided the perfect mixture of what Treadwell needed, and she temporarily quit writing in order to obtain or sharpen skills in all branches of theatre. Visiting observers that summer were impressed by the sense of commitment and collective ensemble which Boleslavsky achieved. Theatre critic Percy Hammond visited the "happy" group of actors and later wrote of finding them sitting "at Boleslavsky's feet, hiving [*sic*] wisdom. . . . The result was that I discovered quite the most interesting adventure in the drama that has come to my notice in what is commonly known as many moons."[10]

Treadwell's summer of study with Boleslavsky rejuvenated her passion for theatre. As the summer months progressed, Treadwell drafted her most exuberant comedy, *Loney Lee*, which depicted the plight of a naive, midwestern girl determined to break into theatre in New York by reviving her successful high school role, Juliet. Treadwell spoke of the play's central character, Appolonia (Loney) Lee, as representing a self-deprecating portrait of "myself as I was when I was not quite sixteen."[11] Innocently believing that success in the theatre involved not so much technique and training as "character . . . And talent! And faith,"[12] Loney subsequently experiences first-hand the coarseness and brutality of the commercial theatre world. Like Loney, Treadwell had discovered she possessed the emotional sensitivity of a theatre artist, but not the requisite technique to communicate that sensitivity. *Loney Lee* was contracted to George C. Tyler in October 1923, and received successful tryouts in Atlantic City and Hartford the following month with Helen Hayes in the title role.

The summer with Boleslavsky also introduced Treadwell to Koiransky, who would become one of her closest friends and trusted mentors. Koiransky remained one of a very select few to whom Treadwell turned for advice on her current writing projects. Deeply distrustful of Broadway managers and agents, Treadwell preferred to retain the guidance of her early Russian tutors, especially Koiransky, for the next three decades. The summer in Pleasantville taught Treadwell that she could rely on Koiransky for insightful and frank feedback. As he stated to her in a letter dated 19 January 1944, "Doubtless, if I had chosen, I could use all kind of diplomatic clapptrapp [in responding to your play]. But I do not choose and never have, to indulge in diplomacy when writing to you."[13]

It was Koiransky who arranged for Treadwell to lecture to students at the American Laboratory Theatre in the winter of 1925.[14] Throughout her career, Treadwell wrote little about her theories or purpose in playwriting, and thus these lectures provide key insights into her views on the art and commerce of New York theatre. In lectures entitled "Writing a Play," "The Playwright as Actor," and "Producing a Play," Treadwell reveals her affinity with Boleslavsky's criticisms of the American commercial theatre. Like Boleslavsky, Treadwell believed this theatre discouraged artistic experimentation, confined the actor to a small range of roles based on physical type, and obfuscated the creative imagination of the playwright.

Treadwell and Boleslavsky both felt that the prevailing consumerism of Broadway theatre directly created many of these inhibiting conditions. In a July 1923 article for *Theatre Arts Magazine*, Boleslavsky lamented that "the contemporary theatre has become a shop, a department store, in which ready-made and labelled goods are sold. But where those goods are created, where their qualities are verified,—nobody cares."[15] In her lectures to the Lab, Treadwell elaborated on this idea as it relates to casting:

The Broadway theatre world of actors is like some big department store in which the producer, the director, the playwright, sample in hand, shops rapidly. I use the word "shops" advisedly. It is the accepted, the usual word for casting. It embraces not only finding the actor for the part but finding out his price and settling terms with him. It is nothing at all for a casting director to ring up an agent and say, "I need a French waiter. Shop around a little for me, will you, and see what you can do at seventy-five"? . . . The agent then looks over his list, an elaborate card index system where the actors are catalogued, picks out such names as seem to him suitable, hands this list to his telephone girl, who seems through some uncanny sense to be able to locate any actor in New York in ten minutes, and the engagement is made. Very often it is made immediately.[16]

For Treadwell, the reduction of the actor to a condition of marketable goods catalogued by exterior packaging represented the first major obstacle to the development of what Boleslavsky called a "creative," as opposed to a "mechanical," performance.[17] As Treadwell concluded to the Lab students: "How any actor face to face with this condition [of casting], really aware of the actuality that confronts and surrounds him, can keep up interest in his work as an art to be developed is beyond me. The answer is, of course, that he doesn't."[18]

Treadwell hinted to the students in an earlier lecture that this condition had prompted her own abandonment of acting in favor of playwriting:

I really gave up being an actor in the first place—years ago—because I love acting so much. I left the stage to write plays because of a hanker, an uncontrollable hanker to go deeper, perhaps soar higher in my work, in the work of acting than just acting afforded me. . . . In writing plays I wasn't limited to just the parts, the stereotyped parts that might be handed out to me. In writing I played, and I played from the beginning of their creation, any and all parts that entered my fancy.[19]

Thus, working for years in what she called a state of "loneliness," Treadwell pursued in her imagination the Boleslavsky and MAT ideal of a versatile actor capable of a range of different characterizations.

In addition to the practice of type casting, Treadwell's lectures also outline other inhibiting conditions. Adhering to the importance of that part of the creative process which Boleslavsky called the "table phase,"[20] the phase in which the acting company conducts careful play analysis, Treadwell notes that Broadway directors' reluctance to discuss the play with the cast ultimately obscures the actor's understanding. "I do not in the least exaggerate when I say that many plays go into their dress rehearsal without the actors knowing . . . what the play is about, what the parts are about and what the words really mean."[21] In addition, Treadwell felt the trend for directors to impose blocking on the actors from the outset of rehearsals resulted in actors incapable and even unwilling to create for themselves: "[The actor] loses respect for the director who cannot tell him immediately in the first day of rehearsal just where he is to go and just what he is to do."[22] If actors subsequently discover in rehearsals that this prescribed business proves emotionally inhibiting, the brevity of the rehearsal period, what Treadwell termed "that terrible four weeks fixed by law,"[23] makes actors and directors reluctant to alter previously planned movements. As influenced by Boleslavsky, Treadwell now stated a preference for a more organic manner of staging in which "the gestures and the movements would follow the thought and the feeling."[24]

The creation by Boleslavsky of the American Laboratory Theatre comprised his attempt to circumvent these typical production constraints and devise conditions that allowed theatre artists collectively to "contemplate, to search, to create."[25] If Treadwell and Boleslavsky both opposed the commodification of Broadway theatre, the obvious question emerges as to why they continued to work for it. Treadwell never publicly addressed the issue, but Boleslavsky felt compelled to answer his critics on this point. To begin, the burgeoning independent theatres in America offered an incomplete alternative to the commerce of Broadway, for they too often failed to emphasize the need for ongoing actor training and development.[26] More important, Boleslavsky stressed an integral connection between his popular work on Broadway and his private work in the lab: "There is no such thing as art for art. Art is for the people from the people and of the people, and art must be studied amongst the people. . . . As long as I know how to [stage successfully on Broadway], I know that I know my 'game' and that I have a right (knowing the old theatre) to look for a new one. . . . To make a theatre of tomorrow, one must know thoroughly the theatre of today."[27] Although Boleslavsky may simply have been voicing an artistic justification for his financial need to work on Broadway, it is worth noting that several of his Broadway efforts met with critical and popular success.

With the exception of *Machinal*, Treadwell could make no such claim. Part of her difficulty in obtaining critical validation resided in the fact that Treadwell refused to adapt her writing to suit popular tastes. As an exasperated Koiransky once stated to her in his typically forthright manner:

sometimes I think that there is in you a definite perversity, with which you insist upon bringing into your plays things and situations which make them unacceptable to the bosses of Broadway. . . . Dearest Sophie, do make up your mind! Do you want your plays to be produced on Broadway? Well, then do not act as Edmond de Goncourt did, in writing beautiful plays, intrinsically obnoxious to the masters of the hour. Or know, that you will write them for the pleasure and admiration of a handful of people who do not count.[28]

It would be decades before Treadwell's lack of commercial success would drive her away from professional theatre.[29] In the years immediately after her study with Boleslavsky, however, Treadwell's enthusiasm for theatre and quest for making change reached its peak. Late in 1924, Treadwell embarked on her first attempt to realize Boleslavsky's teachings by producing and acting in her own drama, *The Love Lady*. Treadwell offered six private performances of the play at New York's Heckscher Theatre in January 1925, with settings by Cleon Throckmorton. This production "convinced her that she could actually put a play she had written upon the stage, that she could assemble a cast of actors, plan sets, drill her company and compose the mental and emotional elements that make a production."[30] The experience provided Treadwell with the confidence to buy out the option of *Loney Lee* from Tyler and offer it herself on Broadway in April 1925 under the new title, *O Nightingale*, a production in which Treadwell acted, directed, and coproduced.

Although far from a financial success, *O Nightingale* reinforced Treadwell's belief that the playwright-regisseur should be the guiding force in the creative process of theatre, a belief that separates her markedly from Boleslavsky, who saw the director as "the single will" shaping the production.[31] According to Treadwell, conflicting views by the playwright and director often constituted "the great chasm that separates the inspiration from the materialization and perhaps prevents any play being finally in the true analysis a work of art."[32] Treadwell concluded, therefore, that the playwright should become "a craftsman, knowing definitely and to the last detail how to make that dream materialize to its fullest within the world of the theatre, a world that can sometimes turn out to be so dull, so mean, so cruel."[33]

Believing her study with Boleslavsky equipped her for success as a playwright-regisseur, Treadwell embarked on an untiring campaign of advocacy for playwrights. In 1924 she brought a celebrated lawsuit against John Barrymore and his wife Michael Strange for plagiarizing her play on Edgar Allan Poe. Months later, Treadwell spoke out in the press after the Broadway opening of *O Nightingale* about the lack of respect afforded playwrights, especially through

the varying motives of producers optioning and holding scripts, directors' demands for quick revisions during rehearsals, and the forced involvement of play
doctors. Treadwell proclaimed that directors and managers "ridicule the playwright and . . . take unwarranted liberties with his script. You see how the
playwright is treated. He is the lowest creature of them all, according to the
Broadway manager. And he isn't. He's the biggest. His is the dream. His the
work."[34] In addition, Treadwell's defense of playwrights continued during her
visit to Russia in 1933. After witnessing Alexander Tairov's production of *Machinal*, she became, at her insistence, the first American playwright to receive
production royalties from the Soviet Union.

Although the injection of confidence, technique, and creative inspiration
Boleslavsky gave to Treadwell appears far ranging, it is at times difficult to
ascertain his influence with a high degree of specificity. Perhaps, for example,
the seeds of Treadwell's best play, *Machinal*, were sown years before its creation
as she sat in the Princess Theatre listening to Boleslavsky's lectures. In one
lecture, Boleslavsky spoke of his vision for the experimental use of sound in the
theatre, a vision which may have prompted Treadwell's expressionistic use of
patterned sounds and offstage voices in *Machinal*. Boleslavsky suggested a
starting point for such experiments:

If we . . . listen carefully to the life that surrounds us and . . . lend our spiritual ear to
all the sounds produced by life, we shall discover an unexpected amount of them and
. . . come to the realization that there are no set instruments to reproduce them. Think
of the city noise, the noise coming from a factory, the clamor of an excited crowd. . . .
The theatre of the future, no matter how funny this may seem to a professional musician, will be filled with new instruments and new sound-combinations. It may even
create a gamut and a new rhythm—not that of the metronome, but the rhythm of human feelings, heart and soul.[35]

Treadwell may not have consciously drawn upon Boleslavsky's ideas in creating
Machinal, but it is not unreasonable to believe they entered into her creative
subconscious, that area to which Boleslavsky liked to refer to his students as the
"golden casket of feelings."[36] Whether or not Boleslavsky influenced the style of
Machinal, Treadwell's summer as an actor under his guidance clearly proved a
summer of self-discovery and artistic challenge that supplied the foundation for
the most innovative period of her career.

NOTES

1. Sharon M. Carnicke, "Boleslavsky in America," *Wandering Stars: Russian
Émigré Theatre, 1905–1940* ed. Laurence Senelick (Iowa City: University of Iowa
Press, 1992): 118.

2. These lecture notes have been recorded in typed form under the title, "The
Creative Theatre." The notes are housed in the New York Public Library for the Per-
forming Arts and are quoted extensively in J[erry] W[ayne] Roberts, "The Theatre
Theory and Practice of Richard Boleslavsky," diss., Kent State University, 1977.

3. Christine Edwards, *The Stanislavsky Heritage* (New York: New York University Press, 1965) 239–240.

4. With a letter of endorsement from Modjeska, Treadwell first submitted one of
her plays to a theatrical manager, Jules Murry, in 1908. Murry's response was encouraging but included a request for revisions. According to Treadwell, Modjeska

prohibited her from altering the playscript to meet Murry's demands. "Better to wait ten years for success," Treadwell quoted Modjeska, "than to make changes at the command of any one. Artists must make their own way in the world" ("Who's Who in the Theatre," *New York Times* 26 April 1925, sec. 8: 2). Murry immediately lost interest in the play. This incident comprises the first of many such encounters between Treadwell and agents and producers.

5. Sophie Treadwell, "Writing a Play," Box 2, ts., Sophie Treadwell Papers, University of Arizona Library Special Collections (UALSC), 6–7.

6. Percy Hammond, "Oddments and Remainders," *New York Tribune* 7 February 1923: 8.

7. Sophie Treadwell, "The Playwright as Actor," Box 2, ts., UALSC, 1–2.

8. There seems to have been no confusion in this group over the Russian pronunciation of the word "bit," unlike those students later trained at Boleslavsky's Lab under Maria Ouspenskaya. Unlike those students, Treadwell recorded "bits" in her notes, not "beats."

9. J[erry] W[ayne] Roberts, *Richard Boleslavsky: His Life and Work in the Theatre* (Ann Arbor: UMI Research Press, 1981) 117.

10. Hammond, "Oddments." Although Playhouse director Alice Lewisohn had serious concerns over the quality of acting the company was able to achieve in the short amount of time, she too noted that "Boleslavsky had induced a fine esprit de corps among the student actors, as well as enthusiasm for continued technical preparation and study distinct from rehearsal" (Alice Lewisohn Crowley, *The Neighborhood Playhouse* [New York: Theatre Arts Books, 1959] 171).

11. Sophie Treadwell, "Miss Treadwell Portrays Herself at 60 in New Play," *New York American.* Undated clipping from the spring of 1925, UALSC.

12. Sophie Treadwell, *Loney Lee,* Box 8, ts., UALSC, 1.21.

13. Alexander Koiransky, letter to Sophie Treadwell, 19 January 1944, Box 1, UALSC.

14. Although the typed lectures in Treadwell's papers are undated, they contain references to her recent return to acting over the past winter. Since Treadwell first returned to the stage in *The Love Lady* in January 1925 and did not act again until the spring of that year, the lectures must have occurred between these two events.

15. Richard Boleslavsky, "The Laboratory Theatre," *Theatre Magazine* July 1923: 245.

16. Sophie Treadwell, "Producing a Play," Box 2, ts., UALSC, 8.

17. Roberts, "Theatre" 193–196.

18. Treadwell, "Producing" 7.

19. Treadwell, "Playwright" 1.

20. Treadwell, "Russian Theory of Acting," Box 2, ts., UALSC, n. pag.

21. Treadwell, "Producing" 11.

22. Ibid. 12.

23. Ibid. 15.

24. Ibid. 12–13.

25. Boleslavsky, "Laboratory" 245.

26. Roberts, *Boleslavsky* 114.

27. Richard Boleslavsky, "Questions to Richard Boleslavsky," *The Pit* 1 (1928): 2. Qtd. in Ronald Arthur Willis, "The American Laboratory Theatre, 1923–1930," diss., University of Iowa, 1968, 240.

28. Alexander Koiransky, Letter to Sophie Treadwell, 7 January 1944, Box 1, UALSC.

29. In 1960, Treadwell admitted to being "awfully bitter" over the critical response to her 1941 drama, *Hope for a Harvest.* She since turned away from the thea-

tre and toward writing novels because it was "easier" (Louis Calta, " 'Machinal' Opens at Gate March 9," *New York Times* 10 February 1960: 42.).

30. "Who's Who in the Theatre."

31. Boleslavsky, "Laboratory" 247.

32. Treadwell, "Producing" 4.

33. Ibid. 4.

34. Percy Stone, "Many-Sided Sophie Treadwell Places Playwright Side First," *New York Herald Tribune* 21 Apr. 1925.

35. Roberts, "Theatre" 187–188.

36. Roberts, *Boleslavsky* 142; Treadwell, "Russian."

13

On "The Verge" of a New Form: *The Cabinet of Dr. Caligari* and Susan Glaspell's Experiments in *The Verge*

Steven Frank

Kicking off the 1921–1922 season of the Provincetown Players, the New York premiere of Susan Glaspell's *The Verge* on 14 November 1921 was perhaps one of the most highly anticipated theatrical events of the year. In his *New York Times* review (15 November 1921), Alexander Woollcott described how spectators "packed the little theater in MacDougal Street to suffocation" to see Glaspell's new work. Perhaps expecting the more conventional realism of Glaspell's earlier successes, such as *Trifles* or *The Outside*, or the political idealism of *Inheritors*, the play that preceded *The Verge,* reviewers and audiences alike were apparently baffled by what they saw on stage. Woollcott called the play "tormented and bewildering . . . a play which can be intelligently reviewed only by a neurologist" and in a follow-up review, noted how audiences were "befogged by the play" (20 November 1921).[1] Similarly, the *New York Herald*, in a review titled "What 'The Verge' Is About, Who Can Tell?" complained the play "is written in code."[2] *The Verge*'s experimental staging left reviewers struggling to put into words what appeared so different from the usual realistic fare on the stage. Intriguingly, two reviews in New York newspapers, the *New York Globe and Commercial Advertiser* and the *Greenwich Villager*, both described *The Verge* as reminiscent of the film *The Cabinet of Dr. Caligari.*[3]

Today considered a classic of the silent-screen era and the first great German expressionist film, *The Cabinet of Dr. Caligari* when it originally came to the United States had already enjoyed considerable acclaim in Europe.[4] When it opened in New York in the spring of 1921, audiences flocked to see the film of which they had already heard such a great deal.[5] In his study of American expressionism, *Accelerated Grimace*, Mardi Valgemae notes that, for American playwrights looking for examples of the new expressionist style sweeping Europe, the film provided an easily accessible introduction.[6] One such playwright to discover the novelty of *Dr. Caligari* was a young Eugene O'Neill. In a letter dated 10 June 1921, O'Neill commented, "I saw Caligari and it sure opened my eyes to wonderful possibilities I had never dreamed of before."[7] He soon reworked an earlier short story into *The Hairy Ape*, a play often noted for its early use of expressionistic devices.[8] While *Dr. Caligari* clearly made an im-

pression on O'Neill, he was not necessarily the first playwright in search of experimental techniques to turn to the film. The original production of *The Verge*
(in November 1921) premiered seven months after *Dr. Caligari* had opened in
New York (in April 1921) but several months before *The Hairy Ape* (which
premiered at the Provincetown on 9 March 1922). Given that two reviewers at
the time compared *The Verge* to *Dr. Caligari*, one may think it reasonable to
consider that Glaspell was also experimenting with this style in her play.[9]

Yet *The Verge*, although widely acknowledged as Glaspell's most experimental work, is still considered by many critics to be a primarily realistic work.
And those critics who have noted that aspects of *The Verge* are expressionistic
have neither explored these elements in detail nor speculated as to what might
have inspired Glaspell to include them.[10] This suggests a critical trend by which
Glaspell has been pigeonholed as a "realist" and *The Verge* read as a realistic
study of a woman's descent into insanity. Such readings tend to devalue the experimental aspects of the play and/or view them as manifestations of the protagonist's disturbed mind-set.[11] However, a close examination of *The Verge* reveals striking similarities between the play and *Dr. Caligari*, indicating that
Glaspell, like O'Neill, was influenced by the film and actively experimenting
with these expressionistic techniques in her work. Viewing *The Verge* as an experiment with expressionism significantly opens up thematic interpretations of
the play and the play's protagonist beyond the limitations of realistic readings.

Most critics consider the second-act setting of *The Verge* to be the most experimental aspect of the play,[12] and it is indeed here that the affinity with *Dr.
Caligari* is most evident. The first and third acts are set within the vast green-
house in which Glaspell's protagonist, Claire, is carrying out a series of experiments to develop a new form of plant life. Sandwiched between these two acts,
the second act is set in a tower in which Claire has sequestered herself in an attempt to escape the family members, her husband and sister, with whom she is
in conflict over her work. The tower setting is clearly not a realistic one; as
Glaspell describes it, the tower "is thought to be round but does not complete the
circle. The back is curved, then jagged lines break from that, and the front is a
queer bulging window—in a curve that leans" (78).[13] In 1921 the *Greenwich
Villager* reviewer, discussing the play's mixture of realism and symbolism, described how the "mystical tower room in the next act suggests *Caligari*." Similarly, Kenneth Macgowan's *New York Globe and Commercial Advertiser* review
noted that the "second act has an expressionistic setting by Cleon Throckmorton.
A tower room with lantern-flecked walls seen through a crazily latticed window,
almost out of 'Caligari.'"[14]

While those reviewers did not elaborate on these superficial comparisons
between the film and the play's second-act setting, a more detailed examination
of the two works reveals striking similarities. Writing on *Dr. Caligari*, Siegfried
Kracauer describes how the settings "abounded in complexes of jagged, sharp-
pointed forms strongly reminiscent of gothic patterns."[15] Lotte Eisner similarly
discusses how the set of the film features "deliberately distorted perspectives
and . . . narrow, slanting streets which cut across each other at unexpected an-
gles."[16] *Theatre Arts* magazine, describing the set of the original Provincetown
Playhouse production of *The Verge*, similarly notes a "distortion" in the setting,
which it terms "expressionistic."[17] Examination of a photograph of the original
second act-setting of *The Verge* as it appeared on the stage of the Provincetown

Playhouse reveals more specific similarities to *Dr. Caligari*. In the photograph, we can clearly see how the circular room and the oddly shaped window through which the stage is viewed create an extremely disorienting perspective. The enormous, distorted window, made up of several curved lines that seem to converge at the top of the stage, seems identical to the oddly shaped windows in *Dr. Caligari*. Moreover, the prominently displayed curvilinear lines here resemble those in *Dr. Caligari,* which Eisner describes as "oblique, curving, or rectilinear lines [that] converge across an undefined expanse towards the background."[18] The tower setting of *The Verge* particularly seems to resemble the prison scene in *Dr. Caligari,* which Eisner describes in detail: "The abstraction and the total distortion of the *Caligari* sets are seen at their most extreme in the prison-cell, with its verticals narrowing as they rise like arrow-heads. The oppressive effect is heightened by these verticals being extended along the floor and directed at the spot where the chain-laden prisoner squats. In this hell the distorted, rhomboid window is a mockery."[19] Eisner's description could easily be applied to Glaspell's set, and comparing the photograph of *The Verge* (see Photo 1) with the prison cell in *Dr. Caligari,* we see that the similarity becomes even more evident. Toward the left of the photograph from *The Verge*, Claire sits crouched on the floor in a similar position as the prisoner in *Dr. Caligari.* The two settings are thus also alike in how they position the actors; in both, the human figures are dwarfed by the harsh lines that extend and converge high above them, creating a metaphor for how the individual is overshadowed by authoritarian forces in the modern industrialized world.

Several other elements included in the second-act setting seem derivative of *Dr. Caligari.* For example, Glaspell stipulates that the tower "is lighted by an old-fashioned watchman's lantern hanging from the ceiling; the innumerable pricks and slits in the metal throw a marvelous pattern on the curved wall" (78). In the photograph, both the lantern and the strange pattern it reflects are evident. The lamp resembles the old-fashioned street lanterns that are prominently displayed throughout *Dr. Caligari.* Similarly, Glaspell instructs that within the tower room a "delicately distorted rail of a spiral staircase winds up from below" (78). Kracauer identifies how *Dr. Caligari* also focuses upon staircases several times to "reinforce the effect of the furniture" in scenes within the police station and the lunatic asylum.[20]

Perhaps the strongest evidence that this setting of *The Verge* was indeed influenced and in many ways based on *Dr. Caligari* is that Cleon Throckmorton, the acclaimed set designer of the original production of *The Verge*, wrote about his regard for the film. In a piece he wrote for the *Little Review* in 1926, Throckmorton discusses the popularity of expressionist settings and mentions "such splendid films as *Dr. Caligari* [which] expresses these mad and exhilarating emotions convincingly."[21] It's important to note, however, that all of the distinctive elements in Throckmorton's set, from the window to the lantern, are included in Glaspell's detailed description of the setting. Throckmorton's design seems to have accentuated those elements that reminded him of the film—elements that Glaspell had already thought to include in the text and made integral to the play. In his *Little Review* piece, Throckmorton discusses his understanding that "the aim of expressionism is not to be crazy for the sake of being crazy, but to intensify the emotions expressed upon the stage by the forms and moods the backgrounds take."[22] This was also a prominent feature of the

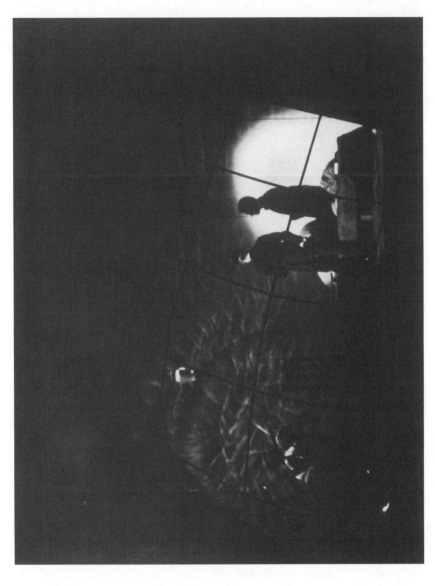

Photo 1. Act 2 of The Verge, Provincetown Playhouse, 1921. Set designed by Cleon Throckmorton. Used by permission of the Billy Rose Theatre Collection, The New York Public Library for the Performing Arts, Astor, Lenox and Tilden Foundations.

Caligari sets, which as Kracauer says, "amounted to a perfect transformation of material objects into emotional ornaments."[23] Glaspell seems to have intended her play's setting to reflect just such an emotional edge when she describes how the "whole structure is as if given a twist by some terrific force—like something wrong" (78).

Moreover, Glaspell's dialogue explicitly aligns the setting with Claire's psychological state. Valgemae describes how the light that Glaspell instructs should escape through slits in the lantern accords with Claire's description of gaiety: "That the playwright is here objectifying the protagonist's inner state becomes apparent when Claire addresses her sister in words that find their counterpart in the stage setting: 'But never one of you—once—looked with me through the little pricks the gaiety made—never one of you—once looked with me at the queer light that came in through the pricks.'"[24] While these lines do establish a connection between Claire's mental state and the setting, there are others that more closely tie Glaspell's metaphoric use of the setting to *Dr. Caligari*. When Claire's sister Adelaide finds her in the tower, Claire discusses their childhood and questions, "Why need I too be imprisoned in what I came from?" to which Adelaide responds, "It isn't being imprisoned. . . . Who's in a tower—in an unsuccessful tower?" (80). This conversation is followed by further references to imprisonment, as Claire fears Adelaide came to "lock [her] in" and claims she "changed the keys" (80). Claire's position in the tower thereby becomes a metaphor for being "imprisoned" by various cultural, sociological, and psychological factors attempting to keep her from completing her work. These references to imprisonment combined with the harsh lines that crisscross the set effectively transform the tower into a physical prison akin to the prison that plays so prominent a part in *Dr. Caligari*.

In the photograph from the second act of *The Verge*, we can also observe the striking contrast between light and shadow, another characteristic expressionist element in *Dr. Caligari*. Toward the right of the photograph, we see the large and imposing shadow of a male figure, probably Claire's lover Tom, hovering over the cot. This use of shadow is also prominent in *Dr. Caligari*, particularly in the scene in which the first murder takes place, as we see an enormous shadow of a male figure above the sleeping victim's head. Kracauer notes that these lighting effects are closely identified with expressionism, that "it was their expressionist nature which impelled many a German director of photography to breed shadows as rampant as weeds and associate ethereal phantoms with strangely lit arabesques or faces."[25] "Strangely lit arabesques" is an apt description for the lighting in the second act of *The Verge*. As we can see in the photograph, the light escaping the slats in the lantern does create, as Glaspell instructed, a "marvelous pattern" on the wall.[26]

Glaspell's description of the lighting in the tower demonstrates that she is clearly interested in experimenting with light and shadow. In addition to the second act, there are other places in the play where she describes unusual lighting, particularly in the opening of the play. Glaspell describes how the "[c]urtain lifts on a place that is dark, save for a shaft of light from below which comes up through an open trap-door in the floor" (58). The play thereby opens with a stark contrast between light and dark, much like those in *Dr. Caligari*. Glaspell also emphasizes shadows in the opening of her play; within the shaft of light, she writes, "Nothing is seen except this plant and its shadow" (58). A moment later,

Claire's assistant, Anthony, emerges from the trapdoor, "his shadow blocking the light" (58). Critics who claim that the play's experimental devices are primarily confined to the second-act setting of *The Verge* have failed to see these similar elements in the opening of the play.[27]

Several other defining characteristics of expressionism seen in *Dr. Caligari* are also evident throughout the play, beyond the second-act setting. For example, a distinct aspect of the film's design, one that is frequently commented upon by critics, is its depiction of highly distorted, sharply angular houses and streets.[28] Similarly, at one point in *The Verge*, Claire relates her fantasy of flying in the air and looking down at houses which she describes as "funny lines and down-going slants—houses are vanishing slants" (69). "Funny lines," "vanishing slants"—one could not find a better way to describe the distorted houses featured prominently in *Dr. Caligari*, indicating that Glaspell might have had them in mind when writing the play. Moreover, *Dr. Caligari's* houses might have shown Glaspell the potential for nonhuman objects to hold human-like qualities and emotions. Eisner describes how the houses in the film "seem to vibrate with an extraordinary spirituality";[29] discussing the German propensity for "animating objects," Eisner goes on to explain how "personification is amplified" in the film, and objects, including houses, street lamps, and chairs, take on human personalities often of a diabolical nature.[30] Glaspell's description of the plants displayed on stage indicates she intends them to achieve a similar effect. Glaspell describes one plant as having "a greater transparency than plants have had. Its leaves, like waves that curl, close around a heart that is not seen" (62). She also describes "a strange vine. It is arresting rather than beautiful. It creeps along the low wall, and one branch gets a little way up the glass. . . . The leaves of this vine are not the form that leaves have been. They are at once repellent and significant" (58). Thus, like the objects in *Dr. Caligari,* Claire's plants are instilled with sinister and disturbing human characteristics.

Expressionism is also associated with depicting the most extreme, intense emotional states, particularly the kind of torment and anguish as found in Edvard Munch's painting "The Cry." The protagonists of both *Dr. Caligari* and *The Verge* experience these kinds of extreme and violent emotions. In the final scene of *Dr. Caligari*, for example, Francis, who has until now been narrating the film's events to an unidentified companion, is revealed to be in a mental asylum. Francis first appears, according to Adkinson's description of the film, with a "childish smile" that "intensifies."[31] However, when the director of the asylum approaches, "Francis screams something out through clenched teeth. The two women on either side of him draw back, their hands raised in fear. Francis clenches his fists above his head, screams and lurches forward."[32] The climax of *The Verge* depicts Claire also rapidly shifting from one emotional extreme to another. Claire at first feels "in ecstasy of rest" with her lover Tom but then "suddenly push[es] him roughly away" and begins to speak "with fury" and "in agony" (99).

These extreme emotional states depicted in expressionist productions invariably affect the physical appearance of the actors, and many of the distinctive traits of expressionist acting are evident in Glaspell and *Dr. Caligari*. For example, expressionist drama frequently emphasizes the appearance of the eyes, which serve as reflections of inner emotional conflict and pain. *Dr. Caligari* features many close-ups of characters' bulging eyes, which stand out even more due to heavy make-up, such as in the scene in which Cesare, the somnambulist, is awakened by Dr. Caligari. In *The Verge* Glaspell also focuses upon her protagonist's eyes. Several times throughout the text, Glaspell describes the appearance of Claire's eyes and the emotion conveyed by them. For example, when Claire meets with the nerve specialist, Glaspell indicates that Claire "look[s] at him with eyes too bright" (91). Similarly, in the play's climax, when Claire realizes that Tom's love cannot redeem her, she speaks "with sight too clear" (99). Related to this emphasis on the emotion expressed by the eyes, the face in expressionist drama is often transformed into a grotesque kind of mask. In *Dr. Caligari*, for example, Cesare's face is covered with heavy white make-up, his eyes darkened with black circles, to appear as a kind of mask. Glaspell at times provides similar descriptions of Claire's facial appearance, describing her at one point as having a "face ghastly" (90).

The positioning and movement of the hands, like the eyes, also often expresses extreme emotional pain. In *Dr. Caligari,* the hands are focused upon just as much as the eyes and often appear tensed and knotted, like claws. For example, in the scene in which Cesare kills Alan, the camera focuses upon the hands of both attacker and victim. Similarly, in *The Verge* Glaspell is also careful to stress the movement of Claire's hands. At the conclusion of act 1, Claire uses her hands in a bitter attempt to destroy her plant; as Glaspell says, she tries "to put destroying hands upon it" (98). The characterization of "destroying hands" suggests Claire's hands are meant to be in the same kind of tight, claw-like position as in *Dr. Caligari.* The attention to Claire's hands is increased when she proceeds to destroy the plant, as Glaspell describes how Claire "buries her hands in the earth around the Edge Vine. . . . grasps it as we grasp what we would kill" (78).

In such elements as its distorted setting, interplay between light and dark, and charged emotional states of its characters, *The Verge* seems highly influenced by expressionist elements in *Dr. Caligari* in terms of production. However, there is a deeper correlation between the two in terms of the thematic meanings that emerge from the works' utilization of expressionistic elements. In *Dr. Caligari* the expressionistic distortions are given a logical explanation by the framing device, which reveals the entire narrative to be told from the point of view of an inmate in an asylum. Similarly, the distorted second-act setting of *The Verge* can be read, as many reviewers and critics have done, as the manifestation of Claire's dementia.[33] Thus, Valgemae lists several of these experimental elements but as serving as "an approximation of how reality must appear to a person on the verge of insanity."[34] As Valgemae's remark indicates, providing this kind of logical explanation for experimental elements ultimately affirms an overall realistic narrative that confines their impact and, in turn, leads to a rather limited reading of character. To read *The Verge* solely as a documentation of Claire's descent into insanity is ultimately to read the play through the confining lens of realistic narrative and characterology by which specific past experiences and inherited traits lead to conflict and tragedy.

In contrast to this kind of limited reading of character, expressionist works, more than depicting the experiences of a specific individual, can serve to express a more collective angst. This was the case with *Dr. Caligari*, which, as Siegfried Kracauer points out, did much more than demonstrate the workings of a sick mind; it also aimed at expressing the "phenomena of the soul," and particularly the collective angst of the German people in the postwar period.[35] This was indeed the intent of the film's writer, as the framing device involving Francis was added later on by the director.[36]

Given the expressionist elements Glaspell included in the play, we may align Claire with the protagonists of expressionism, who, in contrast to the highly specified characters in realist dramas, served as emblems of the struggle of the individual in a cold and oppressive industrialized society. Similarly, Claire's struggle in the play can be read not only as an individual one in which she attempts to hold on to her sanity but as a broader conflict with the various social forces attempting to suppress her creativity. Significantly, Glaspell names the men in Claire's life "Tom, Dick and Harry," thereby giving them a collective, generic status. As a group, they become representative of patriarchal forces preventing Claire from carrying out her project. In "A Stage of Her Own: Susan Glaspell's *The Verge* and Women's Dramaturgy," J. Ellen Gainor suggests that the play reflects Glaspell's own difficulty maintaining her own voice under the influence of her husband and cofounder of the Provincetown Playhouse, George Cook. In attempting to create a "new form," Claire can be viewed as an artist figure who, like Glaspell herself, was experimenting to find new forms of self-expression beyond patriarchal limitations.[37] By viewing the play in expressionistic terms, Claire can be read more representationally, as an emblem of the Woman Artist struggling against the forces of patriarchal oppression and the limiting artistic forms it engenders.

In *The Cabinet of Dr. Caligari,* Glaspell found not only expressionist production elements that help evoke a more collective emotional angst but also a model for Claire as an oppressed artist figure. Claire is less like Francis, the film's insane narrator, and more akin to the film's namesake, Dr. Caligari. Even their names—"C–L–A–I–R–E" and "C–A–L–I–G–A–R–I"—suggest a strong affinity. Both Caligari and Claire are scientists who express an intense passion for and commitment to their work. Just as Caligari pronounces, "I must know everything,"[38] Claire announces her Promethean goals: "I want to give fragrance to Breath of Life—the flower I have created that is outside what flowers have been" (63). Like Caligari, whose work is not condoned by the authorities, Claire hopes, in the process of creating something new, to undo old forms, proclaiming, "But it can be done! We need not be held in forms moulded for us. . . . I want to break it up!" (64). And just as the mad scientist, as represented by Caligari, works outside the realm of conventional scientific inquiry and is therefore exiled, even hunted down, by the community at large, so too is the Woman Artist, in her attempt to subvert patriarchal artistic forms, ostracized and labeled "mad."

The Verge can thus be thought of as an experimental work in terms of both its subject matter and its form. In Claire, Glaspell presents a woman with a passion for experimentation and a fierce determination to create something original. Claire's experiments with creating new forms of plant life find their counterpart in the experimental dramatic devices Glaspell included—the use of shadow and light, the bizarre plants with their diabolical human characteristics, the anguish of the protagonist—which convey the emotional angst experienced by the Woman Artist as she struggles to express herself in the face of strong patriarchal forces. *The Cabinet of Dr. Caligari*, also focusing upon experimentation, both in its "mad scientist" antihero as well as in its expressionistic form, likely served as a source of inspiration for Glaspell, providing specific expressionistic devices she included in her play. Like O'Neill, Glaspell should be credited for seeing potential in the expressionistic form as it appeared in *Dr. Caligari* and attempting to bring it to the American stage with her own daring experiment, *The Verge*.

NOTES

1. Alexander Woollcott, "Second Thoughts on First Nights," *New York Times* 20 November 1921: 23.

2. "What 'The Verge' is About, Who Can Tell?" *New York Herald* 15 November 1921.

3. Kenneth Macgowan, "The New Play: Margaret Wycherly Acts Magnificently in 'The Verge,'" *New York Globe and Commercial Advertiser* 15 November 1921: 20; "Claire—Superwoman or Plain Egomaniac?" *Greenwich Villager* 30 November 1921: 1, 4.

4. Siegfried Kracauer, "Caligari," *The Cabinet of Dr. Caligari: A Film by Robert Wiene, Carl Mayer and Hans Janowitz* (London: Lorrimer, 1972) 15–16, 21.

5. *New York Times* 20 March 1921, sec. 6, 2: 1; *New York Times* 4 April 1921, sec. 18: 1; Kracauer, "Caligari" 15–16, 21.

6. Mardi Valgemae, *Accelerated Grimace: Expressionism in the American Drama of the 1920s* (Carbondale: Southern Illinois University Press, 1972) 9.

7. Eugene O'Neill, *Selected Letters*, ed. Travis Bogard and Jackson R. Bryer (New Haven: Yale University Press, 1988) 156.

8. Valgemae, *Accelerated Grimace* 30–32.

9. Unfortunately, unlike with O'Neill, we do not have definite evidence that Glaspell saw the film. However, one finds it unlikely that the resemblance between the play and the film is merely coincidental given the many similarities between the two I have observed. Gerhard Bach notes that, unlike O'Neill, Glaspell wrote all of her plays during the years in which she was working with the Provincetown group, that "no new play was written and produced until the results of the previous one had been digested" ("Susan Glaspell—Provincetown Playwright," *The Great Lakes Review* 4.2 [1978]: 34). *Inheritors*, Glaspell's play which preceded *The Verge*, was performed at the Provincetown at the end of April 1921, the same month in which *Dr. Caligari* premiered in New York. If Bach is correct that Glaspell did not begin a play until the previous one was produced, then she did not write *The Verge* until well after the premiere showing of *Dr. Caligari* in New York, when the film would have been widely seen and discussed among the Bohemian artist community of Greenwich Village where Glaspell lived and worked. Given the film's tremendous popularity at the time it premiered, it is safe to say that even if Glaspell did not see the film herself, *Dr. Caligari* was very much in the air at the time.

10. Deutsch (Helen Deutsch and Stella Hanau, *The Provincetown: A Story of the Theatre* [New York: Russell & Russell, 1931]: 85), Lewisohn (Ludwig Lewisohn, *Expression in America* [New York: Harper, 1932] 393–401), Waterman (Arthur E. Waterman, *Susan Glaspell* [New York: Twayne, 1966] 83) and Bigsby (C.W.E. Bigsby, Introduction, *Plays by Susan Glaspell* [Cambridge: Cambridge University Press, 1987] 19–25) recognize that the play contains some experimental elements, and Gainor (J. Ellen Gainor, "A Stage of Her Own: Susan Glaspell's *The Verge* and Women's Dramaturgy," *Journal of American Drama and Theatre* 1.1 [1989]) investigates the various experimental elements of the play in detail. However, none mention the play's similarities in form and content to *Dr. Caligari*.

11. See, for example, Valgemae, *Accelerated Grimace*, who calls the play "basically realistic" and says that those experimental devices Glaspell employs are there to provide a "view into the disturbed mind of the protagonist" (25), thereby providing a realistic

rationale for the play's experimental aspects.

12. Waterman, *Susan Glaspell* 82; Valgemae, *Accelerated Grimace* 25.

13. Susan Glaspell, *The Verge* in *Plays by Susan Glaspell*, ed. C.W.E. Bigsby (Cambridge: Cambridge University Press, 1987). Page references appear in the text.

14. Valgemae points out, this review of *The Verge* is historically significant as it marks the first time the word *expressionistic* is applied to a New York theatrical production (26).

15. Kracauer, "Caligari" 13.

16. Lotte H. Eisner, *The Haunted Screen* (Berkeley: University of California Press, 1965) 21.

17. Kenneth Macgowan, "Portrait of a Season," *Theatre Arts Magazine* 6.1 (1922): 12.

18. Eisner, *Haunted Screen* 21.

19. Ibid. 24–25.

20. Kracauer, "Caligari" 21.

21. Cleon Throckmorton, "Overshooting the Mark," *The Little Review* 11 (1926): 97–98.

22. Ibid. 98.

23. Kracauer, "Caligari" 13.

24. Valgemae, *Accelerated Grimace* 25.

25. Kracauer, "Caligari" 25.

26. Interestingly, Valgemae describes how *Dr. Caligari* "contains a scene in a prison cell, with light throwing a grotesque, geometrical pattern upon the crazily leaning walls" (34), but compares it only to *The Hairy Ape*, which features similar lighting effects. Valgemae does not observe the obvious similarity between the "geometrical pattern" in *Dr. Caligari* and the "marvelous pattern" Glaspell describes.

27. Again, Valgemae notes how *Dr. Caligari*, "filled with juxtaposed areas of light and darkness," is similar to *The Hairy Ape* (33), but does not connect it to *The Verge*. As an example, Valgemae notes how in *The Hairy Ape*, whenever "a furnace door is opened, the shadowy stokehold is illuminated by a flash of intense light" (33–34). Although this effect is virtually the same as in the opening of *The Verge*, Valgemae does not make this comparison.

28. Eisner, *Haunted Screen* 21–23; Kracauer, "Caligari" 13–14, 24.

29. Eisner, *Haunted Screen* 21.

30. Ibid. 23.

31. R. V. Adkinson, trans. and description of the action, *The Cabinet of Dr. Caligari: A Film by Robert Wiene, Carl Mayer and Hans Janowitz* (London: Lorrimer, 1972) 98.

32. Adkinson, *Cabinet* 98–99.

33. The trend among reviewers and critics is to identify the play primarily as a study of Claire's insanity and not as a more representational struggle with various psychological and sociological forces. See Lewisohn (396–397), Sievers (W. David Sievers, *Freud on Broadway: A History of Psychoanalysis and the American Drama* [1955; New York: Cooper Square, 1970] 71–72), Waterman, *Susan Glaspell* (80–81) and reviews from the period in the *New York Times* (Alexander Woollcott, Review of *The Verge*, *New York Times* 15 November 1921; Woollcott, "Second Thoughts on First Nights," *New York Times* 20 November 1921), *New York Clipper* ("'The Verge,' The New Play by Susan Glaspell Is Worth Seeing," *New York Clipper* November 1921: 20) and *New York Call* (Maida Castellun, "'The Verge,' Daring Venture in Drama by Susan Glaspell," *New York Call* 16 November 1921).

34. Valgemae, *Accelerated Grimace* 25.

35. Kracauer, "Caligari" 16.

36. Ibid. 9–12.
37. Gainor, "Stage of Her Own" 92–96.
38. Adkinson, *Cabinet* 93.

14

They Knew What They Wanted: American Theatre's Use of Nonverbal Communication Codes to Marginalize Non-Native Characters in the 1920s

Beverly Bronson Smith

The parameters of the American character are an oft-explored topic, harking back to the earliest American dramas. What has not been fully examined, however, are the myriad nonverbal forms that identify these parameters as well as those characteristics that fall outside them. The 1920s is particularly apt for such exploration because the country's reaction to world events resulted in extended self-scrutiny. In spite of usual associations with Roaring Twenties frivolity, the decade of the 1920s in truth was a time of shifts in virtually every aspect of American life. The war had upset the smooth operation of traditional institutions, and in its aftermath a return to proven venues of wealth, power, and isolation within America's borders appeared desirable. "Increasing numbers of Americans came to doubt that the mysterious alembic of American society was actually functioning as it was supposed to—too many immigrants were coming too fast; they were too different from the American national type to be assimilated painlessly or even, many felt, to be assimilated at all."[1]

What was the "American national type?" Clarifying this concept became a fixation, compounded by the fact that "Western man is psycholinguistically dichotomous. That is, he finds it comfortable, logical, and reasonable to divide the universe into paired categories."[2] Dividing the country into "Americans" and "non-Americans" was a natural outgrowth of this tendency to dichotomize, developing into a "them or us" mentality expressed in stereotyping, dominance moves, distancing, and other forms of marginalizing behavior. Native-born Americans certainly knew what they wanted: an elimination of all things "alien," putting the very nature of American society at issue with the institution of Americanization programs. These programs, according to Gleason, confirmed that "conformity to . . . cultural unity was required of all immigrants."[3] Information on American standards is provided not only in the dialogue of the play text but also in the stage directions, technical notes, and photographs from the productions, which encapsulate coding systems such as kinesics, proxemics, and chronemics that communicate relationships, social preoccupations, and the like.

Kinesics is one of the most frequently used and recognizable forms of non-verbal coding. Elam states that the audience tends to interpret individual kinesic behaviors as impersonations of complete acts.[4] In *Welcome Stranger*, the single gesture of one townsperson, Trimble, toward Frankel, an itinerant Jewish sales-man, represents the complete marginalizing act of an entire town in classifying Frankel and his ethnic group as "other."[5] On a blustery evening Frankel is stranded in a small-town hotel. Trimble produces a jug of cider and enough glasses for his fellow townspeople, whereupon Frankel produces a collapsible cup. Trimble tells Frankel to get away and slaps his cup closed. The action is strengthened by the location of the play in New England, the bastion of main-stream America.

Such behaviors often result from accepted stereotypes, which tend to present a highly exaggerated picture of the importance of a few characteristics, in some cases inventing supposed traits and associating them with other true traits to make them seem reasonable. The same characteristics may be ignored or even accepted in the majority population, depending on who uses them and how. Scheflen tells us that even casual observers can distinguish culturally determined behaviors and "may react to the foreignness rather than what is being said or done."[6] Italian and Jewish characters are those most identified with stereotypical gestures, and examples of them abound in such plays as *They Knew What They Wanted, Lombardi, Ltd., Street Scene*, and *39 East*.[7] Use of ethnic-associated mannerisms categorize the character, and the nationality she or he represents, as unacculturated; the individualized and individualizing behaviors of such charac-ters tend to be ignored.[8] As a result, the audience finds it harder to feel empathy for characters who are different from themselves and easier to consider them as objects.

Characters can be also objectified by the way their movements are modified. This can happen by extending a limb with an artifact, visually allying the char-acter with that object and making him or her one with it.[9] In production photos published with the script of *They Knew What They Wanted*, Tony is depicted with either a crutch, connoting helplessness, or a gun, reinforcing the violence stereotype of Italians. In *The Inheritors*, association with artifacts causes even ethnic characters to practice marginalizing behaviors against those not so Ameri-canized.[10] Felix Fejevary, a second-generation Hungarian now a trustee of a local solidly American college, discovers Hindu students passing out handbills advo-cating radical ideas. Felix, along with other officials, plans to expel these stu-dents, who in his eyes become the offending leaflets.

Dominating moves that establish the superiority of the mainstream over the marginality of the foreign-born are clearly encoded in kinesics. In *Street Scene*, for example, Sam Kaplan, a slight, sensitive Jewish youth, is manhandled by Vincent Jones. Surnamed to represent the native-born, Jones pulls Kaplan from where he stands above Jones on the stoop and leaves him face-down on the sidewalk. His behavior demonstrates what Van Zyl calls "redundancy": two or more subsystems (in this case the physical contact, the manner of it, and the vertical levels) convey similar signals, increasing the readability of the commu-nication by heightening its force or weight.[11] As Esslin explains, "it is not the direct appeal, the surface message that is most effective, but . . . the indirect implications of the dramatic action, the meaning that emerges . . . between the lines of the dialogue, from the wider reverberations of the action."[12] Vincent's invective is not the most powerful agent but rather the physicalization of the intent behind it.

Occasionally plays rank characters according to ethnicity, pitting the privileged and accepted (who represent American characteristics) against the merely tolerated or the rejected (who represent non-American characteristics). In *The Bachelor Father* three different ethnicities are characterized (American, English, and Italian), and their relative status is encoded kinesically.[13] Tony, the American daughter, orders her siblings about, and they in turn look to her before taking any action. The Italian Maria, on the other hand, is demure, retiring, and servile. She makes the first overtures of obedience and affection to their stiff British father, although she withholds these when Tony seems to disapprove. She also frequently averts her eyes, a move generally interpreted as shame, evasiveness, or submission.[14] Tony is strongest in her refusal to back down, sense of independence, "spunk," and robust health, all qualities admired and expected of Americans. Maria is the weakest, exemplified in the doctor's examination of her and no one else in the family. Maria is in a no-win situation; if she evinces the same traits as Tony, she would seem brash and lacking proper respect. Her actual reserved behavior is "appropriate" for the foreign-born because it clarifies her inferiority to an American.

Even those qualities appropriated by the mainstream can be interpreted negatively when exhibited by foreign-born characters, especially if the qualities are juxtaposed with their opposites displayed by American characters. The foreign-born stokers in *The Hairy Ape* follow orders and respond promptly to the work call, yet they seem inferior to Yank, who defies authority.[15] Similarly, in *The Detour* Jake Weinstein unquestioningly obeys his father but appears weak and even silly compared to American Kate, who challenges hers.[16]

The conflict for the foreign-born is often one of survival versus conformity. Deviation in any direction could prompt negative reaction. *The Detour*'s Weinstein, a furniture trader, must ingratiate himself with the Hardy family to do business with them; so he appears "bland and smiling," and "friendly," earning grudging acceptance by "bowing politely" at his entrance. Yet he must also be a good businessman to maintain his livelihood; when he plies his trade efficiently, he incurs the wrath and suspicion of the family. Helen carefully counts the money Weinstein pays her for the furniture, and Steve accuses him of swindling them. While business acumen is an American characteristic, when the foreign-born use it in their dealings with the native-born, it becomes a threat.

Children who have rejected their first-generation immigrant parents were fairly common in life as well as in the plays of this period, a phenomenon fostered, some historians claim, by Americanization programs in the schools which marginalized older generations exponentially.[17] The central conflict in *We Americans* focuses on the children's perception of their parents as un-Americanized.[18] A photograph from the original production, published with the script, demonstrates this conflict. The father, pointing to the traditional symbols of the Jewish Sabbath, grasps his daughter's arm as though to hold her to her heritage. The Americanized daughter turns away, her facial expression indicating her distress with her father's unbending attitude. The mother stands nearby showing a supplicating gesture, a more placating approach but still an attempt to return her children to their traditions.

These parents stand alone against a society that attempts to change even their most fundamental behavioral characteristics, homogenizing them into carbon copies of the ideal American. Conformity to American social graces is a hallmark of assimilation; failure to learn or conform to them marginalizes. The Bulgarian Sascha, in *Greatness*, impatiently brushes others out of the way to reach his fiancée.[19] He speaks with his mouth full, as does Count Gionelli in *39 East*. The Count eats noisily, keeps both knife and fork continuously in his hands, and hogs food. He does not rise when Mrs. Smith, with her mainstream appellation, enters the dining room, and he does not show polite attention when he is bored. The consequences for the behavior of these characters is ultimately to be distanced from the play's main action.

The proximity between characters or groups, alignment of vertical and horizontal planes, placement of objects and set pieces, and construction of the spatial environment, among other elements, are parts of the stage picture that make marginalization concrete. The balcony stage right in *See Naples and Die*, for example, demonstrates the effects of architectural proxemics.[20] Used by Skulany, a Rumanian general and would-be dictator, the balcony's distanced position across a road represents an alien way of life. Skulany holds his mistress, Kunie, hostage; several times she entreats her American champion, Charles, for aid, but he can protect her only if she crosses the road. Each of these visual elements represents the world balance of power and American fear of Eastern European political control. Ultimately, however, the distance leads to the triumph of native values such as personal liberty and fair play, since warnings about the assassinations of Skulany and the equally unscrupulous Russian Kosoff go unheard over noise from cars racing between the balcony in the background and the terrace in the foreground. American isolationism is justified.

Territoriality, "identification with an area . . . to indicate ownership and defense of this territory against those who may 'invade' it,"[21] is depicted in both *The Rescuing Angel* and *Welcome Stranger*.[22] In *The Rescuing Angel* Kolinsky is marginalized outside social space, causing Mrs. Deming to behave as if he cannot hear conversation inside it: "Don't urge him to stay, dear, if he really has to go," then "Rose, you're coming to dinner, you and Bill?" Although Mrs. Deming's dialogue is the most obviously negative, Mr. Deming's movements serve as stronger metatransactions by physically channeling Kolinsky's participation. Throughout the play, Kolinsky has no place to sit, nor is he invited to do so, while the others sit or stand as suits them. His movements to approach the family group are aborted, he is ignored unless he breaches territorial limits, and he is always stationed up left of the group, a weak stage position.

Advantageous upstage position, freedom of movement, and distinct verticality should confirm Isidor Solomon's status as the main character in *Welcome Stranger*, according to Knapp.[23] However, lack of a need to move, the foreground location of the table at which Trimble, Tyler, and Whitson sit, and their refusal to turn to face Solomon proxemically convey higher status. Closed body orientation and lack of direct eye contact with Solomon become regulatory functions by denying him access to their circle. In subsequent action vertical planes are reversed and once again normal signals are inverted or modified to deny status. The nonverbal repertoire of this play serves as a more powerful indicator of Solomon's reception than, often cloaked, verbal behavior.[24]

The one-act play *Fog* presents a situation in which normal rules of space usage should break down.[25] Three people are stranded in a lifeboat after their ship has sunk; two figures huddle in the middle with another alone in one end, the mist cloaking identifying details. The dialogue and the gradually increasing light reveal that the isolated figure is a Polish peasant woman and that the bundle in her lap is her dead child. The evolution of their identities, coupled with the attitudes expressed by the men, partially explains how even in these circumstances the ethnic character is distanced. The Business Man marginalizes her on the vertical axis socially and physically by describing steerage as a "filthy sort of hole," while horizontally maintaining distance from her. The Poet, on the other hand, edges toward her, places his coat over her, tries to wake her, feels her pulse, and listens for her heart, "his ear against her breast." He remains with her body in the lifeboat, while the Business Man takes the first opportunity to escape to the rescue boat. The juxtaposition of the two characters—their actions as well as their names—emphasizes the peripheral position of the third.

Time is a further marginalizing signifier in many plays of this era. Pace and rhythm are distinguishing features of a culture and can either bring people together or alienate them.[26] For example, in *The Centuries* the pace of life is markedly different between American and immigrant spheres, signaled by the sewing machines' whir and American bosses' orders to hurry versus the immigrant, old-clothes man's shuffle across the stage.[27] Marginalizing may also result from varying personal tempos, as in *Processional*, where jazz cadences promote a unique emphasis on chronemics.[28] The jazz band becomes a focal point for the range of tempos depicted throughout the play. As with any good musical organization, especially one that marches, the bass drummer (with the American name Smith) sets the beat. "Banging methodically," he illustrates the measured, unvarying pace of the mainstream. Much as the ethnic assortment of musicians might like to deviate from this basic rhythm, they are held in check by it or become conspicuous in their discord. The aura of conformity is augmented by the "monotonous" and "frightening" tread of marching feet. Social harmony is the intended end of the band; a certain degree of variation is permitted, but ultimately little will be allowed to change. Society moves inexorably forward at its unhurried pace "like a train ashufflin' along" on an iron track.

Friction could also occur because of the difference between monochronic and polychronic perceptions of time. Monochronics concentrate on one thing at a time, sealing people off from each other as privacy becomes paramount and short-term relationships become the norm.[29] These characteristics coincide with American tendencies.[30] Conversely, the highly distractible polychronic fosters simultaneity while tending to form lifetime relationships.[31] Tito Lombardi in *Lombardi, Ltd.* is such a character. Although he is loyal and forges lasting alliances, the focus of his characterization is distractibility. He flits capriciously from one idea to the next, lavishly and foolishly spending money he doesn't have. These behaviors place him in conflict with his conservative American accountant and risk bankruptcy for his business, a situation unacceptable by American standards, since Americans tend to find identity in business associations.[32] Tito's alien characteristics result in a never resolved conflict, and he must be saved by outside forces.

Relevant, too, in an analysis of marginalization is the fact that images are difficult to keep in mind; others take their places as the action unfolds.[33] Although Tito displays qualities that challenge American values (unconcern with business, impracticality, lack of self-control, lack of punctuality), many of his traits are solidly mainstream (belief in capitalism, industriousness, confidence, mannerliness, morality). Opinion of him fluctuates with each scene, culminating in a dichotomy for the receiver: audience members can associate amusement and liking with the individual character but generalize negative impressions onto his ethnic group. As Doob writes, "In a series of items, those coming first establish a frame of mind which can affect those coming later, . . . the problem of recency vs. primacy."[34] The first bit of information spectators receive about Tito is that he lacks emotional control.

In some cases the character's status changes during the play. The radical transformations occurring in *We Americans* focus on the fundamental assumption that the foreign-born must change to fit the American mold. Script photographs of *We Americans* in its New York production reveal alterations in clothing, grooming, and set decoration as the first-generation immigrant characters adopt mainstream values. In act 1 apparel is mismatched and unkempt, and the styles, such as headgear, are more Old Country than New. Mr. Horowitz's hair is disheveled and his posture is slouched. The tablecloth and a picture hang slightly askew; other decorations represent quaint, European tastes. Act 3 reveals a metamorphosis. Clothing is neater and more stylish, grooming is more precise (particularly Mr. Horowitz's hair and beard), posture is straighter, and the set decorations have added tastefully patterned draperies, changed the large, loosely hanging tablecloth for a neat, lace-edged one, and replaced old pictures with a cabinet to tidily contain the previously scattered bric-a-brac. The question, of course, is whether such outward manifestations of change would counter marginalization efforts. Therefore, perhaps the most significant signal is the changed nature of the gathering: instead of sharing food and drink, the characters now share books and writing, and all of the characters are now focused on this one activity instead of being scattered in smaller groupings or even sitting in isolation. Americanizers expected this entire transformation process to take place in one generation,[35] evidenced in this play in the intensified time frame of the change from old ways to new.

"The fact of performance as communication must depend on conventions, shared meanings and a common stock of social activity."[36] This chapter explored the ways in which theatrical vehicles produced during the 1920s marginalized the foreign-born through a spectrum of nonverbal coding systems. Contrary to Walter Prichard Eaton's comments that nothing is to be learned about the national character in drama,[37] these samples tell us a great deal about American social conventions. As Bill says in *Processional*, "Everythin' means somethin' if you can only figger it out." "For drama is not a mirror of action. It is a composition. In composing words, gestures, and deeds to form a play, dramatist and performers operate with the constraints . . . of . . . convention . . . [which] amount to a code of rules for the transmission of specific beliefs, attitudes, and feelings in terms of organized social behaviour."[38]

The analysis in this chapter seeks to demonstrate that nonverbal elements are more effective marginalizing devices than the blatant verbalizations present in some of these plays, even though they may not be acknowledged or recognized consciously. In addition, the spectator retains the impact of nonverbal communication longer, as opposed to the fleeting impact of verbal messages. In plays with explicit verbal divisiveness, these signals reinforce; in plays without conspicuous verbalization, they reveal or contradict. Further, verbal messages can be approached on their own terms, agreed or disagreed with, and combated; if the message is transmitted nonverbally, it often works beneath the surface to influence below the level of awareness. As Esslin states, "it must always be kept in mind that this decoding process is only partially conscious: many members of the audience will tend to react instinctively to the 'general impression' produced by the confluence of a multitude of subliminally perceived characteristics."[39] Humans are cognizant, consciously or unconsciously, of many behavioral patterns and their meanings. These patterns are scripts, known in more detailed ways than we could ever know a drama.[40]

Americans, experiencing a sense of dislocation and crisis caused by a war which had overturned their sense of invulnerability, knew what they wanted: a center, a focus—national unity coupled with a clear national identity. This era was one of seeking. Exactly what was America and what things could be called American? The plays cited here seem to simplify the complex issues facing Americans in the 1920s, predisposing audience members to tolerate marginalization and see some in society's midst as "other." Theatre demonstrates the means used to maintain social divisions and inequalities by displaying apparently real life situations using apparently recognized cultural codes. These plays are deceptively innocuous, but analysis of the nonverbal elements reveals the intricacy of their potential signals.

NOTES

1. Philip Gleason, "American Identity and Americanization," *Harvard Encyclopedia of American Ethnic Groups*, ed. Steven Thernstrom (Cambridge: Belknap, 1981) 38–39. The exception is the era of the Know-Nothings, although Gleason asserts that such writers as Ralph Waldo Emerson reaffirmed America's "cosmopolitan faith."

2. R.L. Birdwhistell, *Kinesics and Context* (Philadelphia: University of Pennsylvania Press, 1970) 66.

3. Gleason, "American Identity" 46.

4. Keir Elam, *The Semiotics of Theatre and Drama* (London: Methuen, 1980) 29.

5. Aaron Hoffman, *Welcome Stranger* (New York: French, 1926).

6. Albert E. Scheflen, *Body Language and the Social Order: Communication as Behavioral Control* (Englewood Cliffs, NJ: Prentice-Hall, 1973) 86.

7. Sidney Howard, *They Knew What They Wanted* and Elmer Rice, *Street Scene*, in *Famous American Plays of the 1920s*, ed. Kenneth Macgowan (New York: Dell, 1959); Frederick and Fanny Hatton, *Lombardi, Ltd.* (New York: French, 1928); Rachel Crothers, *39 East*, in *Expressing Willie, Nice People, 39 East* (New York: Brentano's, 1919).

8. George Eaton Simpson and J. Milton Yinger, *Racial and Cultural Minorities: An Analysis of Prejudice and Discrimination* (New York: Harper, 1972) 154.

9. Mary Ritchie Key, *Paralanguage and Kinesics* (Metuchen: Scarecrow, 1975) 116.

10. Susan Glaspell, *The Inheritors*, in *Plays*, ed. C.W.E. Bigsby (Cambridge: Cambridge University Press, 1987).

11. John Van Zyl, "Towards a Socio-Semiotic of Performance," *Semiotic Scene* 3 (1979): 107.

12. Martin Esslin, *The Field of Drama: How the Signs of Drama Create Meaning on the Stage and Screen* (London: Methuen, 1987) 172.

13. Edward Childs Carpenter, *Bachelor Father* (New York: French, 1932).

14. Scheflen, *Body Language* 96. See also Edward T. Hall and Mildred Reed Hall, *Understanding Cultural Differences* (Yarmouth, ME: Intercultural, 1990) 141–142.

15. Eugene O'Neill, *The Hairy Ape*, in *Nine Plays by Eugene O'Neill* (New York: The Modern Library, 1940).

16. Owen Davis, *The Detour*, in *Representative American Dramas*, ed. Montrose Moses (Boston: Heath, 1941).

17. Glenn C. Altschuler, *Race, Ethnicity, and Class in American Social Thought, 1865–1919* (Arlington Heights, IL: Harlan Davidson, 1982) 47. See also Leonard Dinnerstein and David Reimers, *Ethnic Americans: A History of Immigration and Assimilation* (New York: Dodd, Mead, 1975) 49.

18. Milton Herbert Gropper and Max Siegal, *We Americans* (New York: French, 1928).

19. Zoë Akins, *Greatness*, in *Déclassée, Daddy's Gone A-Hunting, and Greatness—A Comedy* (New York: Boni, 1923).

20. Elmer Rice, *See Naples and Die* (New York: French, 1930).

21. Mark L. Knapp, *Nonverbal Communication in Human Interaction* (New York: Holt Rinehart, 1978) 37.

22. Clare Kummer, *The Rescuing Angel* (New York: French, 1923).

23. Knapp, *Nonverbal Communication* 43.

24. P. Ekman and W. V. Friesen, "The Repertoire of Nonverbal Behavior: Categories, Origins, Usage, and Coding," *Semiotica* 1 (1969): 53.

25. Eugene O'Neill, *Fog*, in *Ten "Lost" Plays* (New York: Random House, 1964).

26. Hall and Hall, *Understanding* 18.

27. Em Jo Basshe, *The Centuries: Portrait of a Tenement House* (New York: Macaulay, 1927).

28. John Howard Lawson, *Processional* (New York: Thomas Seltzer, 1925).

29. Hall and Hall, *Understanding* 14–15.

30. Ibid. 144–145.

31. Ibid. 14–15.

32. Ibid. 144–145.

33. Marvin Carlson, *Theatre Semiotics: Signs of Life* (Bloomington: Indiana University Press, 1990) 98.

34. Leonard W. Doob, *Patterning of Time* (New Haven and London: Yale University Press, 1971) 88.

35. Hannibal Gerald Duncan, *Immigration and Assimilation* (Boston: Heath, 1933) 519.

36. Van Zyl, "Socio-Semiotic of Performance" 99.

37. Walter Prichard Eaton, "Broadway and National Life," *Freeman* 1 (27 March 1920): 18.

38. Elizabeth Burns, *Theatricality* (London: Longmans, 1972) 23.

39. Esslin, *Field of Drama* 70.

40. Daniel Stern, "On Kinesic Analysis," *The Drama Review* 17 (1973): 117.

15

The *Poet Lore* Plays: A New Chinese Voice . . . But How New?

Dave Williams

The Chinese have been a significant presence in American society ever since they began to arrive in large numbers in the early 1850s. As their population increased and spread across the country, they carried with them drama performed in their own language. Within a short time, both San Francisco and New York City had many thriving Chinese-language theatres; such venues existed in many smaller cities as well. Lively and well distributed as it was, however, their theatrical activity remained largely apart from the surrounding Euro American culture. With the exception of one script (now lost), it was not until the 1920s that Americans of Chinese descent began to write and distribute plays in English. Between 1922 and 1924, not merely one but three different Chinese playwrights published their works in the literary quarterly *Poet Lore*. Besides appearing roughly simultaneously, they resemble each other in theme and, most importantly, in their image of the Chinese.

One might suppose that after decades of unchallenged misrepresentation by the dominant culture, Chinese playwrights would use the occasion of taking control of their own representation within dramatic literature to strike a blow against racist stereotyping, or at the very least to neutralize the content of the stereotype itself. They did not do this. Although their plays were a significant step forward merely by virtue of their appearance, their content diffuses whatever progressive impact they might have had. The texts do not address the issue of racial stereotyping at all; in fact, their most remarkable feature is their almost complete conformity to the prevalent Euro American image of the Chinese. Two additional generations of Chinese would face distortion (if not outright insult) in Euro American drama before a far angrier group of Chinese dramatists would rebel against such stereotyping in the 1970s.

A bit of historical background will be germane to the situation facing the first Chinese authors to write in English. By the 1920s, two Euro American constructions of the Chinese had each prevailed and then subsided. The first and more popular arose when the Chinese in the Pacific Coast states became sufficiently numerous to be perceived as an economic and social menace to Euro American laborers. The earliest plays which indirectly addressed "the Chinese question" were almost all melodramas set on frontier ranches and mining camps. The Chinese in such plays appeared stereotypically as powerless, emasculated buffoons. They wore the bizarre and effeminate queue, spoke faulty English, held menial jobs, and quite often appeared to be clumsy or stupid. They functioned within their respective texts almost entirely as local color or comic relief. They hardly ever affected the central plot; it is worth noting that the single play that placed such a figure at the center, Bret Harte and Mark Twain's *Ah Sin*, failed both critically and commercially. This image flourished most abundantly during the 1880s, but it did endure sporadically until the 1960s (in a somewhat more humanized manifestation) in the persona of Hop Sing on the televised western *Bonanza*.

A subsequent and considerably less widespread image derived from the urban Chinese criminal, whose supposedly exotic nature had captured the imagination of newspaper reporters and readers. A character constructed according to this stereotype had power his predecessor had lacked, but he used it only for clearly evil purposes. He not only smoked opium (sometimes onstage), but he also used it to seduce Euro American women; hidden from Euro American morality, society, and police in the mysterious catacombs of New York's or San Francisco's Chinatown, he survived by gambling, pimping, blackmail, and violence. In further contrast to the earlier depiction, Chinese characters of the second type often drove the plots of their respective plays by their villainy; they were essential rather than marginalized. Roughly speaking, the popularity of this image flourished in drama before World War I, although the much later Fu Manchu movies demonstrated its wide appeal as well. In short, the Chinese appeared in Euro American drama first as comic outlanders and then as stock villains.

By the early 1920s, however, both these images had largely been supplanted by a third, which portrayed the Chinese as neither ridiculous nor depraved. In this version, all Chinese possessed exquisite sensitivity to morality, ethics, and propriety. Successful plays such as *The Yellow Jacket* and *The Daughter of Heaven* showed Chinese reverently following their ancient Confucian tradition, respecting their families, and speaking in condensed, pithy aphorisms. This change in public opinion is a classic case of a pendulum that had swung too far in one direction swinging back too far in the other.

On the surface this third portrayal would seem to be far more complimentary to the Chinese than the previous two, and hence an improvement. However, even a cursory examination reveals that the case is entirely otherwise. The same Euro American racial animus that had created the Chinese stooge and the Chinese villain found a new expression in creating the Chinese philosopher-dandy. The animus (or at the very least, a sense of insuperable racial difference) does, however, manifest itself with greater subtlety in the third portrayal. A very brief and necessarily superficial discussion of two issues raised by plays propagating this third image of the Chinese, self-sacrifice and modernity, will demonstrate this point quite clearly.

One representative play which prominently features the theme of self-sacrifice is George C. Hazleton and J. Harry Benrimo's piece *The Yellow Jacket*, which premiered in New York City in the autumn of 1912. The play presents a dynastic struggle in ancient China. Chee Moo, mother of the rightful heir to the throne, is forced to flee the court to escape the machinations of her evil rival. Persuaded by a spirit that she must die to save her son, she bites her finger and uses her own blood to write his lineage and destiny on a yellow jacket. Quite slowly and painfully, she then expires from loss of blood. In the remainder of the play, many characters praise her bravery and nobility. The approval of the authors for her action was matched by that of the New York critics and audience. The play received good notices, ran for six weeks, and was successfully revived twice more during the 1920s.

Another 1912 play, Judith Gautier and Pierre Loti's *The Daughter of Heaven*, also features the theme of self-sacrifice, with a slightly more abstract flavor. The title character, the Ming Princess, escapes the invading Qing armies, but later realizes that by not dying with her soldiers, she has irrevocably compromised her integrity. She not only refuses the Qing Emperor's sincere and loving offer of marriage but commits suicide in his presence. Her death scene reaches operatic length and intensity. Instead of laying down her life for an heir, the Ming Princess kills herself purely for the sake of morality and tradition. *The Daughter of Heaven* ran even longer than *The Yellow Jacket*, and exerted greater influence; for example, New York society women copied the hairstyle of the Empress and gave lavish parties using a Chinese theme. These two plays represent simultaneous and somewhat extreme examples, but they were far from the only texts up to the early 1920s to present the supposed tendency of the Chinese to sacrifice themselves. Significantly, such sacrifice appeared as a sign of racial difference, impossible for any Westerners to understand, much less accomplish; moreover, it was usually framed so as to elicit not only wistfulness over lost human potential but admiration as well.

The problematic aspects of the theme of sacrifice are almost too obvious to require comment. First, it derived from an assumption that the Chinese differed from Westerners fundamentally, essentially, and all but incomprehensibly. Such statements are never value free; the implicit comparison always favors the culture that produces it and for whose members its consumption is intended. This overemphasized demarcation almost certainly masks fears that the outlander may attempt assimilation. The connection may seem far-fetched, but it is worth remembering that these fears also found expression in the many state laws forbidding marriage between Chinese and Euro Americans; these remained on the books during the 1920s and beyond. Intentionally or not, by portraying the Chinese mentality as completely alien, Euro American playwrights created (or reflected) a climate hostile to racial and cultural mixture.

Even more important, these plays and others like them explicitly praise the Chinese for using their own destructive impulses against themselves. Quite clearly, the implicit hope is that they would not turn these impulses against Euro Americans. The offering of praise by a dominant culture to a minority for that minority's own suicides can hardly be construed as positive.

A second prejudicial theme in this third image of the Chinese involves China's relation to modernity. As depicted in Euro American drama of the first two decades of the twentieth century, the land remains totally and perpetually static. People contentedly follow the ways of their ancestors, hallowed by decades or even millennia of tradition. In actuality, by the 1920s China had made significant progress in implementing and adopting Western technology in such diverse fields as communication, transportation, aviation, and medicine. No Euro American playwright, however, so much as acknowledged this development by, for example, presenting a character who cuts off his queue and forsakes the classics in favor of engineering. The reason for the disjuncture between China's actual, dynamic modernization and its utterly stagnant image in Euro

American drama is not difficult to find. For years, the West had scorned the backwardness not only of China but also of the East in general. By defeating the Russians in 1905, the Japanese had demonstrated the might of an Asian country equipped with Western technology. But Japan was relatively small; the thought of an Eastern country of over four hundred million people possessing modern equipment seems to have been literally unthinkable. Real China aroused real anxieties; playwrights who hoped to soothe their audiences therefore created the image of China as idyllic, backward, and forever fated to remain so.

One further bit of necessary background involves the sources that led to the emergence of the third image of the Chinese in Euro American drama. There are at least four. First, as the frontier itself disappeared, the entire genre of the frontier melodrama did so as well, largely taking the buffoonish image of the Chinese with it. Second, the 1900 Boxer Rebellion in China furnished extremely unfavorable images of the Chinese. During the actual turmoil journalistic reports of slaughter, mutilation, rape, and cannibalism flooded the newspapers; longer and more detailed accounts appeared for years thereafter. Euro American dramatists who wanted to depict the Chinese unfavorably found it impossible to compete with reality. A third factor, the growing Western disillusionment with Christianity, caused Western spiritual seekers to turn to the East. The infatuation of many Westerners for Lao-tze and Confucius caused them to overlook the realities of China's internal chaos, international helplessness, and low standard of material life. Finally, the emergence of early feminism threatened traditional Western gender roles. As Western women were striving for equality, men opposed to their cause would find relief in portrayals of a traditional, unchallenged, and unchallengeable gender hierarchy. The second-class status of Chinese women in Euro American drama fulfilled two purposes simultaneously; they gratified male fantasies and rebuked rebellious Western women. By the 1920s then the image of the Chinese as refined, polite, deferential, hierarchical, traditional, and philosophical had become the prevalent racial stereotype in the Euro American theatre.

This was how matters stood when three authors of Chinese descent sequentially presented their plays in the early years of the decade in the literary quarterly *Poet Lore*. This periodical was founded in 1889 and continues to publish today. Its circulation has always been minuscule, but it was multicultural in advance of its time, publishing English-language poetry and fiction from authors worldwide. Its eclectic format made it a logical venue for the three works to be discussed in the rest of this chapter with special relation to the issues presented previously.

The first relevant play is *The Wedded Husband* by Shen Hung, which appeared in the spring of 1921. The first of the play's three scenes opens in the summer of 1912 in Tianjian, then besieged by a plague. The situation of the main characters powerfully strikes the thematic note of tradition. Lord Wang, a widower, has arranged the marriage of his twenty-five-year-old daughter, Lady Wang, to Master Chen, the son of an old friend who had helped him escape poverty years ago. She, however, loves another man she has known from childhood, Master Yang. Despite her unhappiness with this marriage, she realizes that her emotions alone cannot guide her actions: "It is a daughter's duty to obey her father. Our ethics teaches us so. If I should refuse him—the people—what would they say?"[1] She has a short conversation with Mr. Yang before he departs on a self-imposed exile to Mongolia. Rather than addressing the situation directly, still less their feelings about it, their talk is completely superficial. After he leaves, she faints from the strain of her repressed emotions.

During the actual ceremony in the next scene, Lady Wang drops a mirror. As in the West, Chinese tradition counts this as an extremely bad omen, especially during a wedding. She then faints once more, but this time, her distress is physical; she has caught the plague. Even though the interrupted wedding remains incomplete, Master Chen counts himself as her husband and chooses to remain with her in her quarantine house. Lady Wang's maid also stays.

Eight weeks later Lady Wang is slowly convalescing from her delirium and does not recall that Master Chen had caught the plague from her and died. After she learns this from her maid, she feels awe for him, displacing her previous disdain. Lord Wang, now willing to permit her to marry the man she truly loves, commands her to wear red clothing (the traditional color for weddings and good fortune) to meet the returning Master Yang. She instead appears in the heavy white clothing symbolizing mourning and tells Master Yang simply but eloquently that she will follow the tradition that a Chinese woman can marry only once. She intends to honor her dead husband by remaining a widow for the rest of her life. All the principals reluctantly accept her decision as the curtain falls.

The play's most prominent theme is the nobility of sacrifice. Practically everyone in the play subordinates his or her own personal desires to received notions of morality. Lord Wang feels he cannot do otherwise than offer his daughter to Master Chen in order to satisfy his debt of gratitude to the young man's father. Purely to protect the wedding festivities from his dejection, Master Yang takes a 600-mile camel journey. Lady Wang, despite her genuine and enduring love for him, first undergoes an arranged marriage to another man in order to uphold the family honor, and then resigns herself to a lifetime of loneliness by insisting on its validity. Young Master Chen makes the greatest sacrifice of all as his sense of duty to Lady Wang costs him his life. Even Lady Wang's maid exemplifies this trait in both deed and word. By choosing to stay with Lady Wang during her quarantine, she jeopardizes her own personal safety; moreover, she strongly protests when Lady Wang at first appears willing to marry Master Yang. The author has constructed his plot so that these sacrifices form a prominent and interlocked pattern.

The secondary theme of the play furnishes the reason for the "necessity" of such sacrifice; this is the postulated importance of tradition to the Chinese. The word *custom* appears in the speech of virtually every character at one point or another; *tradition* is nearly as prevalent. Despite differences in gender, personality, and social class, the characters unanimously consider custom as the only proper guide to behavior, regardless of its harmful effects. With one exception, no one questions, let alone defies, the established Confucian guidelines. The most progressive character in the play is Master Yang, who at one point does comment: "Hm, everything duty and tradition. It's absolute nonsense."[2] Even he, however, makes sure to fulfill his duty to social propriety. *The Wedded Husband* thus presents the Chinese as inhumanly noble and hidebound by tradition. This image of the Chinese is in complete conformity with contemporary plays about the Chinese written by Euro American dramatists.

The second play to be discussed, *The Son Left in the Plantation of Mulberry Trees*, by Chin Lin Chen, appeared in *Poet Lore* in the winter 1922 issue. This brief work presents a single episode rather than an entire story; even so, the themes of sacrifice and tradition show quite strongly. A young father, Teng Po Tao, is on a pilgrimage to his brother's tomb with both his son and the son of his dead brother. During their trip bandits invade the whole area, causing them to flee. The boys become tired, and Teng Po Tao realizes that he has the strength to save only one. He tricks his son into climbing a mulberry tree and then binds him to the trunk. Like Chee Moo, he bites his finger to draw blood and then writes a message on the boy's coat. He reasons as follows: "If the rebels overtake us and kill my son, I must not complain, but if they kill my nephew, how shall I ever meet my brother when I pass to the kingdom of Terrors?"[3] Because a Westerner would probably make the opposite choice for more "natural" reasons, the author presents the Chinese as beings with an entirely different mental constitution. Teng Po Tao then carries his nephew off. Unlike most plays dealing with sacrifices made by the Chinese, this brief piece ends happily. After he and his nephew have left the scene, another relative rescues his son before the bandits can arrive. Despite its brevity and its unexpectedly upbeat ending, the work foregrounds Chinese difference, sacrifice, and subservience to tradition.

The final and most complex play to be discussed is *The Marvelous Romance of Wen Chun-Chin*, by C. C. Hsiung, from the summer 1924 issue. The title character is a young woman who has disguised herself as a man for years to become eligible for the imperial examinations. She has even deluded her two male companions in her studies, Wei Ta and Tu San. Wishing to marry one of them, she shoots a bird and resolves to marry the man who brings it to her; they remain ignorant of both her larger purpose and this specific plan. On the eve of the trio's departure for the capital, Wei Ta brings her the bird.

Before the trip, however, Wen Chun-Chin's mother falls ill. Rather than take the examination for which she has diligently prepared for years, she instead devotes herself to her mother's cure. She goes to seek a special herb on a distant mountain guarded by a demon called the Evil One. She defeats him in battle, obtains the herb, and rests in a nearby inn. Tu San arrives and reveals that *he* had actually found the bird first and given it to Wei Ta to present to Wen Chun-Chin. This throws her into great confusion; in addition, Fu Hsiao-Chai, a young woman staying at the inn, thinks Wen Chun-Chin is a man and has become infatuated with her. Meanwhile, Tu San has defeated Wei Ta on the examination and received an appointment as a provincial viceroy. Despite its reputed powers, Wen Chun-Chin's medicine fails to heal her mother; Fu Hsiao-Chai then appears, and uses magic to cure her. The play ends with the betrothal of Wen Chun-Chin to Tu San and a hasty engagement between Wei Ta and Fu Hsiao-Chai.

The themes of sacrifice and tradition do appear in this play, but they receive less emphasis than in the previous two works. As to sacrifice, Wei Ta praises Wen Chun-Chin's voluntary loss of her years of preparation: "I admire your devotion to your mother. You are the most virtuous fellow I know of."[4] The reliance on tradition occurs in her fight with the Evil One; Wen Chun-Chin encourages herself with the most unusual battle cry of "Filial piety dreads no foe."[5] In addition, before Fu Hsiao-Chai can enter the house of Wen Chun-Chin, the characters discuss whether or not the special circumstances allow them to transgress the custom forbidding a young woman to enter the house of her betrothed before the wedding. Finally, in the background of the play stands the official examination apparatus, an apt representative of millennia of Chinese tradition.

Sacrifice and tradition, though present, are comparatively muted. In their place are two other themes which the other *Poet Lore* plays lack but which also appear in Euro American works such as *The Yellow Jacket*. These aspects of *The Marvelous Romance*, although novel in the work of a Chinese playwright, also conform to the received idea of the Chinese in Euro American culture.

First, crucial points of the plot turn on magic. As in the previous examples, the surface content and the inner content of this idea contain a contradiction. The Chinese are seen to possess special powers Westerners lack. Magic, however, represents prelogical mental processes; when a dominant culture (or gender) defines another as magical, it removes the minority from the domain of reason. The importance of magic in this play is that it caters to the Euro American hope that China and the Chinese would remain "primitive." In this condition, it could constitute no threat to Western logic, technology, or economic dominance.

Second, C. C. Hsiung employs many of the stage conventions of traditional Chinese drama. For example, all the major characters in the play introduce themselves directly to the audience in their first speech. In turn, they all describe their current situations and future aspirations. To take another example, the combat between Wen Chun-Chin and the Evil One is presented as a stylized ballet rather than as a realistic and brutal fight. Upon the defeat and death of the Evil One, the black-clad Property Man waves a red flag in front of him, and he then simply stands up and exits. There is no indication that this play was ever performed, but even on the page these conventions create a powerful alienation effect for the reader. They differ so sharply from Western theatrical practice that they emphasize the difference between Chinese and Euro American cultures. Such an overdetermined demarcation would therefore reassure the Euro American audience of the difficulty, if not the impossibility, of these cultures ever mingling.

One final question regarding the *Poet Lore* plays involves their accuracy. Here they also follow their Euro American models in their lack of fidelity to reality. The Chinese were no more a nation of noble, etiquette-bound esthetes in 1920 than they had been one of clownish coolies or opium-inspired criminals half a century before. Perhaps sensing this, two of the three *Poet Lore* authors do stress the fidelity of their respective pictures of the Chinese to real life. Shen Hung subtitled his piece "A Realistic Chinese Play,"[6] and C. C. Hsiung's brief introduction to his play claims descent from an actual ancient text. The *Poet Lore* plays therefore seem calculated more to assuage Euro American racial anxieties than to portray the Chinese accurately. Evidence of the falsity of these protestations of authenticity can be found by comparing these works to a contemporary play written in Chinese and performed to great acclaim in China. Hu Shih's *The Greatest Event in Life*, written in 1919, presents a situation similar to that of *The Wedded Husband*. In Hu Shih's play, however, the young woman about to be trapped in an arranged marriage defies tradition, augury, and her family, and runs off with a lover of her own choice. Although arranged marriages no doubt continued among the Chinese, this play did represent a new and different spirit which had in fact arisen in the China of the early twentieth century. Its novelty and defiance form a most striking contrast to the complacency of the *Poet Lore* plays.

To conclude, the three *Poet Lore* plays do represent something of an advance in Chinese claiming control of their own representation, but this advance was seriously compromised. It is not surprising that the first American dramatists of Chinese descent would reject the images of the outlandish buffoon and the sinister Chinatown criminal. Their willingness to embrace the third, seemingly positive image, however, seems a questionable strategy at best. By so doing, they acquiesced in images which were twice problematic, first, by reason of their origin within Euro American rather than Chinese culture, and second, by their retrograde and implicitly anti-Chinese content. Perhaps they had no alternative; certainly, Euro Americans of the 1920s would not have accepted a more confrontational self-generated image of the Chinese. Social conditions for such an occurrence would not be ripe until half a century later. Although important trailblazers, therefore, the *Poet Lore* authors largely squandered their opportunity to present a new Chinese voice in drama.

NOTES

1. Shen Hung, *The Wedded Husband*, *Poet Lore* 32.1: 116.

2. Hung, *Wedded Husband* 134.

3. Chin Lin Chen, *The Son Left in the Plantation of Mulberry Trees*, *Poet Lore* 33.4: 595.

4. C. C. Hsiung, *The Marvelous Romance of Wen Chun-Chin*, *Poet Lore* 35.2: 301.

5. Hsiung, *Marvelous Romance* 304.

6. Hung, *Wedded Husband* 110.

Part II:

Theatre and Set Design

16

Against the Tide: Mordecai Gorelik and the New York Theatre of the 1920s—*Processional, Nirvana, The Moon is a Gong*, and *Loudspeaker*

Anne Fletcher

Mordecai Gorelik's Broadway career commenced in the 1920s—decade of *What Price Glory, Desire Under the Elms*, and *They Knew What They Wanted*. This maverick designer and theorist lost his chance at lasting fame, almost before he had begun, as the result of designing sets for plays that would come to fall outside the scope of the accepted dramatic canon—plays that were production dependent, often inchoate in form, and often unpopular in their own time.

In 1925, however, when *Processional* premiered, neither playwright John Howard Lawson nor designer Gorelik had any inkling of how the political or dramaturgical tides would turn. In fact 1925 was a very good year for Gorelik. He became a Broadway designer with *Processional*, "struck out on his own" with a production of *King Hunger*, and was complimented, if not employed, by the "father" of American Expressionism, Elmer Rice.[1]

Gorelik's participation in *Processional* catapulted him into the realm of Broadway design—but his designs for *Processional* caused him to be "typed" and to experience difficulty obtaining future employment. Nevertheless, *Processional* was the ideal production for "Max" Gorelik, and Max Gorelik was the ideal designer for *Processional*.

This production afforded Gorelik the opportunity to put together the popular and the political. His work on it allowed him not only to display his talent for the garish and caricatured design of burlesque but also to test his ideas about the audience-stage dialectic. In designing *Processional*, he could draw on various influences: (1) Burlesque and Vaudeville—where he earned money painting scenery and derision from designers with whom he worked in the legitimate theatre;[2] (2) Expressionism (both American and European)—or his interpretation of it; and (3) the Russian cabaret (which he had learned about through his work with designer Sergei Soudeikine).

Lawson's exposure had been to jazz, vaudeville, and the French cabaret and avant-garde theatre. Both men desired to "break down the fourth wall" and, like Oliver Sayler, were advocates of the "Theatre of Let's Pretend."[3] Lawson and

Gorelik were interested not only in playing directly to the audience, but in provocation as well. Each wanted to goad society into not only recognizing its flaws but also working to alleviate them.

Lawson subtitled *Processional* "A Jazz Symphony of American Life" and described his technique as "vaudevillesque."[4] His characters resemble the stock characters of vaudeville, but they were created with a different purpose in mind.[5] Mordecai Gorelik knew exactly what to do with the sets for *Processional* and could articulate the reasoning behind his nonillusionistic style of production every bit as well as Lawson could explain his dramaturgy—perhaps better. Like Lawson, Gorelik was frustrated with the illusionistic theatre. Thus, for each act of *Processional* he designed a two-dimensional drop.

Although he followed Lawson's stage directions explicitly, Gorelik's designs were his own invention. The advertisements, for example, in act 1—symbolic of a capitalistic society—were Gorelik's addition. These advertisements served as a frame, not only for act 1, but for the entire production.[6] He explained his style: "Leaf tormentors are a tradition in burlesque houses . . . no matter what the design is, the color has the kick of a stallion mule. Loud color, wrong color, dirty, heavy, wicked, and alive."[7]

An early pencil sketch for *Processional* shows that Gorelik erased the traditional straight line that indicated where the stage ends and wings begin, replacing it with a wavy line and indicating, again, that he wished to utilize the cut-wing convention of vaudeville.[8]

The *Processional* set was a success, even if the play was not: "As realized, Gorelik's setting amplified the inherent theatricality of Lawson's script."[9] The actors were literally forced into a presentational style: "And when . . . Lawson saw the acting styles were beginning to coalesce, he credited Gorelik's sets."[10] Gorelik's effort did not escape the critics, either. Even Lee Simonson, the Theatre Guild's regular designer, often at odds with Gorelik, championed the designs in an article subtitled "Scenic Director of Theatre Guild Explains Effect of Bizarre Scenery by Gorelik."[11]

Gorelik believed that he was developing an indigenous American style of production, one that incorporated aspects of popular entertainment with elements of the legitimate stage. "I think I am on the road to become eventually the first scene designer with anything that might be called an American technique."[12]

Despite his successes in 1925, 1926 started as a lean year for Gorelik. In his own words, "The comedown was terrific" as he made the rounds of producers' offices.[13] Gorelik was repeatedly turned away with comments such as "when we start doing burlesque shows we'll let you know."[14] His designs for *Processional* and *King-Hunger* were even called, disparagingly, "nut stuff."[15] So at the age of not yet twenty-five Gorelik found himself typed and unemployed. Little did he know then that this typing would persist throughout his career, prompting him to comment in 1988, " 'overshadowed' may be the word for my existence on Broadway, where no one ever asked me to design a musical. I was considered 'special' and told 'Don't call us; we'll call you.' "[16]

In the spring of 1926 Lawson and Gorelik were reunited professionally for Lawson's new play, *Nirvana*. Through Lawson, Gorelik came to know John Dos Passos. As *Nirvana* and Dos Passos's *The Moon is a Gong* were being written and produced, the seeds were being sown for a much more political theatre company, the New Playwrights.

The production process for *Nirvana* began with a sound rejection from the Theatre Guild on the grounds that the play was "too offensive."[17] The Guild had been wary even of *Processional*, and *Nirvana* lacked the humor and popular entertainment elements that saved the former from being didactic. In *Nirvana*, Lawson unilaterally satirized almost every Western religion—and modern literature and science to boot.

Nirvana is a difficult play with a nebulous dramatic form. The production, despite an elaborate program note in which Lawson set forth his intentions, met with derision from the critics. Lawson has been said to have "baffled the critics . . . with an expressionistic exploration of sex and religion."[18]

Nirvana's plot revolves around the characters Dr. Alonzo Weed, a ruthless experimenter with electric shock who seems to earn his living largely though performing illegal abortions; Bill, his brother, a hopeless philanderer and modern novelist; Janet Milgrim, one of Bill's lovers; and Priscilla, his cousin whose youth and innocence attract Bill to her. The cast is completed by Aunt Bertha, a devout Christian Scientist; Miss Pendergast, Dr. Weed's very Catholic nurse; Dr. Gulick, an Evangelist preacher; Holz, a philanthropist of sorts who made his money in opium trade; and a host of cocktail-party-goers. Janet's husband is killed; she is accused and arrested. Priscilla falls from Dr. Weed's rooftop garden; Dr. Weed tries to save her through electric shock therapy; and Bill finds religion and prays for her recovery. As Priscilla lies unconscious, near death, each of the characters, each deplorable for one reason or another, espouses his or her particular religious or scientific beliefs.

Apart from the cocktail-party scene, when Lawson is at his satirical best, the dialogue is weak (and trite) throughout. Even a close reading fails to disclose whether the characters' truisms are intended by the playwright as tongue in cheek or are meant to be taken seriously. In his introduction to Lawson's *Loud Speaker*, Joseph Wood Krutch refers to *Nirvana* as a tragedy. The script begs for production to illuminate the author's intent; but in production it failed as well. Lawson withdrew the play after four performances, never permitting publication of the text.[19] While, with the aid of the popular entertainment idiom, Lawson had managed to combine a number of themes fairly successfully in *Processional*, he was incapable of unifying *Nirvana* into a coherent piece.

Despite *Nirvana*'s shortcomings, some attributes of the play were of obvious appeal to Gorelik. The theme of science versus religion and the concept of an afterlife were ideas Gorelik would explore much later in his own plays. *Nirvana*'s references to shooting men into space bore the kind of science fiction quality Gorelik admired in *R.U.R.*, for example.

Technically speaking, the sound and lighting effects necessary for the depiction of Dr. Weed's office/laboratory would interest Gorelik. Lawson's description of the setting for act 1 refers to "all sorts of lighting and electrical apparatus: Alpine ray, X-ray, rhythmic current generator, high frequency generator, fluoroscope, galvanic table for electrical control," and "an enamel operating table of the latest mode."[20]

Once again Lawson gave Gorelik an enormous amount of leeway and credit. Critics did too. Echoing Lawson's praise, Alexander Woollcott even averred that "the best contribution . . . is young Mordecai Gorelik's scenery."[21]

In terms of Gorelik's development, *Nirvana* is far more important with regard to his theory than his practice. The settings for the production were appropriate and functional, and the rooftop scene was quite beautiful; but the show did little to test, challenge, or strengthen Gorelik's skill as a designer. It did offer him an opportunity to further his theory of the theatre, and the production program gave him a forum in which to publish his latest thoughts.

John Dos Passos's *The Moon is a Gong* (also titled *The Garbage Man*) opened at the Cherry Lane Theatre a scant ten days after *Nirvana* opened. Gorelik worked on the two designs simultaneously, a practice common among designers. What is unique about this situation is the fact that Lawson and Dos Passos (and by now Gorelik) were not only friends but also men who were fighting together to create a new form of dramatic literature and a new style of production.

The Moon is a Gong was Dos Passos's first play, deeply affected by his admiration for Lawson. In *Dialogue in American Drama*, Ruby Cohn pinpoints the major problem with the piece: "Dos Passos . . . saw Expressionism as a more viable form than realism in which to register social protest. German Expressionist plays tend to be stridently social . . . or, stemming more directly from Strindberg, to focus on the poetic quest of the protagonist. . . . Dos Passos mixes the two streams, and writes a confusing play."[22]

Not only does Dos Passos mix these two strains of expressionism, but he also adds, emulating Lawson, a presentational, musical theatre element to his play as well.

The Moon is a Gong is cast in two acts, each comprising four short scenes. It chronicles the escape of Tom and Jane from their stuffy, privileged upbringing; their separation (during which time Jane becomes a Broadway star and Tom a bum); and their reunion. Upon his return, Tom recounts his adventures, and he and Jane agree that all they ever wanted was right there in their own backyard. The play is a *Bildungsroman* of sorts and anticipates the widely acclaimed growing-up musical, *The Fantasticks*. However, one gets the sense that Dos Passos's characters are just a little too old to be experiencing such adolescent nonsense.

Very little has been written on the play, and, as is the case with Lawson's *Nirvana*, it is difficult to ascertain the degree of intentional comedy inherent in the script. Dos Passos's production note for the printed text praises Edward Massey's spirited and presentational staging of the original production at Harvard, indicating the playwright's desire to foreground comedy and stylization.[23]

Most often, characters in *The Moon is a Gong* dance their entrances. Sometimes groups of characters break into the equivalent of production numbers. Dos Passos, from his association with Lawson (and Gorelik), knew very well the effect such techniques can have on the audience-stage relationship. (Dos Passos's adulation of *Processional* and its audience-stage dialectic is illustrated in his article "Is the Realistic Theatre Obsolete?")[24] The similarities between *The Moon is a Gong* and *Processional* did not go unnoticed by critics whose consensus was that the Dos Passos piece fell short of Lawson's work. Burns Mantle, for example, described the play as "out of 'Processional' by 'Dr. Caligari.' "[25] Once again, Gorelik's sets were singled out for praise, for example, by Gilbert Gabriel, who described them as "stunning, quite, all of them."[26]

The Moon is a Gong is not a good play, but, like *Nirvana*, it is significant in a study of Gorelik. The repeated image of the moon as a gong would have set Gorelik's metaphor mind going. The recurrent sounds of the power plant and industry that serve as an auditory backdrop to the piece would have intrigued him. The "prosperity parade" and other social class issues were in keeping with Gorelik's proletariat leanings. (Nobody loved a parade more than Max Gorelik!) Of course, the destruction of the "fourth wall" was compatible with Gorelik's theoretical work to date. All this coupled with his chance to share ideas with Lawson and Dos Passos would have prompted Gorelik to design the piece.

Nirvana and *The Moon is a Gong* foreshadow the involvement of Lawson, Dos Passos, and Gorelik in the New Playwrights Theatre. It is fitting to begin a discussion of the New Playwrights Theatre at its end, for not only was the entire enterprise short-lived, but Gorelik's direct participation in it was even briefer. He designed only *Loud Speaker* by Lawson, the company's initial letterhead and logo, and the costumes for Michael Gold's *Fiesta*. His experience with the company helped him to further develop his theory of the theatre, but, practically speaking, his dismissal from it left him high and dry once again in terms of employment.

Lawson's *Loud Speaker*, the company's first production, is more in the spirit of *Processional* than *Nirvana*. With the New Playwrights' blessing, Gorelik pulled out all the stops for the setting of the broad political farce with *commedia dell'arte* characterizations. The set was a maze of chutes and ladders and a series of red and green multileveled platforms with connecting stairs. Only the fourth example of constructivism to reach the American stage,[27] the setting was more widely acclaimed than the script. Critics recognized the inherent humor in Gorelik's design far more readily than that of Lawson's script. Words and phrases such as "cheerfully painted,"[28] "amusing,"[29] "good-natured abandon,"[30] and "poking fun"[31] permeate criticism of the piece. Even John Anderson from the *New York Post*, who found fault with the play, acknowledged Gorelik's use of "the stage in opulent satire itself."[32]

Loud Speaker's plot concerns politician Harry Collins's bid for the office of governor of the state of New York. Collins represents the hypocrisy of those in power in the American government. He is a man with a past—namely, a cheap mistress from Atlantic City who appears and provides a dream sequence of sorts for Collins. Collins is a sometimes humorous, often pathetic, example of someone who lives by situational ethics. The entire Collins clan is composed of stereotypical characters of the 1920s, providing a collectively unflattering backdrop to Collins's candidacy. His wife is accompanied by an occult guru to whom she is devoted; his daughter is a flapper of the first degree. The play's straight man is the inept but personable Johnnie Dunne, an investigative reporter whose mission is to uncover the smut behind the Collins façade. In a neat plot twist Dunne not only turns out to be the mysterious and intriguing "Viscount" Clare Collins met on one of her world cruises, but he falls in love with her.

Collins meets his demise as he is about to give a speech. He becomes befuddled and walks right off the platform. The scene switches abruptly to Johnnie and Clare in a boat, in China, on their honeymoon. The honeymoon is over, and they are brimming with recriminations. They plan to return to New York and become carbon copies of Collins and his wife—a sorry proposition and apparently the message of the play.

The play's professed style is farce, and in two scenes in particular the script succeeds in achieving the fast pace necessary for this form. The script is blessed with some terrifically funny lines. However, Lawson's style is characteristically inconsistent. As with his other works, *Loud Speaker*'s potential could be truly reached only in performance. In his introduction to the printed text Joseph Wood Krutch alludes to this production-dependency.[33]

Precisely those elements that confounded critics and confused audiences would have fascinated Mordecai Gorelik. The same sort of experimentation with presentational theatre that had served as the underpinning for *Processional* and *The Moon is a Gong* applied to *Loud Speaker*: an orchestra playing in full view of the audience, characters exiting and entering through the house aisles, and dance numbers. Original music was composed for the production, and the cast was backed up by a black jazz band, the Imperial Serenaders.[34] Clare and Johnnie sing one love duet that is humorously juxtaposed with their playing craps. A romantic ballad, "Creamy Moon, Dreamy Moon," provided the ironic background for their quarreling in the last scene.[35]

Given the encouragement of the playwright once again, Gorelik could experiment all he liked with the constructivist setting and with the relationship of the audience to stage.

By the time *New Theatres for Old* was published in 1940, Gorelik had come to be considered America's primary advocate of presentational staging as the method of the future—and of the Epic theatre of Bertolt Brecht. But the American theatre even by the 1920s was entrenched in a tradition of realism. American drama would find its force in Freud, not Marx, and in Stanislavski, not Meyerhold. As the dramaturgical tide turned, Mordecai Gorelik would continue to swim against it for the duration of his seventy-five-play-year career.

NOTES

1. In 1925, Gorelik completed sketches and models for Elmer Rice's *The Subway*. While Rice approved of them, and Gorelik went so far as to have Throckmorton (because of his shop) draw up an estimate, Throckmorton was awarded the job. ("1925" Floder, p. 365 red pencil; p. 406 lead pencil, Gorelik Papers, Sarasota, FL, now housed in Special Collections, Morris Library, Southern Illinois University at Carbondale).

2. Gorelik's diary entries indicate Cleon Throckmorton's attitude toward his work at the Novelty Scenic Studio (6 May 1922) and Robert Edmond Jones's disdain for the "old vaudeville stuff" (1 January 1925).

3. Oliver Sayler, *Our American Theatre* (New York: Brentano's, 1923) 220–232.

4. John Howard Lawson, Preface to *Processional* (New York: Thomas Seltzer, 1925) Title page and v.

5. Beverle Bloch, *John Howard Lawson's Processional: Modernism in American Theatre in the Twenties*, diss., University of Denver, 1988, 54: "The presence of these characters on the legitimate stage calls attention to their Theatricality, and . . . reminds the audience that they are watching a theatrical performance."

6. Bloch, *Lawson's Processional* 118.

7. Mordecai Gorelik, "On 'Processional,'" *New York World* 8 February 1925: 8–9.

8. William Brasmer, "Early Scene Designs of Mordecai Gorelik," *Ohio State University Theatre Collection Bulletin* 12 (1965): 46.

9. Bloch, *Lawson's Processional* 119.

10. Ibid. 122.

11. Lee Simonson, "Sets for 'Processional' Came from Satire on Vaudeville Method," *New York Post* n.d., Special Collections, Morris Library, Southern Illinois University at Carbondale.

12. Gorelik, Diary, January n.d., 1925.

13. Gorelik, *Toward a Larger Theatre* (Lanham, MD: University Press of America, 1988) 6. Diary entries from 1925 and 1926 indicate that Gorelik was under consideration for several design assignments which he lost to Throckmorton, Geddes, and Mielziner. Unable to obtain work for several months, Gorelik was "in a slump" and often compared his social and financial status to that of the aforementioned designers and others.

14. Gorelik, "Up From Burlesque," *New York Evening Post* 8 October 1932: S5

15. Ibid.

16. Letter from Mordecai Gorelik to the author, 27 November 1987.

17. James Palmer, "Mordecai Gorelik's Theory of the Theatre," diss., Southern Illinois University at Carbondale, 1967, 64.

18. W. David Sievers, *Freud on Broadway: A History of Psychoanalysis and the American Drama* (1955; Cooper Square, 1970) 142.

19. Gary Carr, *Left Side of Paradise: The Screenwriting of John Howard Lawson* (Ann Arbor, MI: UMI Research Press, 1984) 6.

20. John Howard Lawson, *Nirvana*, ts., courtesy Special Collections, Morris Library, Southern Illinois University at Carbondale.

21. Palmer, "Gorelik's Theory" 66–67; and Lawson, *Rebellion in the Twenties*, ts., as cited in Palmer.

22. Ruby Cohn, *Dialogue in American Drama*, (Bloomington: Indiana University Press, 1971) 179.

23. John Dos Passos, *The Garbage Man* in *Three Plays* (New York: Harcourt Brace, 1934) 75.

24. John Dos Passos, "Is the Realistic Theatre Obsolete?" *Vanity Fair* 19 May 1925.

25. Burns Mantle, "The Moon is a Gong is a Jazz Nightmare," *New York Daily News* 13 March 1926.

26. Gilbert W. Gabriel, "Of All the Things Under the Moon," *New York Sun* 13 March 1926.

27. Roberta Lynn Lasky, "The New Playwrights Theatre: 1927–1929," diss., University of California at Davis, 1988, 66; Mordecai Gorelik, *New Theatres for Old* (1940; New York: E. P. Dutton, 1962) 307.

28. Review of *Loud Speaker*, *Wall Street News*: N. pag., in Gorelik Scrapbook, Special Collections, Morris Library, Southern Illinois University at Carbondale.

29. Review of *Loud Speaker*, *The Theatre* 4 March 1927: N. pag., in Gorelik Scrapbook, Special Collections, Morris Library, Southern Illinois University at Carbondale.

30. Review of *Loud Speaker*, *New York Herald Tribune*, 12 March 1927: N. pag., in Gorelik Scrapbook, Special Collections, Morris Library, Southern Illinois University at Carbondale.

31. Review of *Loud Speaker*, *New York Times*, 20 March 1927: N. pag., in Gorelik Scrapbook, Special Collections, Morris Library, Southern Illinois University at Carbondale.

32. John Anderson, "New Playwrights Dedicate Their Own Theatre with Mr. Lawson's Play, *Loud Speaker*," *New York Post* 3 March 1927: N. pag.

33. Joseph Wood Krutch, Introduction to John Howard Lawson, *Loud Speaker* (New York: Macauley, 1927) xiii.

34. Lasky, "New Playwrights Theatre" 64.

35. Ibid.

17

"Another Revolution to Be Heard From": Jane Heap and the International Theatre Exposition of 1926

John Bell

Twentieth-century theatre operates on an aesthetic continuum that, on one side, features text- and actor-based drama, and on the other focuses on what Roland Barthes calls "Image-Music-Text." One interesting topic is tracing the developing traditions of this latter form, which is often called "experimental" or "avant-garde" theatre, and one question to be answered is how and when the United States became a center for this type of theatre. The western European avant-garde, starting with Symbolism in the 1890s, made the most innovations in avant-garde theatre through the 1930s, but after World War II, experimental activity seems to have shifted to America. One question is how and why that shift takes place; a more specific question is when and how Americans become aware of European avant-garde theatre, which is where the 1926 International Theatre Exhibition comes in.

THE LITTLE REVIEW AND AMERICAN MODERNISM

Broadway had a boom year in 1926. The Gershwin musical *Oh Kay* opened with Gertrude Lawrence; *The Shanghai Gesture* starred Florence Reed in a performance of exotic orientalia; Basil Rathbone and Helen Menken performed in *The Captive*, "a sensitive study in abnormal psychology"; and Mae West's *Sex* was closed down by the authorities, its star spending ten days in the workhouse. *Earl Carroll's Follies* featured white comedians in blackface and clown shoes, and Sigmund Romberg's *Desert Song* presented Morocco as an exotic realm of pageantry, love, and intrigue. On Fourteenth Street Eva Le Gallienne opened her Civic Repertory Company, whose first season presented *The Three Sisters*, *The Master Builder*, *Twelfth Night*, and other classics at low prices. Moscow's Habima Theatre played *The Dybbuk*, and it had been only four years since the first American appearances of the Moscow Art Theatre.[1]

In January of that year, farther downtown at the Greenwich Village Theatre, Kenneth Macgowan, Robert Edmond Jones, and Eugene O'Neill produced the *Great God Brown*, which, despite its innovative use of life-sized masks, was a

surprising commercial success. The previous year the Theatre Guild had produced John Howard Lawson's *Processional*, a jazz- and vaudeville-tinged production Lawson had written in Paris under the direct influence of Diaghilev's
Ballets Russes. In 1926 the Theatre Guild offered eight different productions; it
was one of the last years of operation for the Provincetown Playhouse at the
Greenwich Village Theatre.

John Howard Lawson, the author of *Processional*, was one of many Americans, including Jones and Macgowan, who had been exposed to European avant-
garde theatre. Another was Mike Gold, a leftist activist who returned from Russia enthusiastic about the very different theatre he had seen there—different
from either the experimental or realistic theatre in New York: "Acrobatic actors
race up and down a dozen planes of action. The drawing-room play has been
thrown on the junk-pile of history. Things happen—broad, bold physical things,
as in the workers' lives. There are dangers and the feel of elementals. . . . Machinery had been made a character in the drama. City rhythms, the blare of modernism, the iron shouts of industrialism, these are actors."[2]

In this atmosphere of general ferment the International Theatre Exhibition
of 1926 appeared for two weeks in February at the Steinway Building on West
57th Street. Heap, at this moment the editor of *The Little Review*, was one of the
"lesbian modernists" who helped shape this century's concepts of modernist art,
literature, and performance. The International Theatre Exhibition's two-week
presentation of stage and costume designs had enormous implications for the
entire form and content of American avant-garde theatre. It is interesting that it
should be the result of the efforts of a woman who was not a "theatre person"
per se, and perhaps even more interesting that this woman defined herself publicly, in 1926, as a lesbian.

Heap had been an early supporter of the original Little Theatre started by
Maurice Browne and Ellen Van Volkenburg in Chicago. A native of Topeka,
Kansas, Heap graduated from the Art Institute of Chicago in 1905, studied
painting in Germany, came back to Chicago to learn costume jewelry design,
and in 1916 had met Margaret Anderson, another Little Theatre supporter, who
had begun *The Little Review*. *The Little Review* was the first—and perhaps
best—of the "little magazine" movement that started early in the century. Devoted to "radically experimental" writing, it featured works by writers in America such as Hart Crane, Sherwood Anderson, Ernest Hemingway, Hilda Doolit-
tle, William Carlos Williams, and Emma Goldman; and writers in Europe including Gertrude Stein, T. S. Eliot, Ezra Pound, Wyndham Lewis, James Joyce,
Jean Cocteau, Laszlo Moholy-Nagy, Tristan Tzara, Francis Picabia, Constantin
Brancusi, Guillaume Apollinaire, El Lissitsky, Kurt Schwitters, Igor Stravinsky,
and Edgar Varèse.[3] In short, it represented a whole range of the modernist contributions to literature, theatre, music, sculpture, painting, and architecture.

Heap and Anderson became lovers and worked in close association on the
magazine for the next decade. Heap changed the magazine's appearance by introducing modern typographical design and reproductions of contemporary artists' works, but she otherwise preferred to stay in the background, appearing on
the masthead only as "jh." In 1917 the magazine moved to New York. Ezra
Pound, an early *Little Review* supporter, became its foreign editor, and brought

in new examples of modernist literature from Europe, including Joyce's *Ulysses*, which ran in installments for three years. *The Little Review*'s publication of *Ulysses* is, of course, its own dramatic story, including official censorship, the confiscation and incineration of whole issues of *The Little Review*, and a landmark obscenity trial in 1921.

By 1922 Margaret Anderson had grown tired of being editor of *The Little Review*, and Heap took over the job. Heap changed the magazine's concentration "from literature to an emphasis on international experimental art movements" such as Dada, Surrealism, Futurism, Constructivism, and Bauhaus.[4] Heap became particularly interested in the relationship of art and the machine, and her efforts began to direct themselves toward "bringing the art of the Machine Age to New York." In a 1922 issue of *The Little Review* she wrote:

> The artist . . . must establish [his] social function. . . . He must affiliate with the creative arts in the other arts, and with the constructive men of his epoch; engineers and scientists etc. Until this is established a great spiritual waste is going on through the dispersed unrecognized or unattained energy of the true artist. *The Little Review* has long been working on a plan to promote this idea, and to bring the artist into personal contact with the consumer and the appreciator.[5]

Heap's interest in the Machine Age was influenced by the mystical teachings of G. I. Gurdjieff, whom she began to study in 1923. As a result Heap's embrace of the machine had an important spiritual component: she saw the whole importance of machines in metaphysical terms. Although, Heap wrote, the United States more than any other western country had achieved its "legitimate pursuit," the "acquisition of wealth, enjoyment of the senses, and commercial competition," there was something missing. "No nation," she wrote, "can progress beyond our present state, unless it is 'subjected to the creative will.' " "A great many people cry out at the Machine," she continued, "as the incubus that is threatening our 'spiritual life.' " But, Heap wrote, western spirituality was already in trouble, since its materialist goals had "bred an incomplete man," whose "outer life is too full, his inner life empty." "The world is restless with a need to express its emotions," she wrote; "the desire for beauty has become a necessity." "THE MACHINE," she concluded in capital letters, "IS THE RELIGIOUS EXPRESSION OF TODAY."[6]

THE EXHIBITION

The International Theatre Exhibition of 1926, organized with Austrian stage designer Friedrich Kiesler and under the auspices of the Theatre Guild, the Provincetown Playhouse, the Greenwich Village Theatre, and the Neighborhood Playhouse, brought the full force of avant-garde modernism to the attention of the American theatre. It combined 1,541 examples of stage and costume design from Europe and the United States and featured the major theatrical works of constructivist, futurist, expressionist, and Bauhaus design.[7]

In addition to the Exhibition itself, Heap turned the Winter 1926 issue of *The Little Review* into an exhibit catalogue as well as a platform for articles explaining these new experiments in theatre. The writing, by Friedrich Kiesler, Fernand Léger, Hans Richter, Herwarth Walden, Anton Giuglio Bragaglia, Remo Bufano, Alfred Döblin, Luigi Russolo, and Enrico Prampolini ranged from overviews of the contemporary Russian, Polish, and Parisian theatre scenes to Friedrich Kiesler's wild introductory manifesto proclaiming the death and rebirth of theatre. Fernand Léger contributed an analysis of the object in theatre, Remo Bufano a re-evaluation of puppet theatre's potential on the modern stage, Luigi Russolo a technical explanation of the "art of noise," and Prampolini a description of his utopian "Magnetic Theatre." Herwarth Walden defined his expressionist vision of theatre, avant-garde theatre patron (and Gurdjieff follower) Otto Kahn offered an analysis of "the American Stage," and Alfred Döblin contributed a short play about the *Lusitania*. *Theatre Arts Monthly* editor Sheldon Cheney organized extensive and successful press coverage for the event, including a four-page preview in his journal, in which he said the Exhibition would confront New York

with a new challenge to the imaginativeness of its stage artists. It seems—if advance reports may be credited—that while the American stage decorators have been busy developing the simplified plastic setting into a thing of taste, charm and dramatic effectiveness, with only a rare gesture on the part of [Norman Bel] Geddes or [Herman] Rosse toward a more radical inventiveness, a group of European artists, in league with the Expressionists, Constructivists and Dadaists of the other arts, have abandoned representation and created new and strikingly theatrical backgrounds for acted plays.[8]

And Kenneth Macgowan, in a preview article in the *New York Times Magazine*, wrote that the exhibit, "fathered by the rebel theatres of New York," is "given up to new work that demonstrates three fresh heresies in stage design . . . : Futurist and cubist scenery from Russia and Italy; constructivist scenery from Russia and Germany; actorless theatres from Italy, Germany and France." Macgowan asked rhetorically, "why an International Theatre Exposition? What is it going to show us that we don't see nightly along Broadway and throughout the little theatres of the provinces?" His answer was that "the fact that the names associated with this exposition are new names—Friedrich Kiesler, organizer of the show, with the aid of Jane Heap; Léger, Prampolini, Meyerhold, Tairoff, Depero, Exter—ought to suggest that here is still another revolution to be heard from."[9]

The exhibition included stage models, photographs, and designs but also full-scale examples of this new theatre. For example, there were Picasso's flat, over-life-sized cut-out puppets for *Mercure*, a dance-theatre piece he conceived himself, with choreography by Léonide Massine and music by Erik Satie, for Étienne de Beaumont's 1924 "Soirées de Paris." Also on display were masks, costumes, and over-life-sized figures by Fernand Léger for the *Creation of the World*, produced in Paris by the Ballets Suédois in 1923. The production had an orchestral score by Darius Milhaud influenced by Harlem jazz and a scenario by Blaise Cendrars inspired by an African creation myth he had just published in an anthology of African folklore. *The Creation of the World* was, like *Mercure*, a movement theatre piece using life-sized performing objects, arm and leg stilts, masks, and three fifteen-foot-tall flat giant puppets. Léger's direct de-sign inspiration was obviously African art, yet he saw the show as an aspect of a "machine aesthetic" which, as he explained in his essay in *The Little Review* catalogue, was poised to make theatrical use of the plastic qualities of objects and the human body.[10] The exhibition included contributions by five Bauhaus designers, including Xanti Schawinsky's designs for mechanical puppets, Kurt Schmidt's sketches of his *Mechanical Ballet*, and Oskar Schlemmer's designs and choreographic plan for the *Triadic Ballet*.

In addition to Enrico Prampolini's "Magnetic Theatre" manifesto, the Ital-ian futurists were well represented by Prampolini's masks, stage models, and scene plans; photographs and drawings of Fortunato Depero's *Balli Plastici*, and a photograph of Luigi Russolo's "new mechanical instruments," with which, as he explained in his *Little Review* essay, he produced "sounds with new timbres that are different from other musical instruments," and that imitate "wind, water, . . . frogs, cicadas."[11]

Perhaps the most impressive contributions to the International Theatre Ex-hibition were Soviet stage designs showing the radical innovations of construc-tivism. They included Alexander Vesnin's stage model and costume designs for Racine's *Phèdre*; Vesnin's stage model and costume designs for *The Man Who Was Thursday*; photographs and designs by Lyubov Popova of the mechanical stage and functional workers' clothes she designed for the history-making pro-duction of *The Magnanimous Cuckold* (directed by Meyerhold, and the first example of constructivism on stage); and fifteen photographs and a stage model of *Tarelkin's Death*, another Meyerhold production, designed by Varvara Ste-panova. Although he admitted that the ideas behind constructivism were "very hard to state in the columns of a general newspaper," Kenneth Macgowan briefly summarized them, and it is interesting to note how what he then de-scribed as a novel, alien form, has now become commonplace: "constructivism banishes the canvas room and the canvas exterior. In its place it provides a sin-gle structure of different levels, steps and runways, which remains exposed throughout the evening upon a naked, brick-walled stage."[12]

RESPONSE TO THE EXHIBITION

The International Theatre Exposition defined what the *New York Times* called "the newest ideas in scenic design" at a cultural moment when the term *modernist* was still novel enough to demand bracketing with quotation marks and the attached adjective "so-called."[13] The two floors of exhibits were open from 10 A.M. to 10 P.M. and featured "daily lectures on phases of the modern theatre," organized by a twenty-one-member "lecture committee" including Macgowan, Moscow Art Theatre veteran Richard Boleslavsky (who had co-founded the American Laboratory Theatre the previous year), Neighborhood Playhouse designer Aline Bernstein, theatre writer Barrett H. Clark, Theatre Guild actor Dudley Digges, and Neighborhood Playhouse cofounder Irene Lewisohn; in short, some of the leading figures of 1920s "art" theatre.[14] The fact that well-connected exhibition participants like Cheney or Macgowan (who spoke at the exhibition on its opening day) were in a position to set a favorable spin on it from platforms like *Theatre Arts Monthly* and the *New York Times* shows that the downtown "experimental" theatre scene in New York was in fact well connected to uptown media outlets. But support for the "rebel theatre" movement and the Machine Age ideas represented by Heap's exhibition was not necessarily widespread.

The *Times*'s Brooks Atkinson, for example, reviewed the exhibit with a kind of bemused mystification that worked itself out in print as satire. Focusing on Friedrich Kiesler's hyperbolic manifesto statement that "the theatre is dead" (and ignoring, until his review's last sentence, the positive implications of Kiesler's call to work "for the theatre that has survived the theatre"), Atkinson shied well away from any analytical consideration of the hundreds of radically different theatre works represented in the exhibit and their implications for the stage.[15] Although wary of nonrealistic text, gestural theatre, masks, and dynamic lighting effects, Atkinson decided he could in fact support the idea of "abstract settings" but only because he could cite the reassuring authority of George Bernard Shaw. It is as if Atkinson did not yet have an analytical framework from which to examine exactly what Prampolini, Meyerhold, Popova, Stepanova, Schlemmer, and the other exhibitors were doing.[16]

An unsigned *Times* editorial was more critical—and sarcastic. Misunderstanding the import of the event as Atkinson had, it focused on the dire threat the exhibit supposedly posed to the central importance of the actor:

The International Theatre Exposition, sponsored by our various Guilds and Playhouses, shows a stage populated only by lights, colors, and mechanical objects, all controlled by a switchboard. The music also is mechanical. If ever speech is needed, it is megaphoned. To an enquirer who doubted whether an audience would catch the human significance of all this the inventor [Kiesler?] retorted: "A man struck by lightning doesn't have to be told what has happened." It's as direct and powerful as that, the actorless theatre. Another inventor [Fortunato Depero], more nature-loving than mechanistic, has a stage peopled only by flowers, the accessories being shifted lights and varied perfumes—all guaranteed to lift the audience to ecstasies of beauty and tears.[17]

The *Times* editorialist, not quite willing to take the entire exhibit into account, or to accept that the actor had a very important—if different—role to play in expressionist, constructivist, futurist, and Bauhaus theatre, obliquely rejected the innovation represented by the exhibition by arguing that it had nothing new to say anyway. According to the editorial, Edward Gordon Craig, Maurice Maeterlinck, Max Reinhardt, Constantin Stanislavsky, and Mrs. Patrick Campbell had all called for the same thing years ago. Taking advantage of the moment to knock Macgowan and Jones's comparatively timid experiment with abstraction in O'Neill's *The Great God Brown* (whose "obvious . . . painted and immobile" mask is "so ugly, and it so painfully distorts human speech, that one begins to be reconciled to actors"), the editorial cites P. T. Barnum to conclude that the premises of the so-called "actorless theatre" are bunk, and the final salvo that "the actorless theatre . . . tends to become authorless too."[18]

SUBSEQUENT INFLUENCE

Clearly many in the New York theatre world of the 1920s did not quite yet understand the "modernist" way of viewing the world, despite the fact that "modernists" like Heap, Kiesler, Macgowan, and Cheney were living and looking at the same environment Brooks Atkinson and the *Times* editorialist were—the modern American city. At the exhibition's opening night Friedrich Kiesler said to those gathered at Fifty-seventh Street,

I represent the youth movement in the theatres of Europe. There is a special fitness in this, because we who consider ourselves architects in the theatres look to America as the originator of a new-world architecture, and therefore in a sense the originators of the new types of staging that are here demonstrated. We are bringing you a thing that is in a sense new to you, and yet it is yours. Especially it is your spirit that has brought this new art into the theatre.[19]

This, of course, was not news to people like Jane Heap who, long imbued with the modernist spirit, understood and supported the power of its formal message. But it is difficult to pinpoint the direct effects of the 1926 International Theatre Exhibition. John Howard Lawson, Em Jo Basshe, Michael Gold, and Francis Faragoh met as an indirect result of the event, and together with John Dos Passos and the financial support of Otto Kahn, they formed the leftist New Playwrights Theatre later that year, to create productions heavily influenced by the techniques represented in the International Theatre Exhibition.[20] The influence of Soviet experiments reappeared in the Federal Theatre Project's "Living Newspapers" of the late thirties, and Bauhaus designer Xanti Schawinsky himself wound up at West Virginia's Black Mountain College in 1936, where he taught John Cage and Merce Cunningham. Boris Aronson, Aline Bernstein, Remo Bufano, Norman Bel Geddes, Mordecai Gorelik, Robert Edmond Jones, Louis Lozowick, Jo Mielziner, Donald Oenslager, Lee Simonson, and Cleon Throckmorton, who were all represented in the exhibit, adapted elements of it as they redefined American set design in the thirties.

The role of women in the development of modernist art movements is an important, fascinating, and highly problematic subject, given the aggressive male domination of most modernist art movements; and the role of declared lesbians like Jane Heap and her partner Margaret Anderson has only recently been acknowledged. What conclusions might be drawn about the example of Jane Heap's International Theatre Exhibition? First of all, the exhibition shows the consistency of Anderson and Heap's *Little Review* philosophy, which, as Anderson put it, was to create "a free stage for the artists."[21] Heap, a dedicated anarchist more than a socialist or feminist, created a stage with her exhibition where the full spectrum of modernist theatre ideas from Europe could reach an American audience. Heap understood something about the nature of machines, society, and theatre which quite clearly eluded established critics like Brooks Atkinson. And Heap was open enough to understand that the effects of Machine Age performance would be wide ranging, expanding or breaking the previously existing bounds of theatre—something quite obvious to us in the post-McLuhan age, but not so obvious in the twenties. Moreover, Heap found a way not only to accept and celebrate the contributions of technology to modern culture, but also to find a spiritual dimension in their union, a subject which in the 1990s is often treated as if it were brand new. How much all of this had to do with Heap's lesbian identity is an intriguing question. Perhaps a sense of social marginality allowed her to examine and understand American society both inside and outside its current bounds.

Finally, a measure of Heap's keen, critical, and realistic sense of American society can be seen in her understanding of the far reach of the kinds of communication undertaken by the work represented at the International Theatre Exhibition. While a mainstream critic like Atkinson could see only what he saw there in relation to the staid canon of British drama and its heirs, Heap easily made the kind of genre leaps that now characterize today's cultural studies. Heap understood that even if traditional theatre makers did not understand the possibilities of the Machine Age, other communicating aspects of modern capitalist society would, especially in the world of advertising, whose innovators employed all the theatrical effects of Machine Age imagery in their works. As a committed anarchist, Heap did not celebrate advertising's use of Machine Age forms, but she did realize its importance. In the final issue of *The Little Review* Heap wrote, "Modern Art. It has come into its own: advertising."[22]

NOTES

1. Daniel Blum, *A Pictorial History of the American Theatre* (New York: Chilton, 1960) 223.

2. Michael Gold, qtd. in George A. Knox and Herbert M. Stahl, *Dos Passos and "The Revolting Playwrights"* (Uppsala: Lundequistska Bokhandeln, 1964) 8–9. About Meyerhold Gold wrote:

His bare, immense stage . . . stripped for action, like a steel mill or a factory. . . . Intricate structures, like huge machines created for a function, furnish the scaffold on which actors race and leap and walk from plane to plane. All that was static in the old theatre has been stamped out. This is the theatre of dynamics. This theatre is the battle-field of life; it is a trench, a factory, the deck of a ship in a storm. (9)

3. Shari Benstock, *Women of the Left Bank: Paris, 1900–1940* (Austin: University of Texas Press, 1986) 363.

4. *Notable American Women: The Modern Period. A Biographical Dictionary*, 1980 ed., s.v. "Anderson, Margaret Carolyn," by Matilda M. Hills.

5. Qtd. in Susan Noyes Platt, "Mysticism in the Machine Age: Jane Heap and *The Little Review*," *Twenty/One* 1 (Fall 1989): 28.

6. Jane Heap, "Machine-Age Exposition," *The Little Review* (Spring 1925): 22.

7. Heap's catalogue edition of *The Little Review* (Winter 1926) listed the exhibitors by country (spelling as in the original):

Austria: Camilla Burke, Hans Fritz, Cary Hauser, Friedrich Kiesler, Alfred Roller, Oscar Strand, Harry Täuber, Fritz Treichlinger, Treichlinger and Rosenblum.
Belgium: Studio L'Arsault, M. L. Baughiet, Jean Delecluze, P. Flouquet, Geo., J. de Meester Jr., Rene Moulard, Van de Pawerb, F. Scouflair, M. Stoubbaerts, Theatre Catholique Flamand, James Thiriar.
Czechoslovakia: Josef Capek, B. Feuerstein, V. Hofman, A. V. Hrska, Wenig.

France: Ive Alix, Count Étienne de Beaumont, Nicolas Benois, Georges Braque, André Derain, Maxime Dethomas, Guy Dollian, Walter René Fuerst, Jean Hugo, Jean Janin, Irene Lagut, Pierre Laprade, Fernand Léger, R. Mallet Stevens, Luc Morreau, Audrey Parr, Helene Perdriat, Francis Picabia, Robert Rist, Tristan Tzara, Léon Zack.

Germany: Willy Baumeister, Hans Blanke, Marcel Breuer, Felix Cziossck, Heinrich Heckroth, Vera Idelson, Ludwig Kainer, Adolf Mahnke, Constantin V. Mitzscheke-Collande, Caspar Neher, Hans Richter, Dr. Eduard Löffler, Xanti Schawinsky, Oskar Schlemmer, Kurt Schmidt, Hans Strohbach.

Holland: Vilmos Huzar.

Hungary: Ladislas Medgyes, Laszlo Moholy-Nagy, Farkas Molnar.

Italy: M. Ago, Ludovico Bragaglia, Fortunato Depero, Dottori, Marchi, De Pistoris, Enrico Prampolini, Luigi Russolo, Tato, Valente.

Yugoslavia: Ljubo Babic, Sergius Glumac.

Latvia: Libertis, Muncis.

Poland: Vincent Drabik, J. Colus, Stanislas Yarocki, K. Kobro, Kard Krynski, Nawroczynski, Mme. Nicz-Borowiakowa, André and Zbigniew Pronaszko, Alexandre Rafalowski, Stanislaw Sliwinski, Stazewski, Simon Syrkus, Stanislaw Wyspianski, Stanislas Zaleski.

Russia: Nathan Altman, Michel Andreenko, Léon Bakst, Boris Bilinsky, Chestakoff, Chtchouko, Egeroff, Erdmann, Alexandra Exter, Fedorovsky, Ferdinandoff, Erdmann and Ferdinandoff, Gontscharova, Jakouloff, Kardovsky, Komardenkoff, Konstodieff, Larionow, Lentouloff, Libakoff, Simon Lissim, Meller, Meierhold Theatre, Moscou Art Studio, Nivinsky, Henriette Pascar, Petrisky, L. Popova, Popova and Vesnine, I. Rabinovitch, Rodtschenko, Slovtsova, Somoff, V. and G. Sternberg, V. and G. Sternberg and K. Medounetsky, Stepanova, Alexander Tairoff, Theatre Beresil, Theatre for Children, The Revolution Theatre, The Imperial Theatre, Pavel Tchelietcheff, Vesnine, Vialoff.

Spain: Rafael Barradas, Louis Massiera, Pablo Picasso.

Sweden: Nils de Dardel, Isaac Grunewald, Bertel Nordstrom, Swedish Ballet: Foujita.

Switzerland: G. and W. Hunziker.

America: Boris Aronson, Bradford Ashworth, Aline Bernstein, Claude Bragdon, Remo Bufano, Allan Crane, George Cronyn, Warren Dahler, Ernest De Weerth, Manuel Essman, Joseph Fossko, Norman Bel Geddes, Mordecai Gorelick, Carolyn Hancock, Mrs. Ingeborg Hansell, Nathan Israel, Frederick Jones, Robert Edmond Jones, Jonel Jorgulesco, Louis Lozowick, R. Sibley Mack, Jo Mielziner, Joseph Mullen, Donald Oenslager, Irving Pichel, Esther Peck, James Reynolds, Herman Rosse, H. Schultz, Lee Simonson, Raymond Sovey, Woodman Thompson, Cleon Throckmorton, R. Van Rosen, Sheldon K. Viele, Rollo Wayne, John Wegner, Anna Wille, Russell Wright.

England: Arnold O. Gibbons, Terrence Gray, Victor Hembrow, Isabel Horn, Albert Rutherston, R. Schwabe, George Sheringham, Sheldon K. Viele, Christina Walsh.

8. Sheldon Cheney, "The International Theatre Exhibition," *Theatre Arts Monthly* 10.3 (March 1926): 203.

9. Kenneth Macgowan, "Stagecraft Shows Its Newest Heresies," *New York Times Magazine* 14 February 1926: 9.

10. Fernand Léger, "A New Realism—The Object (Its Plastic and Cinematographic Value)," *The Little Review* (Winter 1926): 7–8.

11. Luigi Russolo, "Psofarmoni: New Musical Instruments," *The Little Review* (Winter 1926): 51.

12. Macgowan, "Stagecraft" 23.

13. "A number of exhibitions of so-called 'modernist art' are holding different portions of the New York [art] field," wrote the author of "Academy of Design Reaches a New Age," *New York Times Magazine* 21 March 1926: 16.

14. "Exposition Reveals New Theatre Ideas," *New York Times* 28 February 1926: 16. The "Lecture Committee" is listed in *The Little Review* (Winter 1926): 4.

15. Friedrich Kiesler, "Foreword," *The Little Review* (Winter 1926): 1.

16. Brooks Atkinson, "Bourgeois Laughter," *New York Times* 14 March 1926, sec. 8: 1.

17. "An Actorless Theatre," *New York Times* 24 February 1926, sec. 18: 5.

18. Ibid.

19. "Exposition Reveals New Theatre Ideas," *New York Times* 28 February 1926: 16.

20. Jay Williams, *Stage Left* (New York: Scribner's, 1974) 19–20.

21. Qtd. in Benstock, *Women of the Left Bank* 377.

22. Jane Heap, "Wreaths," *The Little Review* (May 1929): 62.

18

Architecture for the Twentieth Century: Imagining the Theatre in the 1920s

William F. Condee

The foundation of current American theatre architecture lies in the reform movement of the 1920s. Thrusts, arenas, flexible theatres, and apron stages were all advocated in the "New Movement," which was most active from 1915 to 1930. While these theatre forms were not actually built during that period, theatre reformers established the theoretical, historical, and artistic basis for the "open stages" of the post–World War II era.

American theatre reformers, influenced by Appia, Craig, Reinhardt, Copeau, and others, had a vision of new forms of theatre architecture that would promote social, artistic, and religious reform. The usual purpose of theatre architecture, to house an existing performance style as well as possible, was reversed. Instead, architecture would provide a fertile environment in which a new drama could flourish. While critical studies have focused on the design, directing, and drama of the New Movement, the reformers themselves viewed architecture as central to their goals. In fact, these architectural reforms are central to understanding American theatre of the 1920s.

The American reform movement was opposed to the then-dominant realistic theatre and its associated architectural form, the picture-frame proscenium theatre, which enforced an architectural boundary between audience and performance. The "peephole" theatre, as the reformers loved to call it, was considered to be a modern "house of bondage."[1]

The New Movement sought an invigorated, noncommercial theatre in which artistic decisions would be determined by the "art of theatre," not the box office. The reformers wished to produce nonillusionistic drama in which the theatricality of the performance was frankly acknowledged. Theatrical production was to be governed by the "New Stagecraft" guidelines of simplicity, suggestion, and synthesis. But these goals could not be achieved in the existing theatres. In fact, the reformers believed that these goals could be achieved only by altering the place of the performance.

The reformers saw the picture-frame proscenium theatre as perfectly suited to nineteenth-century illusionism, but inadequate for all nonillusionistic drama and production methods—past, present, or future. While painted canvas scenery was appropriate to the frontal perspective of the proscenium theatre, the plastic, sculptural forms of the New Stagecraft implied a three-dimensional, "in-the-round" relationship with the viewer. According to Kenneth Macgowan, the New Stagecraft itself contained "the implication of a new physical playhouse and a new way of looking at the problems of production. Realism is at a discount; the convention of the fourth wall is discarded; the picture frame proscenium ignored. . . . All this is in very obvious transition towards a new playhouse built for a style of production utterly unrealistic, quite apart from representation or illusion."[2]

For the new theatre architecture the reformers wanted to strip away the encrustation of nineteenth-century gewgaws. Sheldon Cheney called these theatres "ornate, overdecorated, and vulgarly gorgeous,"[3] having the "fat obscenity of the Paris Opera."[4] This reaction is part of the Modernist call for simplicity, in which form is to follow function and any decoration is to be expressive of structure. Cheney clearly reflected this desire in his call for "naked construction" in theatre architecture, analogous to the qualities of "the designed machine," with a "clean line" and "sheer surfaces."[5] The auditorium was to provide a serene sanctuary for the contemplation of the mood created onstage.

For the audience-performance relationship, the reformers called for the "open stage," in which the audience and the performers occupy the same architectural volume with no proscenium bisecting the theatre into auditorium and stage. The reformers stressed that they were merely restoring the true theatrical harmony of the Greek and Elizabethan theatres. As Roy Mitchell put it, "We are now beginning to suspect that our people of the theatre missed the turn three centuries ago and that in order to go forward . . . we may have to retrace our steps to the place where the mistake was made . . . and go on from there."[6]

The "apron stage" was a slight reform of the existing theatre: It consisted simply of a narrow portion of the stage extending beyond the proscenium arch as had generally been the case in the pre-picture-frame proscenium theatre. While this would now be considered only a slight variation—if a variation at all—on the old-fashioned theatre, Mordecai Gorelik said that in the 1920s "this little space became, with good reason, a battleground of dramatic theory."[7]

The "Shakespeare stage" was a far greater departure from the existing theatres. It contained a permanent "architectural" setting on a simple platform stage, with little or no production-specific scenery. The audience could be on three sides (a thrust stage) or all on one side (an end stage). The oft-noted European examples were Copeau's Théâtre du Vieux Colombier (see Photo 1), Reinhardt's Redoutensaal, and the various attempts at reconstructing the Elizabethan theatre.

The "circus theatre," so called because the early examples were converted from former circuses, abandoned the proscenium altogether. American reformers lauded Reinhardt's "Theatre of the Five Thousand" and the Grosses Schauspielhaus (see Photo 2). In its pure form, such as the Cirque Medrano (see Photo 3), the circus stage was an arena theatre stripped to the reformers' essentials: actor, stage, and audience.

For the American New Movement the effects of these reforms would extend far beyond architecture. Socially the reformers saw the pit-box-gallery auditorium as a creation of the European aristocracy with comfortable seats and good sightlines for the upper classes and neither for the lower. For Hiram Moderwell the existing theatres were "a remnant, a 'hang-over,' from the days when art was a mere ornament for the aristocracy." Moderwell believed that theatre

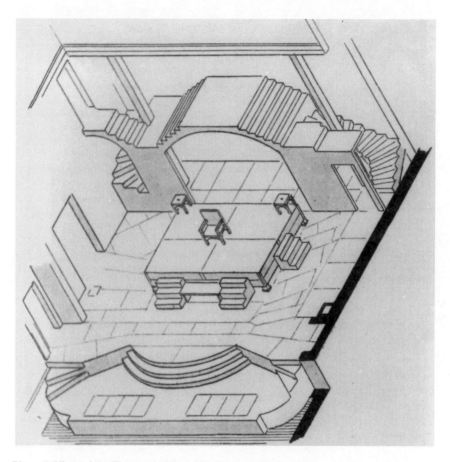

Photo 1. View of the Theatre du Vieux Colombier, Paris. From *Twentieth Century Stage Decoration* by Walter Rene Fuerst and Samuel J. Hume. Copyright 1967 (Reprint). Reprinted by permission of Dover Publications.

Photo 2. View of the Grosses Schauspielhaus, Berlin. From *The Theatre of Tomorrow* by Kenneth Macgowan. Copyright 1921 by Boni & Liveright, Inc., renewed 1949 by Kenneth Macgowan. Reprinted by permission of Liveright Publishing Corporation.

Photo 3. "An impression of the Cirque Medrano in Paris." Illustration from *Continental Stagecraft* by Kenneth Macgowan, copyright 1922 by Harcourt Brace & Company, reproduced by permission of the publisher.

architecture needed to reflect democratic, not aristocratic, social ideals: "Democracy says . . . that if possible nobody shall have a bad seat in a theatre, no matter how few pennies he has paid for admission."[8] Politically and socially architecture was essential to the reformers: Existing theatres harbored a European and aristocratic social structure while the architecture of the future contained a vision of American democracy.

The reformers also believed that these new theatre forms would engender a new body of nonillusionistic drama. The reason this new drama had not yet emerged, the reformers argued, was the straitjacket imposed on playwrights by the picture-frame proscenium arch. The reformers contended that this type of theatre building, like any other, largely determined the nature of the play and its performance style. The only theatres in which playwrights could have their plays produced had picture frames, and only illusionistic productions worked in this type of theatre. Thus, the reformers believed, playwrights continued to write illusionistic drama. According to Norman Bel Geddes: "The conventional theater with its proscenium frame is adaptable only to the peep-show type of play, which has adapted itself to the peep-show type of theater. . . . These restrictions which are now generally taken for granted impose very confining limitations on the dramatist, clipping the wings of inspiration and depriving drama of the freedom."[9]

The reformers believed that when playwrights could see plays produced in the "theatre of tomorrow," their imaginations would be liberated so as to produce the "drama of tomorrow." Mitchell traced the evolution from New Stagecraft to new drama: "The development of the scene may go to new and nobler forms of building based on a new theory of theatre. It could . . . become so majestic and so moving as to provoke a new dramaturgy altogether."[10]

The greatest—perhaps grandiose—result of these architectural reforms was that the theatre would become the instrument of the "New Spirit" the reformers saw emerging in society. These reformers were addressing the perceived spiritual crisis of the time, what Eugene O'Neill described as "the sickness of today . . . the death of the Old God and the failure of science and materialism to give any satisfying new One."[11]

These new theatre forms would promote a mystical communion among the audience and with the performers, and theatrical production would take on a religious quality. Macgowan wrote: "It is the conviction of some of us that there has resided in the theater—and our hope that there may reside once more—something akin to the religious spirit. . . . It is not: Can religion make itself theatrical? But: Can the theater make itself—in a new sense—religious?"[12]

This theatrical-religious basis led to the notion that the new theatre would be the cathedral of the future—the locus of humankind's spiritual aspirations. Cheney believed that the reformers were beginning to create "a theatre that will be, indeed, not less than a new cathedral in its appropriateness to the uses of the soul."[13]

These ultimate goals of the New Movement have a metaphysical quality, but, ironically, the means of achieving them were—literally—concrete.

The theatrical revolution that the reformers prophesied did not occur. While many theatres were built in America during the 1920s, they were not designed according to the reformist guidelines. These were traditional, picture-frame proscenium theatres built as commercial ventures. During the Depression and through World War II, few new theatres were built at all.

Despite this lack of major progressive theatres, there were unbuilt projects and little theatres designed along reformist lines in the 1920s and 1930s. These theatres are important in that they provided prototypes for post–World War II American theatre architecture.

Some of the earliest apron stages in America were designed by Joseph Urban, an Austrian émigré. His theatres, which include the Ziegfeld Theatre in New York (1926) and an unbuilt project for Reinhardt, are fairly traditional in form, but each did contain an apron, proscenium doors, and means of carrying the performance into the auditorium.

Norman Bel Geddes designed the first American modernist thrust stages, and his projects had widespread influence. His are the first fully developed plans to incorporate the architectural ideas of the American reform movement. Bel Geddes was also the first American theatre architect to design with the now-common idea that every aspect of the theatre building should be based on a clearly defined artistic program.

In his "Theatre Number Six," first exhibited in 1914, Bel Geddes rotated the usual auditorium-stage axis—a longitudinal line of a rectangle—to a diagonal axis of a square (see Photo 4). The stage is a quarter circle set in one corner of the square plan with concentric rows of seats radiating outward from the curved front of the stage.

A central goal of Bel Geddes's design is to provide a space that unifies stage and auditorium. There is no proscenium, and a set of curving steps eases the transition from stage to auditorium. The domed ceiling over the audience continues over and behind the stage, tying the space together and providing a "cyclorama" or "sky dome" that can be lit for the production. The single, unbroken bank of seats contained within a unified space addresses the reformist goals of a democratic seating plan and promoting a mystical communion among the participants. According to Bel Geddes, "a sense of unity, intimacy, and audience-participation pervades the theater, arising in part from the fact that the same great domed ceiling spans actors and audience."[14]

Unlike many open stages, the diagonal theatre has a capability—however complex and expensive—for changing scenery. The onstage scenery would be on a wagon and could be lowered on an elevator to the basement level; there it would roll into a storage area, another wagon with scenery would roll on, and the elevator would rise again to stage level.

This semi-thrust may have influenced Frank Lloyd Wright's theatre designs.[15] Wright worked on a project for Aline Barnsdall from 1916 to 1920, and its major features persisted in all of his subsequent theatre designs. These include the theatre in the Imperial Hotel, Tokyo (1922), and the New Theatre, which was originally designed in 1928 and underwent many design changes before it was finally built as the Kalita Humphreys Theatre at the Dallas Theatre Center in 1959.

The common elements in Wright's designs are a stage extending across the full width of the auditorium; a large, curved apron with continuous steps leading into the auditorium; and a continuous ceiling extending over the stage and auditorium. Like Bel Geddes, Wright designed his theatres to be incapable of handling conventional scenery. Wright's theatres had a curving plaster cyclo-

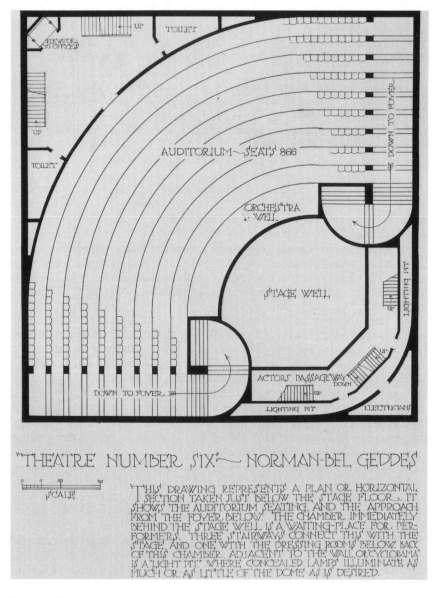

TOILET

ELEVATORS
TO OFFICES

UP

UP

TOILET

AUDITORIUM~SEATS 866

DOWN TO FOYER

ORCHESTRA
WELL

STAGE WELL

LIGHTING PIT

UP

ACTORS' PASSAGEWAY
DOWN

UP

DOWN TO FOYER »»>

LIGHTING PIT

UP

ELECTRICIANS

"THEATRE NUMBER SIX"~ NORMAN·BEL GEDDES

SCALE

THIS DRAWING REPRESENTS A PLAN OR HORIZONTAL
SECTION TAKEN JUST BELOW THE STAGE FLOOR. IT
SHOWS THE AUDITORIUM SEATING AND THE APPROACH
FROM THE FOYER BELOW. THE CHAMBER IMMEDIATELY
BEHIND THE STAGE WELL IS A WAITING-PLACE FOR PER-
FORMERS. THREE STAIRWAYS CONNECT THIS WITH THE
STAGE, AND ONE WITH THE DRESSING ROOMS BELOW. BACK
OF THIS CHAMBER, ADJACENT TO THE WALL, OR "CYCLORAMA"
IS A "LIGHT PIT" WHERE CONCEALED LAMPS ILLUMINATE AS
MUCH OR AS LITTLE OF THE DOME AS IS DESIRED.

Photo 4. Theatre Number Six, Norman Bel Geddes. By permission of the Norman Bel Geddes Estate, Performing Arts Collection, The Harry Ransom Humanities Research Center, University of Texas at Austin.

rama at the rear of the stage and a complex system of curving ramps and eleva-tors for moving scenery. In these theatres one can see Wright's concern, evi-denced throughout his architecture, for the continuous flow of space.

The "corner stage," "diagonal-axis theatre" or "semi-thrust" is the basis for many American theatres of the 1960s and 1970s, including the Actors Theatre of Louisville, Cincinnati Playhouse in the Park, the Alley Theatre in Houston, and the Kreeger Theatre at the Arena Stage in Washington, D.C.

Bel Geddes was also the first American to design a theatre-in-the-round with his intimate "Theatre Number Fourteen" (see Photo 5). Instead of the common type of arena theatre today, in which the stage floor flows with little interruption into the first row of seating, this theatre had a moat around the stage: concentric rings of steps led down to the basement level. The steps served as an apron and a continuous, circular "vom" entrance to the stage. The theatre is unique in that it allows for scenic spectacle in an arena theatre: scenery could be moved on and off the stage by the same wagon-and-elevator arrangement as in the diagonal-axis theatre.

The earliest actual arena stage in America was the Penthouse Theatre, founded in 1932 by Glenn Hughes in the penthouse of a Seattle hotel. In 1940 he then opened the first modern American theatre built expressly as an arena. Differing from the other reformers, Hughes aimed for "extreme realism of ac-tion" and favored light, conventional drama. Hughes also differed in his mod-esty: rather than aiming to revolutionize theatre, drama, society, and religion, he wrote that the Penthouse Theatre was a "supplementary" and "secondary" thea-tre.[16] It is ironic that while Hughes was able to build the kind of theatre for which reformers yearned, ideologically and artistically he was a reactionary.

Frederick Kiesler, another Austrian émigré, designed the first American "multiform" theatre project. His "Universal Theatre," which he worked on from 1926 to 1961, contained two separate, back-to-back theatres, one intimate and the other large; the two could also be combined to form a single two-sided arena. The seating platforms were movable so that many different arrangements were possible, including thrust and arena. This project is a "multiform" theatre in that it employs mechanical means to convert the theatre into a few predeter-mined configurations, such as has been built at the Loeb Drama Center in Cam-bridge, Massachusetts, and the Vivian Beaumont Theater in New York City.

There was one small flexible theatre built in America during this period. In 1924 Gilmor Brown began producing plays in a studio in which he rearranged the stage and audience from one production to the next. And in 1929 he built the Playbox, seating only fifty people, which could be reconfigured for each performance:

The central room . . . serves as both stage and auditorium. . . . It has two adjustable floor levels, with narrow recesses or alcoves on three sides raised another step or two. There are real fireplaces on two sides. The action of the play may take place in the centre of the room, on one side or another, or on all sides. The comfortable armchairs are arranged to suit the scheme of action, wherever it may be.[17]

Though the theatre was tiny, it had enormous appeal for reformers. It lacked a proscenium, eschewed conventional scenery, and could be transformed from production to production. This theatre set the model for the countless "black-

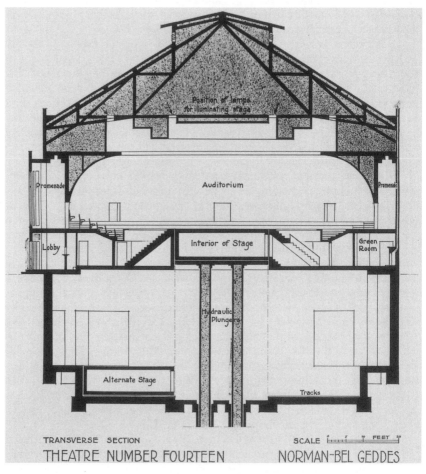

Photo 5. Theatre Number Fourteen, Norman Bel Geddes. By permission of the Norman Bel Geddes Estate, Performing Arts Collection, The Harry Ransom Humanities Research Center, University of Texas at Austin.

box" flexible theatres that were built all over the country in the 1960s and 1970s.

The reformers understood that these new theatres would not suit every play. They wanted many theatre forms for the many dramatic forms they wished to produce, which led Bel Geddes to design a theatre complex. His "Repertory Theatre" contained large and small performance spaces with various audience-performance configurations. Implicit in the architecture is the idea that different performances require different spaces and that a fully functioning performing arts center, such as was later built at Lincoln Center and around the country, requires multiple auditoria.

The New Movement did not achieve its goals in the ways the reformers had predicted: the New Stagecraft did not immediately give birth to new forms of theatre architecture, theatre buildings did not engender new drama, and the theatre did not replace the church. Nevertheless, the goals of the New Movement did provide the theoretical and aesthetic basis for the radical changes in theatre after World War II. While these reforms were carried out by a new generation of theatre artists, often without acknowledging the New Movement, their accomplishments did bring to fruition its goals. No doubt, many proscenium theatres have been built, and the pendulum may be swinging back in that direction, but open stages are now part of the theatre vernacular.

New theatres of the post–World War II era, including thrust, arena, and flexible, contain the audience and performers within a single, unified volume. The encircling audience emphasizes a sculptural, three-dimensional use of space. Auditoria are usually designed in a restrained—even severe—modernist style. These theatre forms are designed on a basis of good sightlines, acoustics, and seating for all. Audiences now readily accept nonrealistic dramaturgical techniques. While drama does not aim to supplant religion, many directors, including Tyrone Guthrie, Jerzy Grotowski, Richard Schechner, and Peter Brook, have emphasized the ritualistic aspect of the dramatic event.

The New Movement did burn out without achieving its goals, yet it imagined a new theatre that we now have built.

NOTES

1. Edith Isaacs, ed., *Architecture for the New Theatre* (New York: Theatre Arts, 1935) 10.

2. Kenneth Macgowan, *The Theatre of Tomorrow* (New York: Boni and Liveright, 1921) 46.

3. Sheldon Cheney, *The New Movement in the Theatre* (New York: Kennerley, 1914) 208.

4. Sheldon Cheney, *The New World Architecture* (New York: Longmans, Green, 1930) 349.

5. Sheldon Cheney, "The Theatre in the Machine Age," *Theatre Arts* 10 (1926): 507.

6. Roy Mitchell, "The House of the Presence," *Theatre Arts* 14 (1930): 575.

7. Mordecai Gorelik, *New Theatres for Old* (New York: Samuel French, 1941) 286.

8. Hiram Moderwell, *The Theatre of To-Day* (New York: John Lane, 1914) 238, 243.

9. Norman Bel Geddes, *Horizons* (Boston: Little Brown, 1932) 152–153.

10. Roy Mitchell, *Creative Theatre* (New York: John Day, 1929) 212–213.

11. Eugene O'Neill, "On Man and God," in Oscar N. Cargill, N. Bryllion Fagin, and William J. Fisher, eds., *O'Neill and His Plays* (New York: New York University Press, 1961) 115.

12. Kenneth Macgowan and Robert Edmond Jones, *Continental Stagecraft* (New York: Harcourt, Brace, 1922) 215, 218.

13. Cheney, *New World* 351.

14. Bel Geddes, *Horizons* 150.

15. Wendell Cole, "The Theatre Projects of Frank Lloyd Wright," *Educational Theatre Journal* 12 (1960): 88.

16. Glenn Hughes, *The Penthouse Theatre* (New York: Samuel French, 1942) 10, 46, 52.

17. Harriet L. Green, "Gilmor Brown's Playbox," *Theatre Arts* 19 (1935): 514.

Selected Bibliography

The following is a selected bibliography of book-length studies devoted in whole or in part to American history, the American drama, and theatre as it relates to experimenters, rebels, and disparate voices in the theatre of 1920s America.

American Heritage. *The American Heritage History of the 20s and 30s*. New York: American Heritage, 1970.

Atkinson, Brooks. *Broadway*. New York: Macmillan, 1970.

Beacham, Richard C., ed. *Adolph Appia. Essays, Scenarios, and Designs*. Tr. Walther R. Volbach. Ann Arbor: UMI Research Press, 1989.

Ben-Zvi, Linda, ed. *Susan Glaspell: Essays on Her Theater and Fiction*. Ann Arbor: University of Michigan Press, 1995.

Black, Eugene Robert. *Robert Edmond Jones: Artist of the New Stagecraft*. Ann Arbor: University Microfilms, 1956.

Bolin, John Seelye. *Samuel Hume: Artist and Exponent of American Art Theater*. Ann Arbor: University Microfilms, 1970.

Bordman, Gerald. *American Theatre, A Chronicle of Comedy & Drama, 1914–1930*. New York: Oxford University Press, 1995.

———. *The Oxford Companion to the American Theatre*. New York: Oxford University Press, 1984.

Brown-Guillory, Elizabeth, ed. *Wines in the Wilderness: Plays by African American Women from the Harlem Renaissance to the Present*. New York: Praeger, 1990.

Bryer, Jackson R., ed. with the assistance of Ruth M. Alvarez. *The Theatre We Worked For: The Letters of Eugene O'Neill to Kenneth Macgowan*. New Haven: Yale University Press, 1982.

Cashman, Sean Dennis. *America in the Twenties and Thirties: The Olympian Age of Franklin Delano Roosevelt*. New York: New York University Press, 1988.

Craig, Edward. *Gordon Craig: The Story of His Life*. 1968. New York: Limelight Editions, 1985.

Crowley, Alice Lewisohn. *The Neighborhood Playhouse*. New York: Theatre Arts Books, 1959.

Demastes, William W., ed. *American Playwrights, 1880–1945: A Research and Production Sourcebook*. Westport, CT: Greenwood, 1995.

Derleth, August. *Still Small Voice: Biography of Zona Gale*. New York: D. Appleton Century, 1940.

Deutsch, Helen, and Stella Hanau. *The Provincetown: A Story of the Theatre*. 1931; New York: Russell & Russell, 1972.

Dickey, Jerry. *Sophie Treadwell: A Research and Production Sourcebook*. Westport, CT: Greenwood, 1997.

Douglas, Ann. *Terrible Honesty: Mongrel Manhattan in the 1920s*. New York: Farrar, Straus, and Giroux, 1995.

Dukore, Bernard F. *American Dramatists, 1918–1945*. Grove Press Modern Dramatists. New York: Grove Press, 1984.

Durham, Weldon B., ed. *American Theatre Companies, 1888–1930*. Westport, CT: Greenwood, 1987.

Gale, Zona. *Miss Lulu Bett*. New York: D. Appleton, 1921.

Glaspell, Susan. *Plays*. Ed. C.W.E. Bigsby. Cambridge, England: Cambridge University Press, 1987.

Gorelik, Mordecai. *New Theatres for Old*. 1940. New York: Dutton, 1962.

Hatch, James V., and Leo Hamalian, eds. *Lost Plays of the Harlem Renaissance, 1920–1940*. Detroit: Wayne State University Press, 1996.

Hatch, James V., and Ted Shine, eds. *Plays by African Americans, 1847 to Today*. Rev. and expanded ed. New York: Free Press, 1996.

Heller, Adele, and Lois Rudnick, eds. *1915: The Cultural Moment. The New Politics, the New Woman, the New Psychology, the New Art, and the New Theatre in America*. New Brunswick, NJ: Rutgers University Press, 1991.

Hill, Errol, ed. *The Theater of Black Americans*. 2 vols. Englewood Cliffs, NJ: Prentice-Hall, 1980.

Huggins, Nathan Irvin. *Harlem Renaissance*. New York: Oxford University Press, 1971.

Isaacs, Edith J. R. *Theatre: Essays on the Arts of the Theatre*. Boston: Little, Brown, 1927.

Kinne, Wisner Payne. *George Pierce Baker and the American Theatre*. Cambridge, MA: Harvard University Press, 1954.

Klein, Carole. *Aline*. New York: Harper and Row, 1979.

Knox, George A., and Herbert M. Stahl. *Dos Passos and "The Revolting Playwrights."* Essays and Studies on American Language and Literature, XV. Ed. S. B. Liljegren. Uppsala: A. B. Lundequistska Bokhandeln, 1964.

Leiter, Samuel L., ed. *The Encyclopedia of the New York Stage, 1920–1930*. 2 vols. Westport, CT: Greenwood, 1985.

Macgowan, Kenneth, and Robert Edmond Jones. *Continental Stagecraft*. New York: Harcourt, Brace, 1922.

Mantle, Burns, and Garrison P. Sherwood, eds. *The Best Plays of 1909–1919 and the Year Book of the Drama in America*. New York: Dodd, 1933.

Mantle, Burns, ed. *The Best Plays of 1919–1920 and the Year Book of the Drama in America*. New York: Dodd, 1920.

———. *The Best Plays of 1920–1921 and the Year Book of the Drama in America*. New York: Dodd, 1921.

———. *The Best Plays of 1921–1922 and the Year Book of the Drama in America*. New York: Dodd, 1922.

———. *The Best Plays of 1922–1923 and the Year Book of the Drama in America*. New York: Dodd, 1923.

———. *The Best Plays of 1923–1924 and the Year Book of the Drama in America*. New York: Dodd, 1924.

———. *The Best Plays of 1924–1925 and the Year Book of the Drama in America*. New York: Dodd, 1925.

———. *The Best Plays of 1925–1926 and the Year Book of the Drama in America.* New York: Dodd, 1926.

———. *The Best Plays of 1926–1927 and the Year Book of the Drama in America.* New York: Dodd, 1927.

———. *The Best Plays of 1927–28 and the Year Book of the Drama in America.* New York: Dodd, 1928.

———. *The Best Plays of 1928–29 and the Year Book of the Drama in America.* New York: Dodd, 1929.

———. *The Best Plays of 1929–30 and the Year Book of the Drama in America.* New York: Dodd, 1930.

Markowsky, Veronica A. *Susan Glaspell's Century of American Women: A Critical Interpretation of Her Work.* New York: Oxford University Press, 1993.

Meserve, Walter. *An American Drama. 1920–1941.* The Revels History of Drama in English: American Drama 8. Ed. T. W. Craik. London: Methuen, 1977.

Papke, Mary E. *Susan Glaspell: A Research and Production Sourcebook.* Westport, CT: Greenwood, 1993.

Parrish, Michael E. *Anxious Decades: America in Prosperity and Depression, 1920–1941.* New York: Norton, 1992.

Pendleton, Ralph, ed. *The Theatre of Robert Edmond Jones.* Middletown, CT: Wesleyan University Press, 1958.

Perkins, Kathy A., ed. *Black Female Playwrights: An Anthology of Plays Before 1950.* Bloomington: Indiana University Press, 1989.

Perry, John. *James A. Herne: The American Ibsen.* Chicago: Nelson-Hall, 1978.

Peterson, Bernard L., Jr. *A Century of Musicals in Black and White: An Encyclopedia of Musical Stage Works By, About, or Involving African Americans.* Westport, CT: Greenwood, 1993.

The Provincetown Plays. First Series. New York: Frank Shay, 1916.

The Provincetown Plays. Second Series. New York: Frank Shay, 1916.

The Provincetown Plays. Third Series. New York: Frank Shay, 1916.

Richardson, Willis, comp. *Plays and Pageants from the Life of the Negro.* 1930. Jackson: University of Mississippi Press, 1993.

Schanke, Robert A. *Shattered Applause: The Lives of Eva Le Gallienne.* Carbondale and Edwardsville: Southern Illinois University Press, 1992.

Schleuter, June, ed. *Modern American Drama: The Female Canon.* Madison: Fairleigh Dickinson University Press, 1990.

Shafer, Yvonne. *American Women Playwrights, 1900–1950.* New York: Peter Lang, 1995.

Sheehy, Helen. *Eva Le Gallienne: A Biography.* New York: Knopf, 1996.

Sievers, W. David. *Freud on Broadway: A History of Psychoanalysis and the American Drama.* 1955. New York: Cooper Square, 1970.

Smith, Page. *Redeeming the Time: A People's History of the 1920s and the New Deal.* Vol. 8. New York: McGraw-Hill, 1987.

Time-Life Books. *The Roaring Twenties, 1920–1930.* This Fabulous Century, vol. 3. Alexandria, VA: Time-Life Books, 1969.

Valgemae, Mardi. *Accelerated Grimace: Expressionism in the American Drama of the 1920s.* Carbondale: Southern Illinois University Press, 1972.

Wainscott, Ronald H. *The Emergence of the Modern American Theater, 1914–1929.* New Haven: Yale University Press, 1997.

Waterman, Arthur E. *Susan Glaspell.* New York: Twayne, 1966.

Woll, Allen. *Black Musical Theatre: From Coontown to Dreamgirls.* Baton Rouge: Louisiana State University Press, 1989.

Index

Abbott, George, 5, 17

Acting: ensemble, 96; ideal of versatility in, 114; Stanislavsky's system for, 111, 112

Actors Equity, 98

Actors' Theatre, 97

Adams, Franklin P., 8

Addinsell, Richard, 98

African American actors, 41, 42; in black-authored plays, 67, 68; on Broadway, 33; as traditional stage "darky," 73–74; in traditional white roles, 73

African American arts and culture: advocacy of national theatre for, 48, 52–53; black aesthetic in, 48, 49, 50, 51–52; characterizations of blacks in, 42, 45, 47–49, 53; community support for, 53; and Krigwa Players' manifesto, 48; of New Negro/Harlem Renaissance movement, 39–40, 47–54, 71–90; literature in, 85, 87–88; role of black colleges and universities in, 85–86. *See also* Du Bois, W.E.B.

African American drama, 33, 39, 40–45; assimilationist versus nationalist debate in, 50–51; black aesthetic in, 51–52, 54; Broadway productions of, 39, 45, 53, 71–90; comedy/comic relief in, 72–73, 74; community drama movement and, 83–85, 89; folk expression in, 49, 50, 53, 74, 75, 83, 86–87; form and content debate in, 48–52; of Howard Players, 49–50, 83–90; and New Negro movement, 47–48, 71; sensationalism in, 78; social and political subject matter in, 48–49, 75; taboos in, 48–49; use of dialect in, 52, 72; white audience for, 45, 50–51, 78, 79; by white playwrights, 48, 52–53. *See also* Anderson, Garland

African American playwrights, 39–45, 47, 49, 55–69, 71–90; avant-garde, 24; female, 50, 88; racial messages of, 72, 74, 74, 77, 79; radical, 23; Theatre Guild and, 3–4. *See also* Thurman, Wallace

African Americans: portrayals of, 42–43; white stereotyping of, 50, 59; as theatre critics, 47–54, 74, 76

African Grove Theatre and Company, 71

About the Editors and Contributors

ESTELLE ADEN, a retired Adjunct Professor of Drama at Hofstra University, has been concerned with the performing voice and the performance of literary and dramatic text. Focused research has contributed to her performance, writing, and teaching. She has lectured extensively on the careers and writings of Ellen Terry, Edith Wharton, and Eva Le Gallienne. These great talents have made contributions to academia, literature, and the commercial theatre. Her numerous articles include studies in the creative interpretation of the actor/actress in Pirandello plays, poems, and short stories. She is the recipient of the 1996 Excellence in Teaching Award from University College for Continuing Education at Hofstra University.

JOHN BELL teaches theatre and performance theory and practice in the Performing Arts Department at Emerson College, and is a member of Great Small Works theatre company. His latest publication is "Landscape and Desire: Bread and Puppet Pageants in the 90s."

BEVERLE BLOCH is an Assistant Professor of Theatre/Comunications at Lewis University, and previously chaired the Department of Communication and Theatre at St. Andrews College in North Carolina. She is primarily interested in the intersection of theatre history and performance theory and is currently writing about glimpses of Asian theatre training in fiction and nonfiction film. She is the co-Editor of *Scholia: The Journal*, a journal connected to the Scholar's Program at Lewis University.

WILLIAM F. CONDEE is Associate Professor and Associate Director in the School of Theater at Ohio University. He is the author of *Theatrical Space: A Guide for Directors and Designers*, and is currently studying the relationship of the opera house and local culture in Appalachia.

JERRY DICKEY is Associate Professor of Theatre Arts at the University of Arizona. He is the author of *Sophie Treadwell: A Research and Production Sourcebook* (1997), as well as essays on Treadwell in *Theatre History Studies* (1995), *Women & Theatre: Occasional Papers 4* (1997), *Speaking the Other Self: American Women Writers* (1997), and the forthcoming *Cambridge Companion to American Women Playwrights*.

ANNE FLETCHER teaches in the Theater Department at Southern Illinois University at Carbondale. Her principal research interest involves the examination of theatre companies whose work can be viewed as "production dependent"—namely, the New Playwrights Theatre and, presently, the Omaha Magic Theatre. She is collaborating on a study of Mordecai Gorelik and John Howard Lawson.

STEVEN FRANK is a full-time professional writer who received his M.A. from New York University, where he has taught dramatic literature for the College of Arts and Sciences and Tisch School of the Arts.

ARTHUR GEWIRTZ is associate professor of English emeritus at Hofstra University, Hempstead, New York. From 1962 to 1992 he taught at the New School for Social Research, New York City. He is the author of *Restoration Adaptations of Early 17th-Century Comedies* (University Press of America, 1982); "Arthur Wing Pinero" and "Alfred Sutro" in *British Playwrights, 1880–1956* (Greenwood Press, 1996); and "Sidney Howard" in *American Playwrights, 1880–1945* (Greenwood Press, 1995). He has also written for *Shakespeare Quarterly*, *The New Leader*, *Newsday*, and *The Mediterranean Review*. He was codirector of the three-day conference "Art, Glitter and Glitz: The Theatre of the 1920s Celebrates American Diversity," which took place at Hofstra University, November 1994.

FREDA SCOTT GILES is Assistant Professor of Drama at the University of Georgia, and has served on the faculty at the University at Albany, New York and the City College of the City University of New York. Her principal research interest is African American drama and theatre, particularly during the Harlem Renaissance period. She has published articles in *African American Review*, *Womanist Theory and Research*, *Theatre Journal*, and numerous other journals and books.

JAMES J. KOLB is Professor of Drama at Hofstra University, Hempstead, New York, where he teaches dramatic literature and theatre history, and is Chair of the Department of Drama and Dance. He is a frequent stage director, and is a regular lecturer on American musical theatre. As a "Speaker in the Humanities," he has lectured extensively for the New York Council for the Humanities throughout New York State. He was codirector of the three-day conference "Art, Glitter and Glitz: The Theatre of the 1920s Celebrates American Diversity," at Hofstra University, November 1994, and also coauthored *"Runnin' Wild": A Musical Revue of the 1920s* for the conference.

ALAN KREIZENBECK is an Associate Professor of Theatre at the University of Maryland, Baltimore County and formerly held appointments at several other universities. He has published extensively in scholarly journals and has presented papers at numerous academic conferences. His research efforts are focused on American theatrical productions and playwriting during the 1920s and 1930s.

JEANNE-MARIE A. MILLER is Professor emerita of English at Howard University and is the former Director of the Graduate Studies Program in English. A specialist in African American drama, Dr. Miller has published numerous articles on the subject in a variety of journals and books and has taught courses in American and African American literature and drama at Howard. For ten years she edited *The Black Theatre Bulletin* for the now defunct American Theatre Association and is a former associate editor of the *Theatre Journal*. She has been a fellow of the Ford Foundation and the Southern Fellowships Fund as well as a grantee of the American Council of Learned Societies, the National Endowment for the Humanities, and the Howard University Faculty Research Fund.

MICHAEL C. O'NEILL is Director of Theater at Lafayette College and Adjunct Associate Professor at New York University. He has written extensively on modern drama and has directed plays both in the United States and abroad. A former Fulbright Fellow, he is the recipient of N.E.H. and C.I.E.S. grants and is the three-time winner of Purdue University's Cordell Playwrighting Prize.

JANE T. PETERSON is Assistant Professor of Theatre at Montclair State University of New Jersey. She is coauthor of *Women Playwrights of Diversity* in addition to having articles in *Notable Women of the American Theatre* and the forthcoming *American National Biography*. She has published and presented several articles reflecting her interest in Robert Edmond Jones and the theatre of the 1920s.

JOHN D. SHOUT is Professor of Theatre and English at the State University of New York at Plattsburgh and most recently has spent a year teaching at the American University in Cairo. He has published in such areas of theatre history as Edwardian drama, contemporary Irish theatre, and the American political theatre of the 1930s.

BEVERLY BRONSON SMITH is Assistant Dean of Liberal Arts at Cuyahoga Community College. She has previously been Director of Performing Arts at Urbana University (Ohio) and on the faculties of Ohio State University–Newark, Kent State University, University of Akron, and Youngstown State University. Her studies of nonverbal representations of ethnic characters have been presented at a number of national conferences and published in such works as *Staging Difference*. Several articles on twentieth-century playwrights will appear in the *Encyclopedia of American Literature* and the *Encyclopedia of World Literature*.

KORNELIA TANCHEVA recently defended her Ph.D. dissertation on American dramatic and theatrical modernism at Cornell University. She is currently living in Ithaca and teaching part-time at Ithaca College. Her most recent research is on contemporary East European theatre and drama.

DAVE WILLIAMS teaches at Ohio State University, Newark campus. In addition to pursuing his main academic interests of Asian and Asian American Drama, he also performs, designs, and directs. He is the editor of the recently published *The Chinese Other, 1850–1925: An Anthology of Plays*.

SCOTT ZALUDA is Assistant Professor of English at Westchester Community College and previously served on the faculty of the City University of New York and Nassau Community College. His research and writing have been directed to exploring how social and cultural change influences and is influenced by American literature as well as education in literature and in literacy, especially during the first years of the twentieth century.